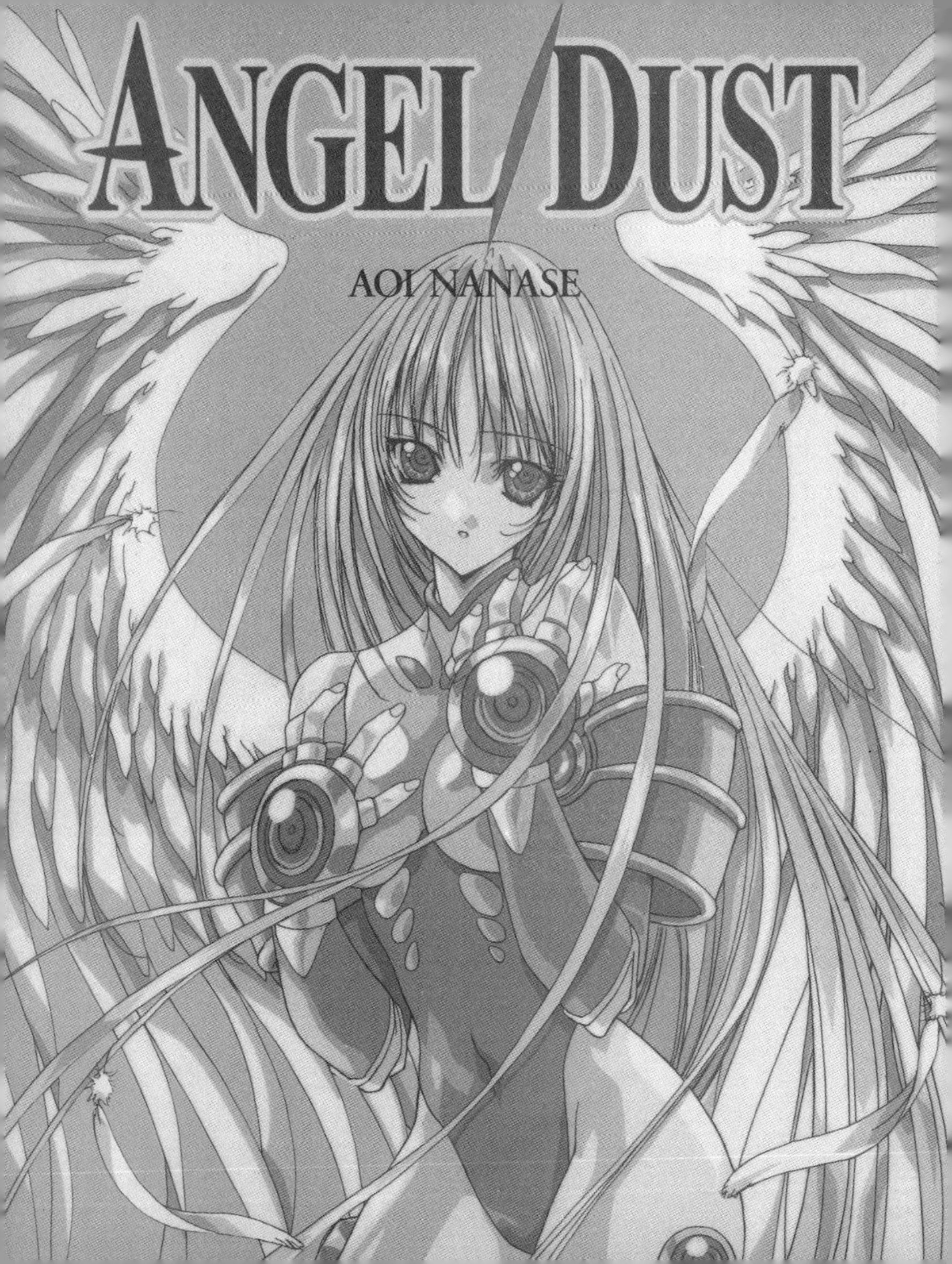
ANGEL DUST
AOI NANASE

# contents



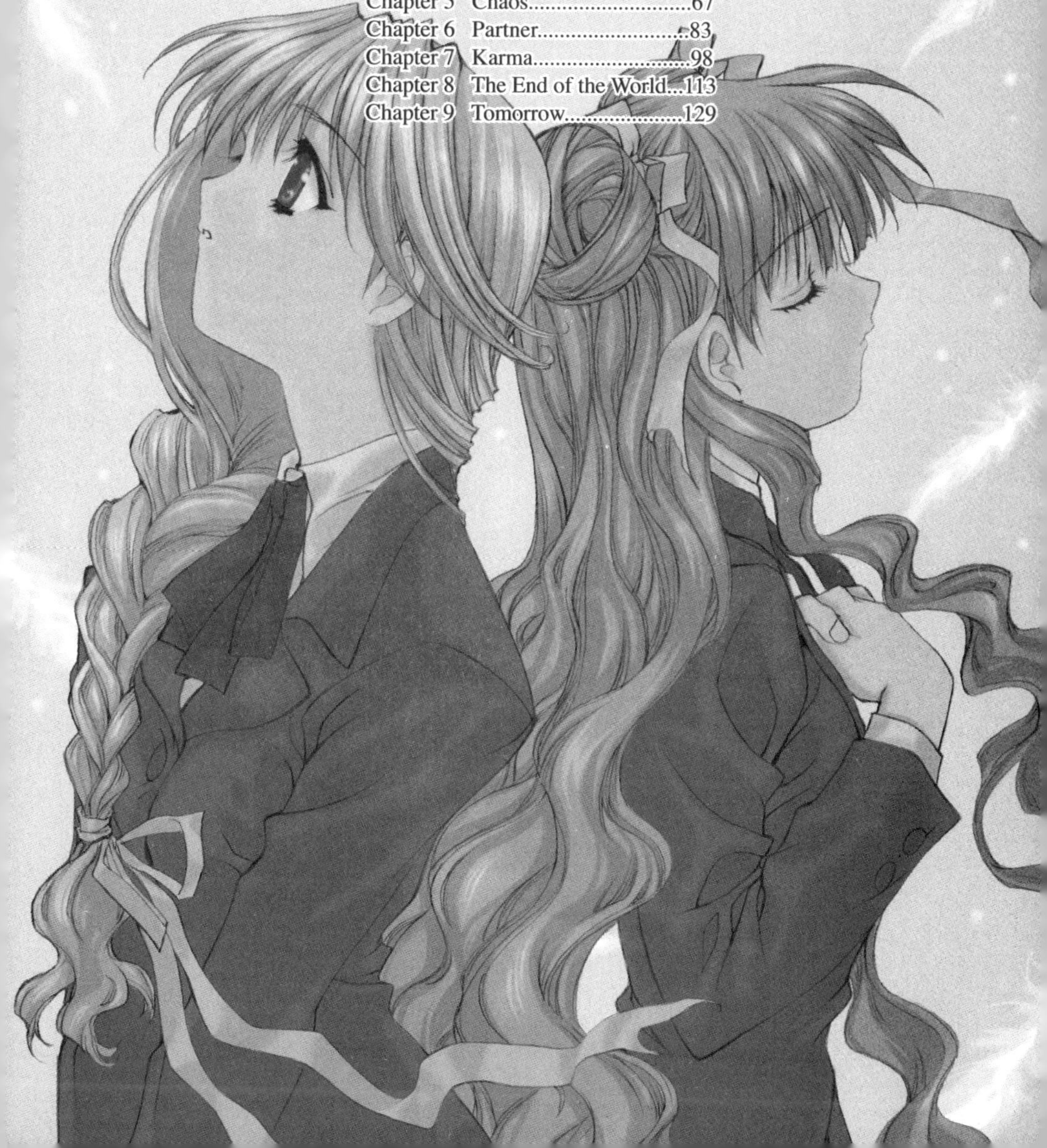

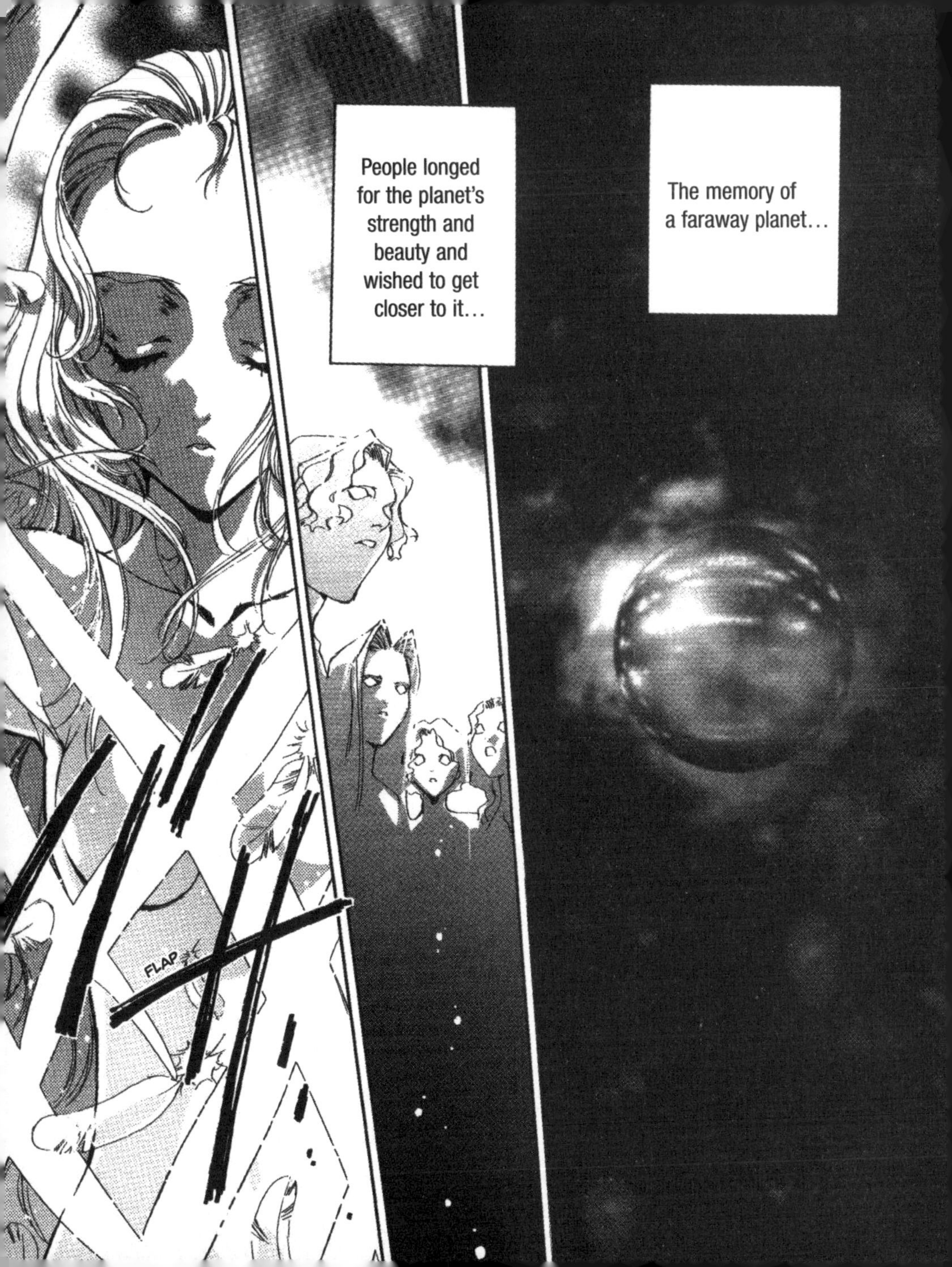

The memory of a faraway planet…
People longed for the planet's strength and beauty and wished to get closer to it…
FLAP

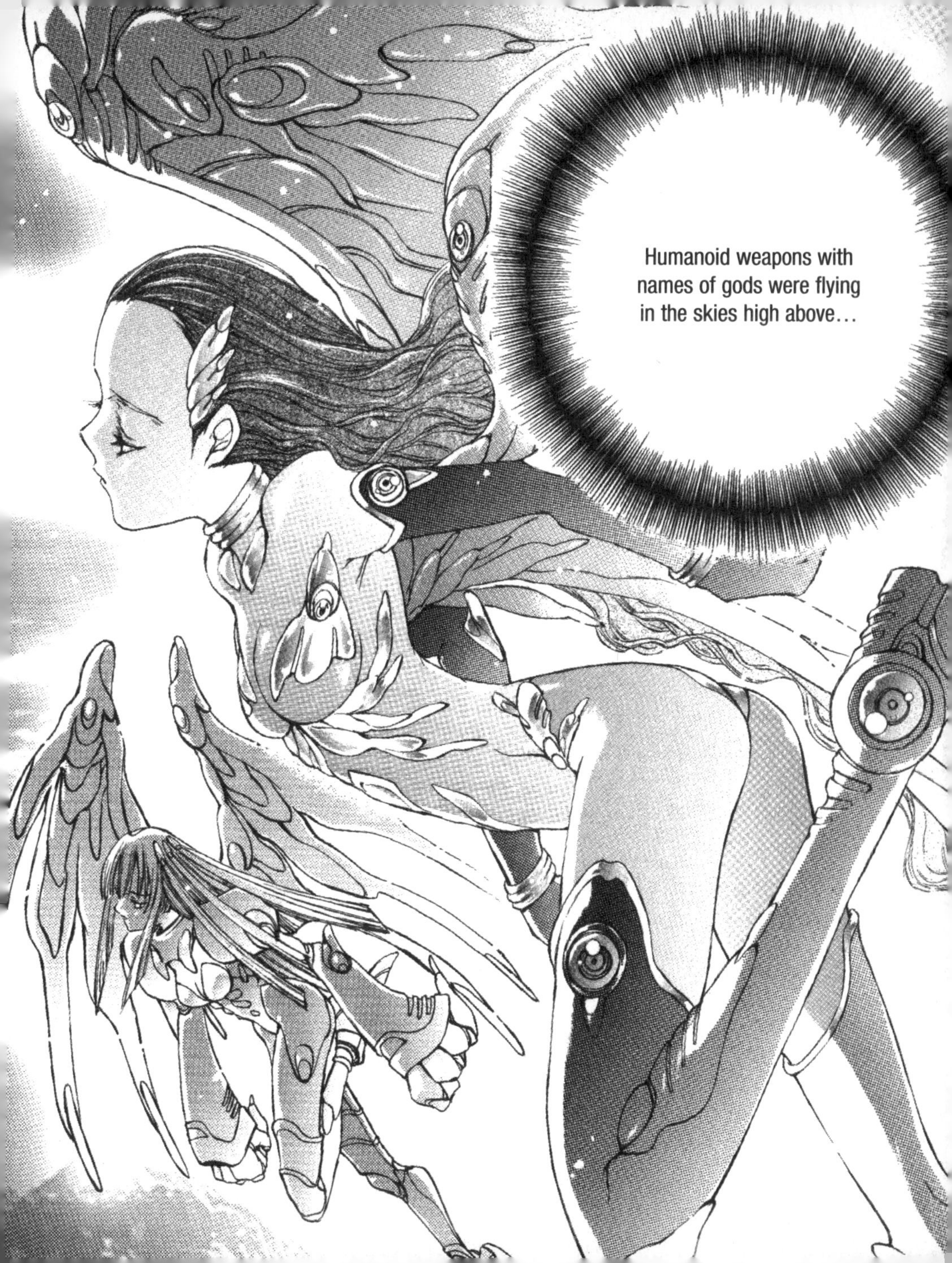
Humanoid weapons with names of gods were flying in the skies high above…

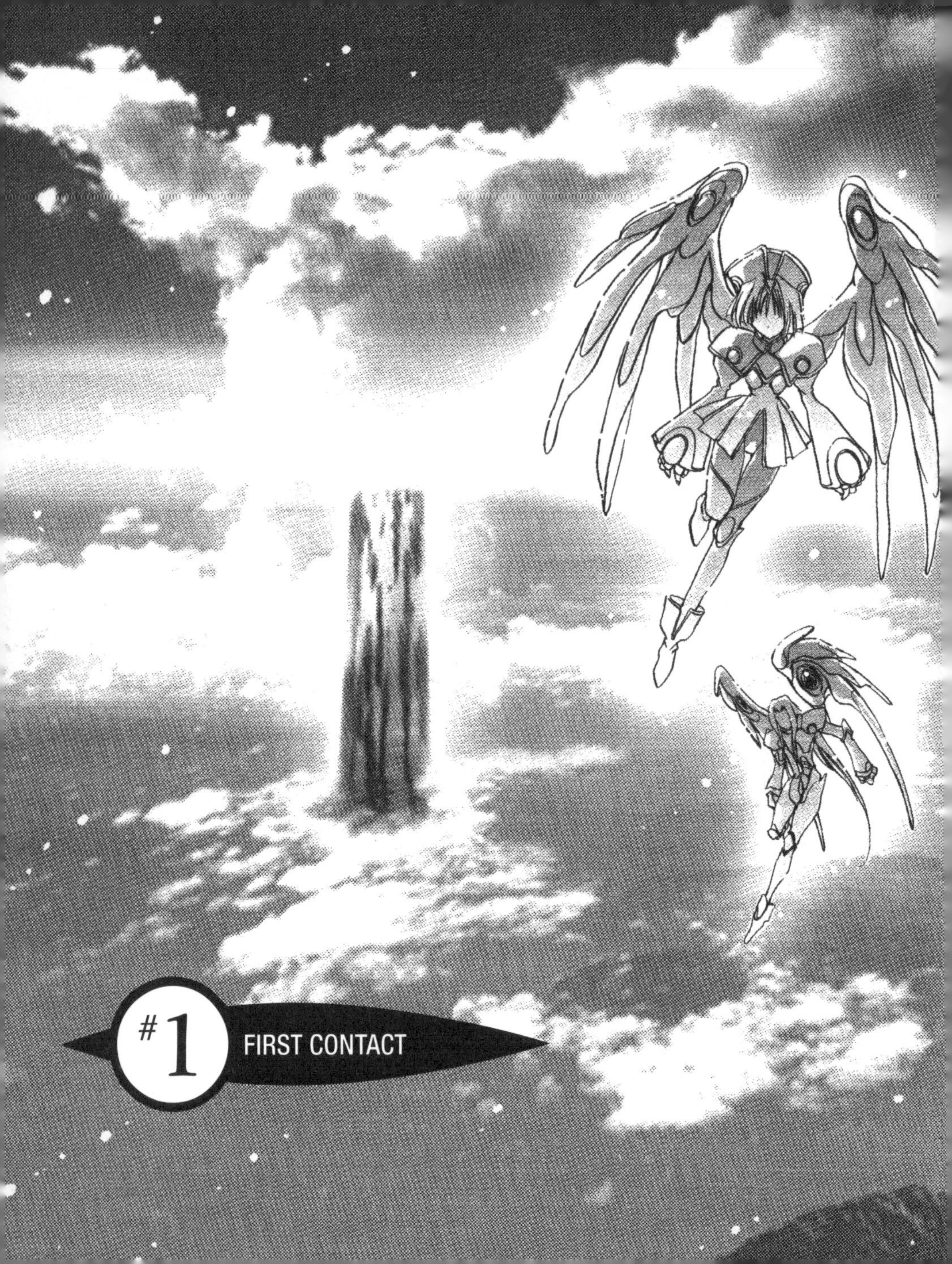
#1
FIRST CONTACT

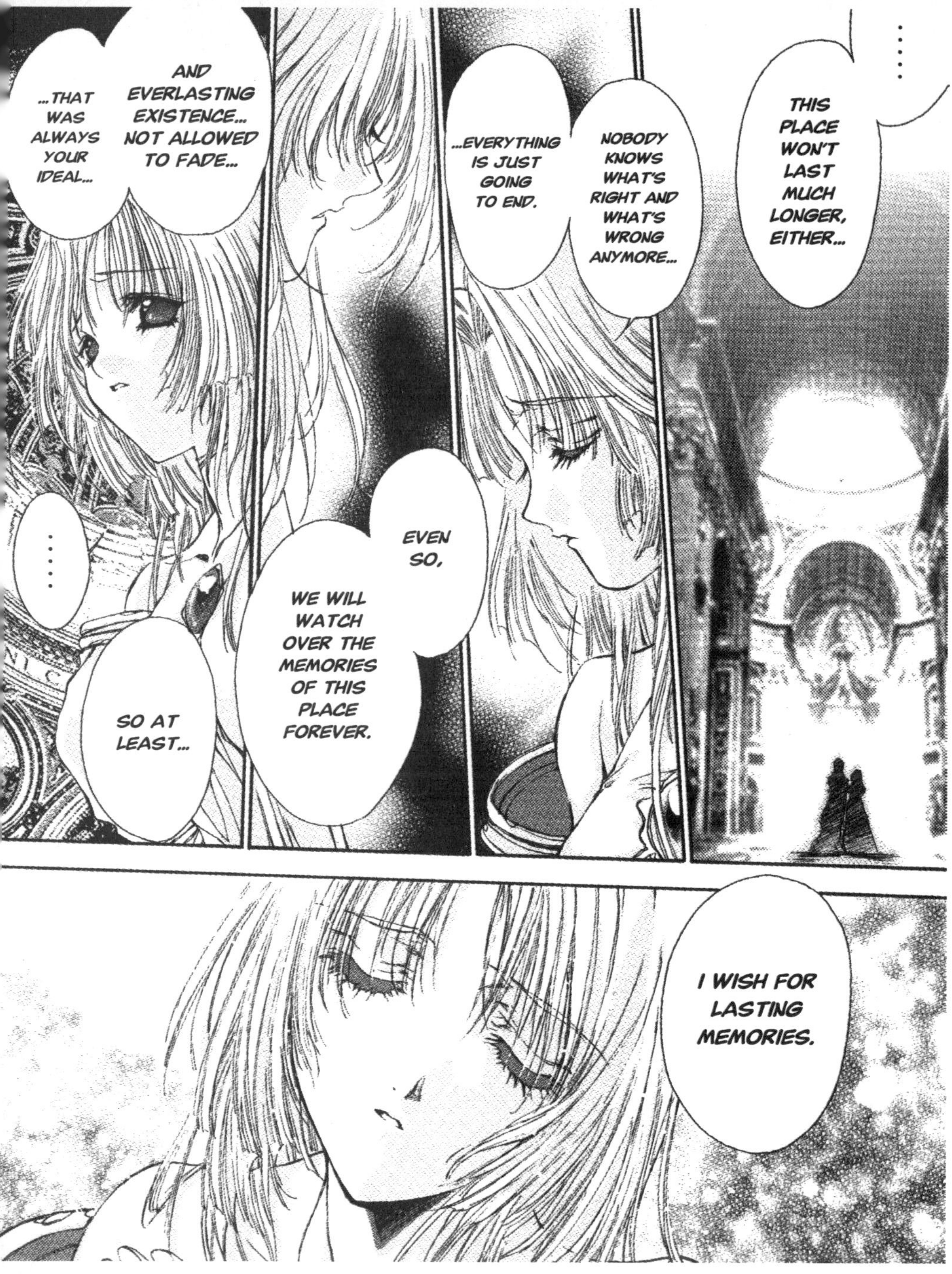
.....
THIS PLACE WON'T LAST MUCH LONGER, EITHER...
NOBODY KNOWS WHAT'S RIGHT AND WHAT'S WRONG ANYMORE...
...EVERYTHING IS JUST GOING TO END.
AND EVERLASTING EXISTENCE... NOT ALLOWED TO FADE...
...THAT WAS ALWAYS YOUR IDEAL...
......
EVEN SO,
WE WILL WATCH OVER THE MEMORIES OF THIS PLACE FOREVER.
SO AT LEAST...
I WISH FOR LASTING MEMORIES.

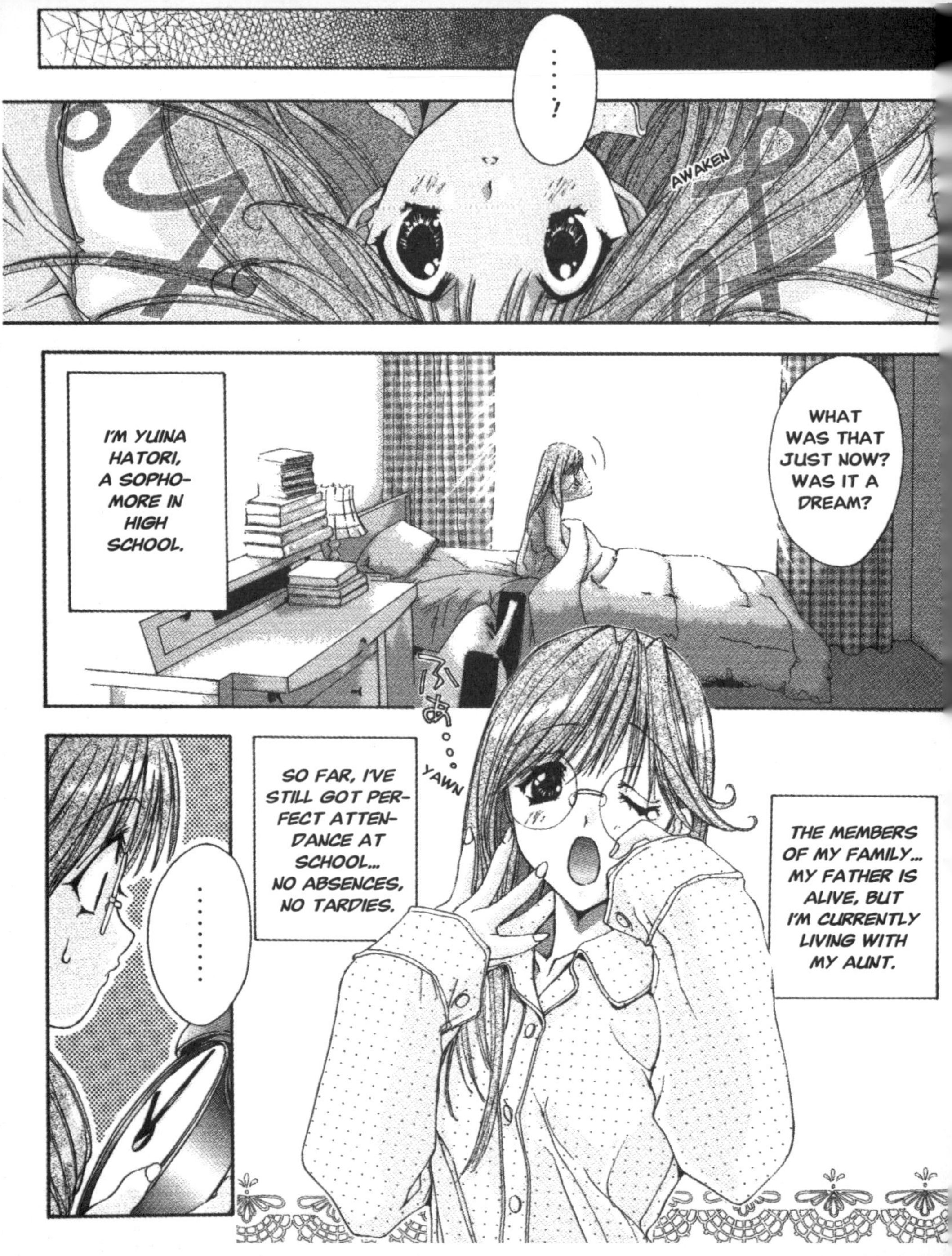
......!
AWAKEN
WHAT WAS THAT JUST NOW? WAS IT A DREAM?
I'M YUINA HATORI, A SOPHOMORE IN HIGH SCHOOL.
YAWN
THE MEMBERS OF MY FAMILY... MY FATHER IS ALIVE, BUT I'M CURRENTLY LIVING WITH MY AUNT.
SO FAR, I'VE STILL GOT PERFECT ATTENDANCE AT SCHOOL... NO ABSENCES, NO TARDIES.
.........

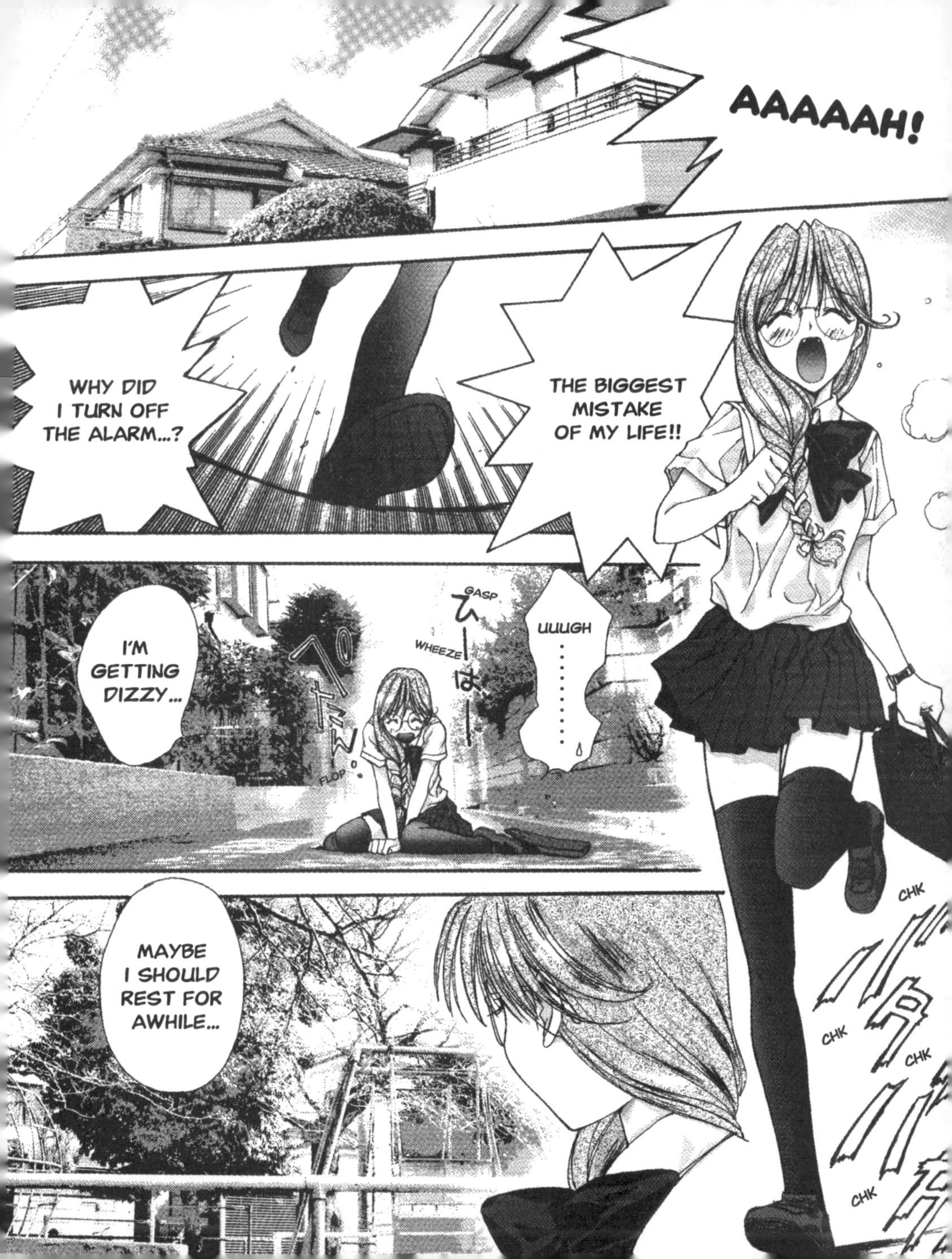

AAAAAH!
THE BIGGEST MISTAKE OF MY LIFE!!
WHY DID I TURN OFF THE ALARM...?
CHK
CHK
CHK
CHK
UUUGH
GASP
WHEEZE
FLOP
I'M GETTING DIZZY...
MAYBE I SHOULD REST FOR AWHILE...

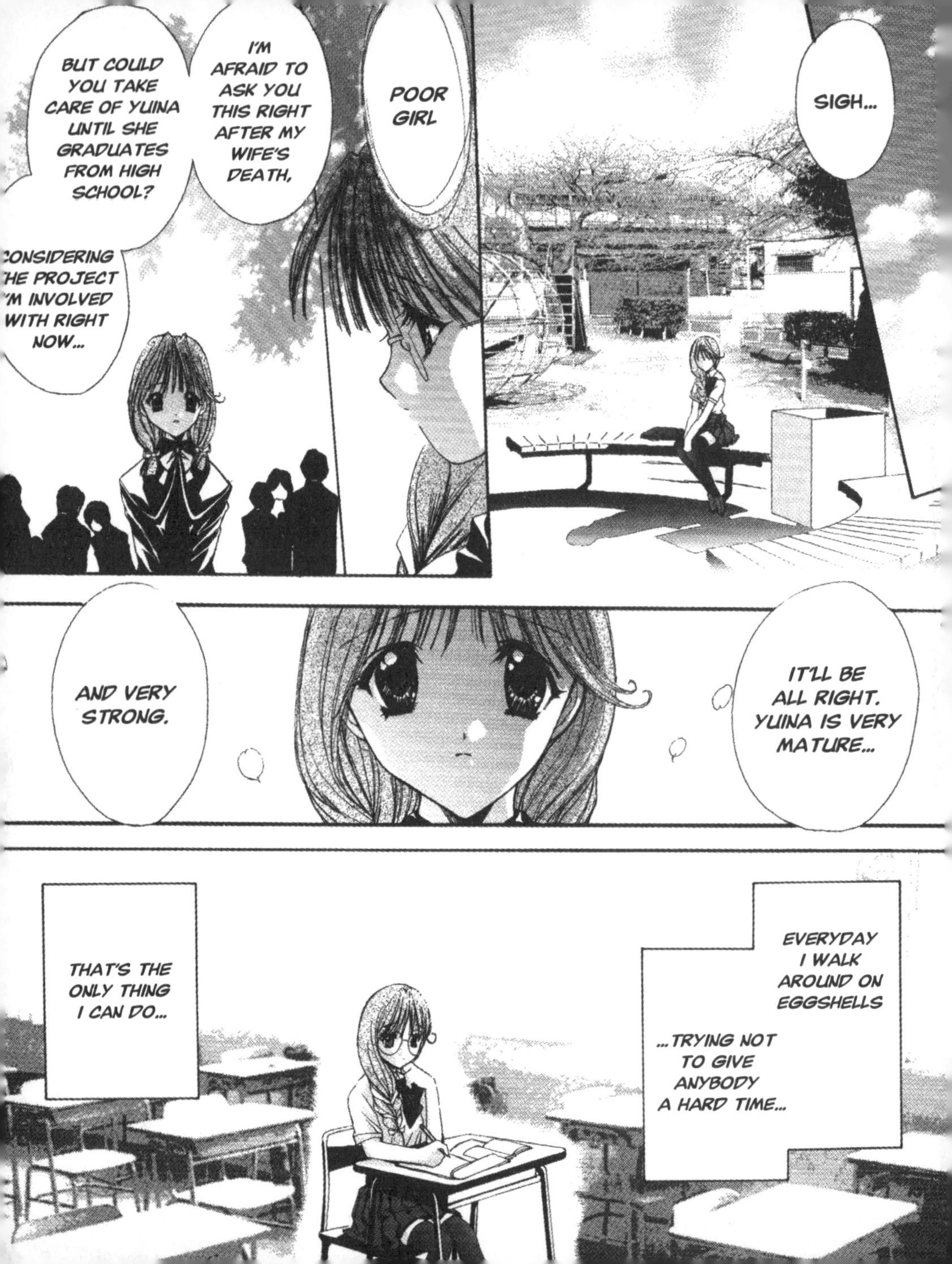
SIGH...
POOR GIRL
I'M AFRAID TO ASK YOU THIS RIGHT AFTER MY WIFE'S DEATH,
BUT COULD YOU TAKE CARE OF YUINA UNTIL SHE GRADUATES FROM HIGH SCHOOL?
CONSIDERING THE PROJECT I'M INVOLVED WITH RIGHT NOW...
IT'LL BE ALL RIGHT. YUINA IS VERY MATURE...
AND VERY STRONG.
EVERYDAY I WALK AROUND ON EGGSHELLS
...TRYING NOT TO GIVE ANYBODY A HARD TIME...
THAT'S THE ONLY THING I CAN DO...

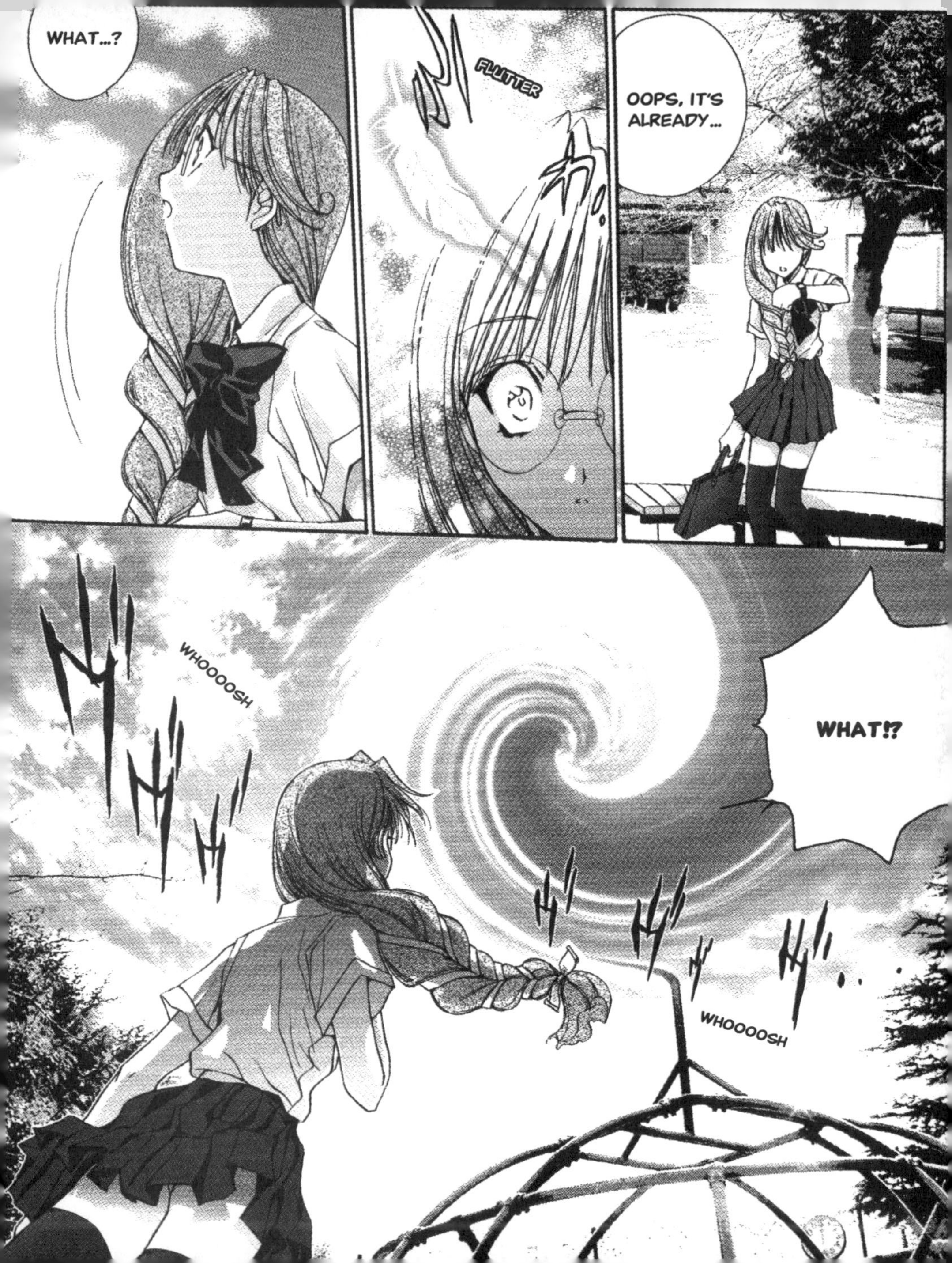
OOPS, IT'S ALREADY...
FLUTTER
WHAT...?
WHAT!?
WHOOOOSH
WHOOOOSH

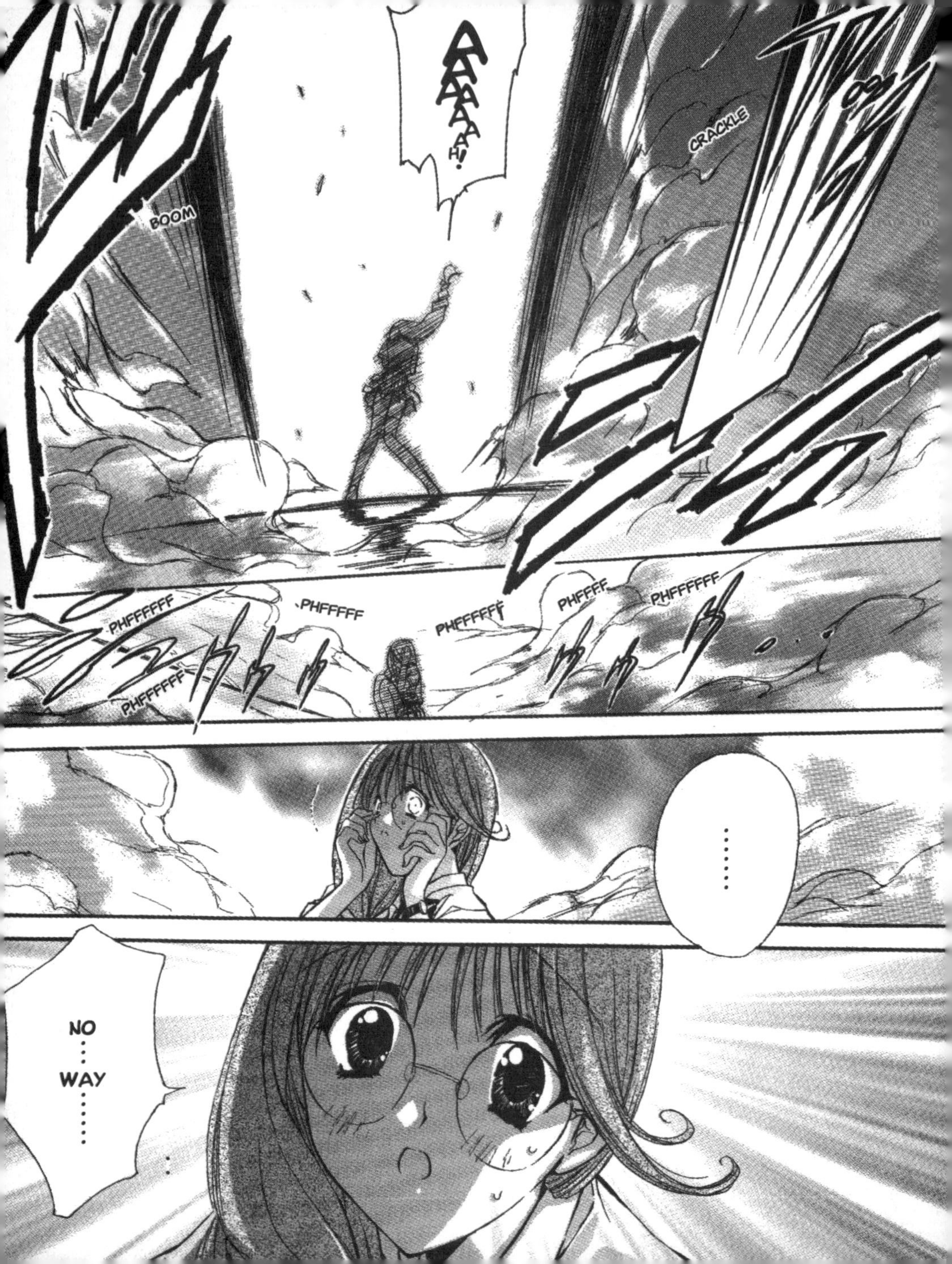

CRACKLE
AAAAAAAH!
BOOM
PHFFFFFF
PHFFFFFF
PHFFFFFF
PHFFFFF
PHFFFFFF
PHFFFFFF
PHFFFFFFF
......
NO... WAY.......

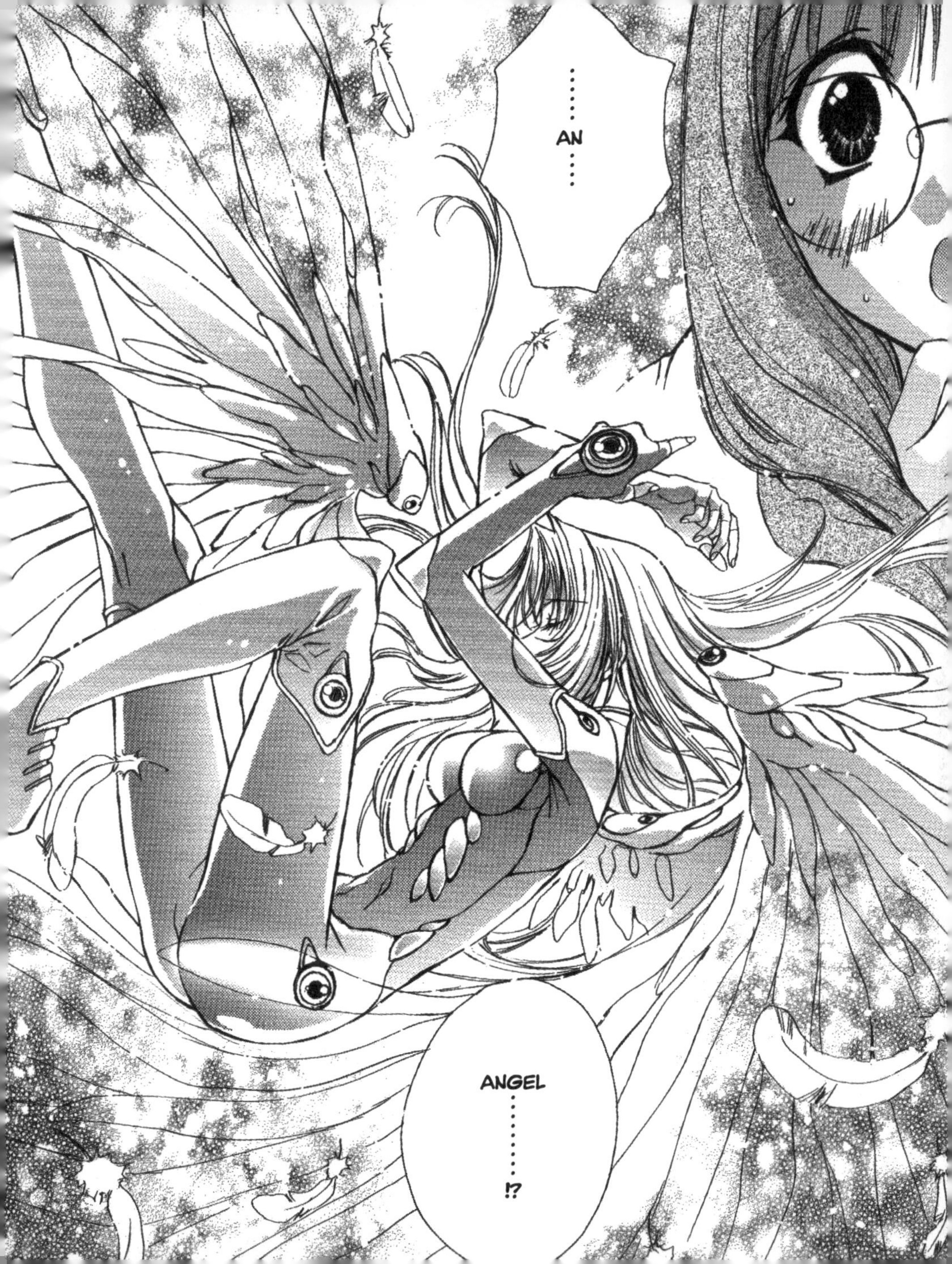

......AN......
ANGEL..........!?

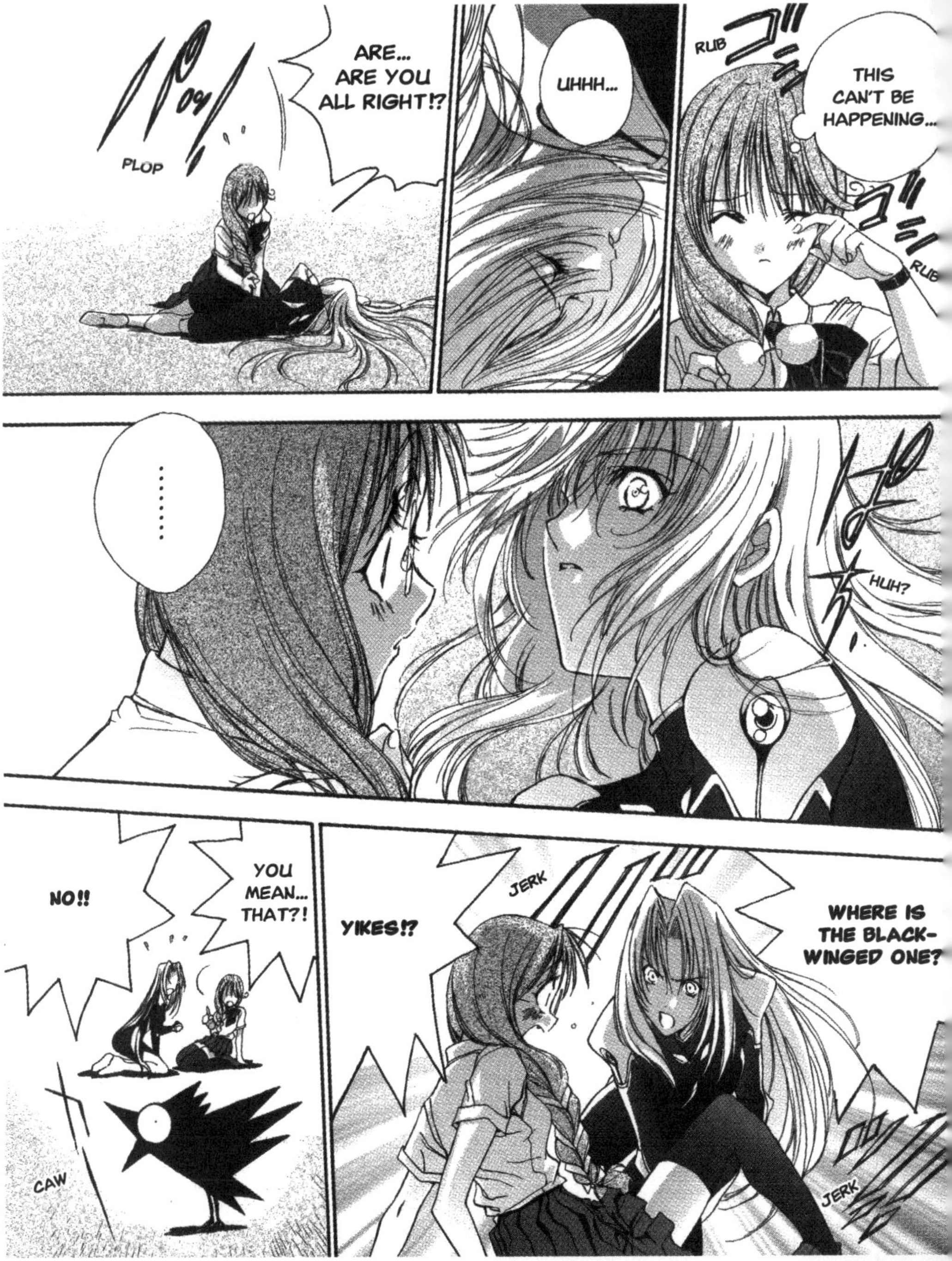
RUB
THIS CAN'T BE HAPPENING...
RUB
UHHH...
ARE... ARE YOU ALL RIGHT!?
PLOP
........
HUH?
WHERE IS THE BLACK-WINGED ONE?
JERK
YIKES!?
JERK
YOU MEAN... THAT?!
NO!!
CAW

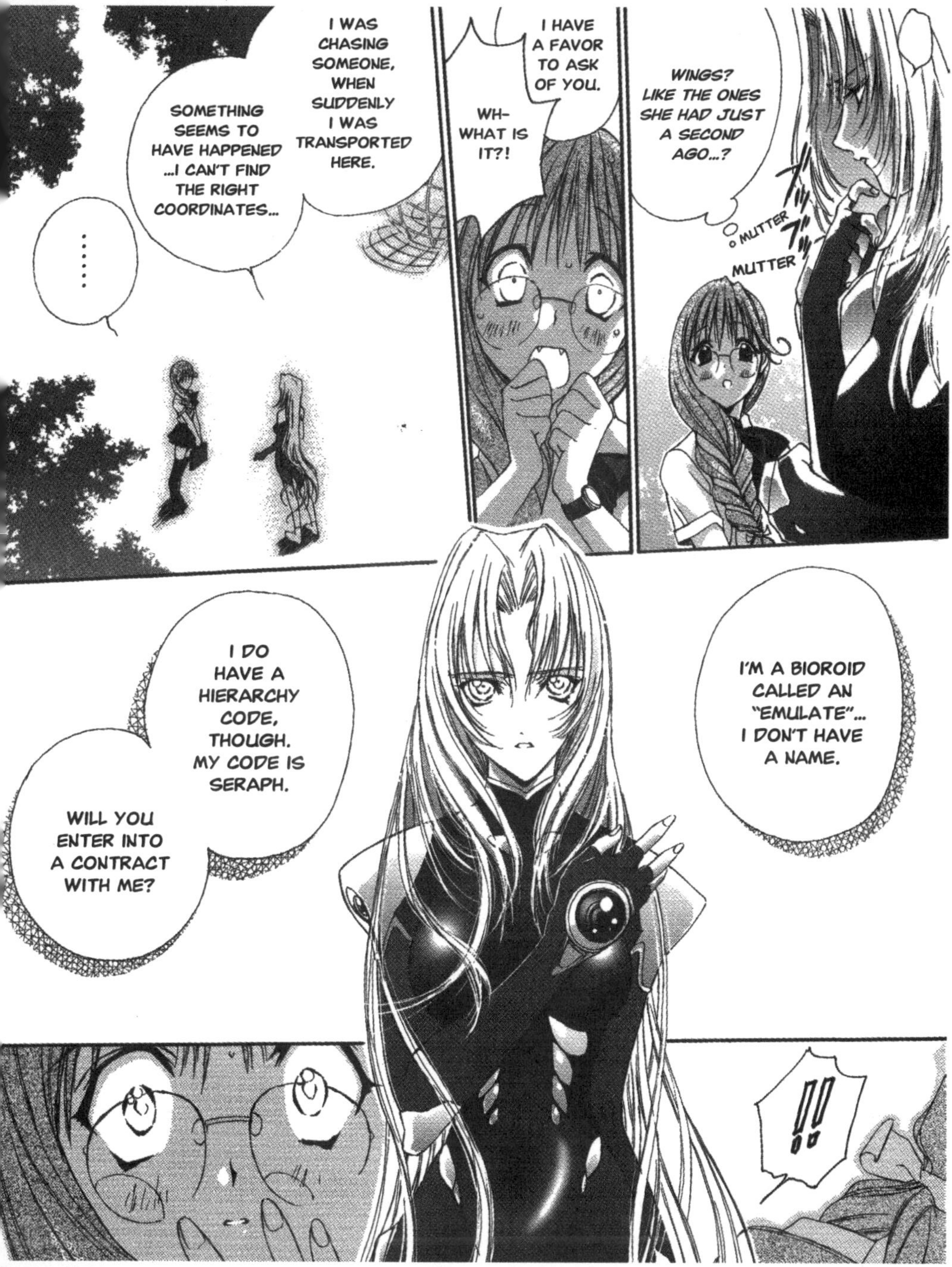

WINGS? LIKE THE ONES SHE HAD JUST A SECOND AGO...?
MUTTER
MUTTER
I HAVE A FAVOR TO ASK OF YOU.
WH-WHAT IS IT?!
I WAS CHASING SOMEONE, WHEN SUDDENLY I WAS TRANSPORTED HERE.
SOMETHING SEEMS TO HAVE HAPPENED ...I CAN'T FIND THE RIGHT COORDINATES...
......
I'M A BIOROID CALLED AN "EMULATE"... I DON'T HAVE A NAME.
I DO HAVE A HIERARCHY CODE, THOUGH. MY CODE IS SERAPH.
WILL YOU ENTER INTO A CONTRACT WITH ME?
!!

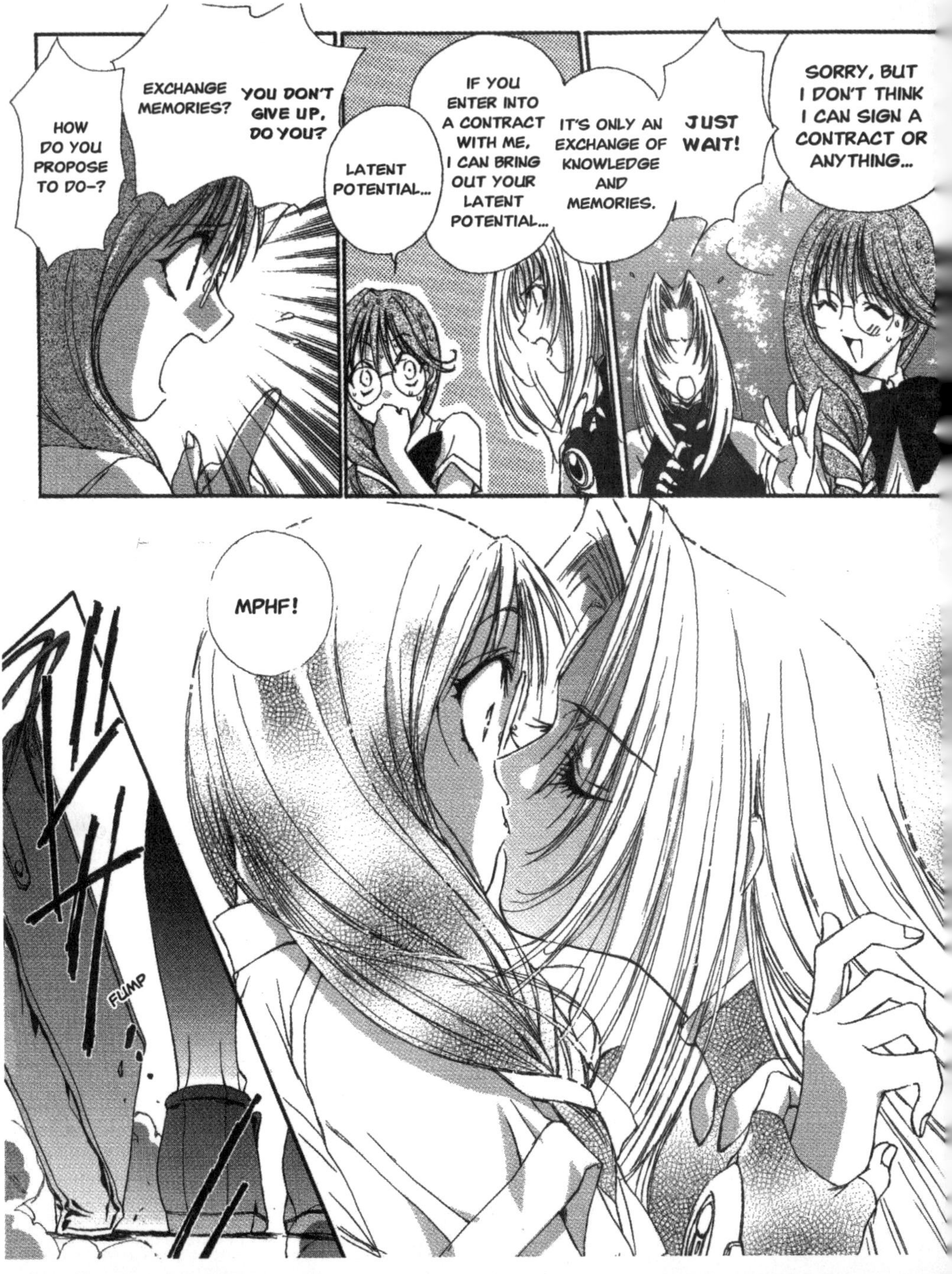
SORRY, BUT I DON'T THINK I CAN SIGN A CONTRACT OR ANYTHING...
JUST WAIT!
IT'S ONLY AN EXCHANGE OF KNOWLEDGE AND MEMORIES.
IF YOU ENTER INTO A CONTRACT WITH ME, I CAN BRING OUT YOUR LATENT POTENTIAL...
LATENT POTENTIAL...
YOU DON'T GIVE UP, DO YOU?
EXCHANGE MEMORIES?
HOW DO YOU PROPOSE TO DO-?
MPHF!
FLUMP

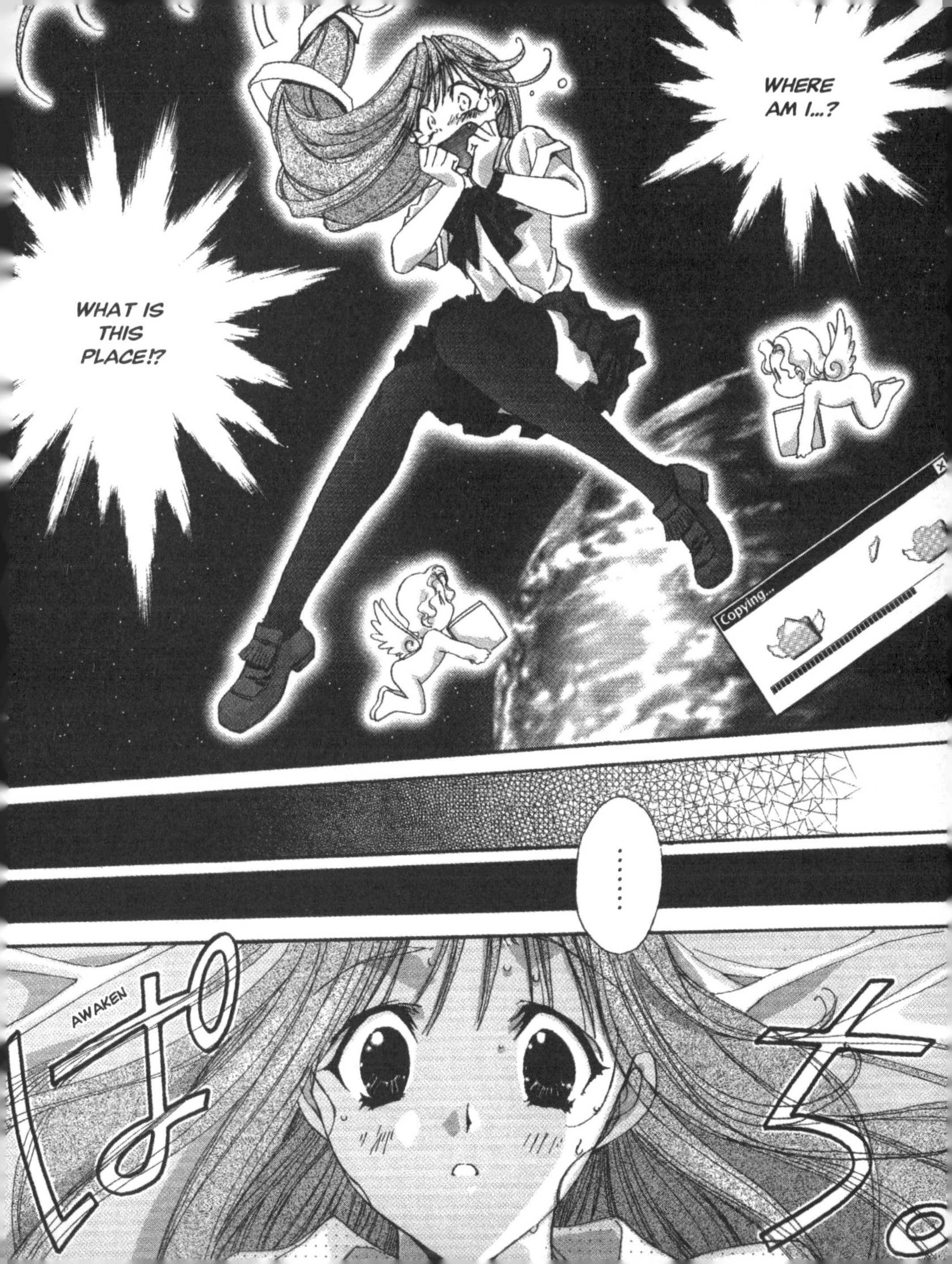
WHERE AM I...?
WHAT IS THIS PLACE!?
Copying...
......
AWAKEN

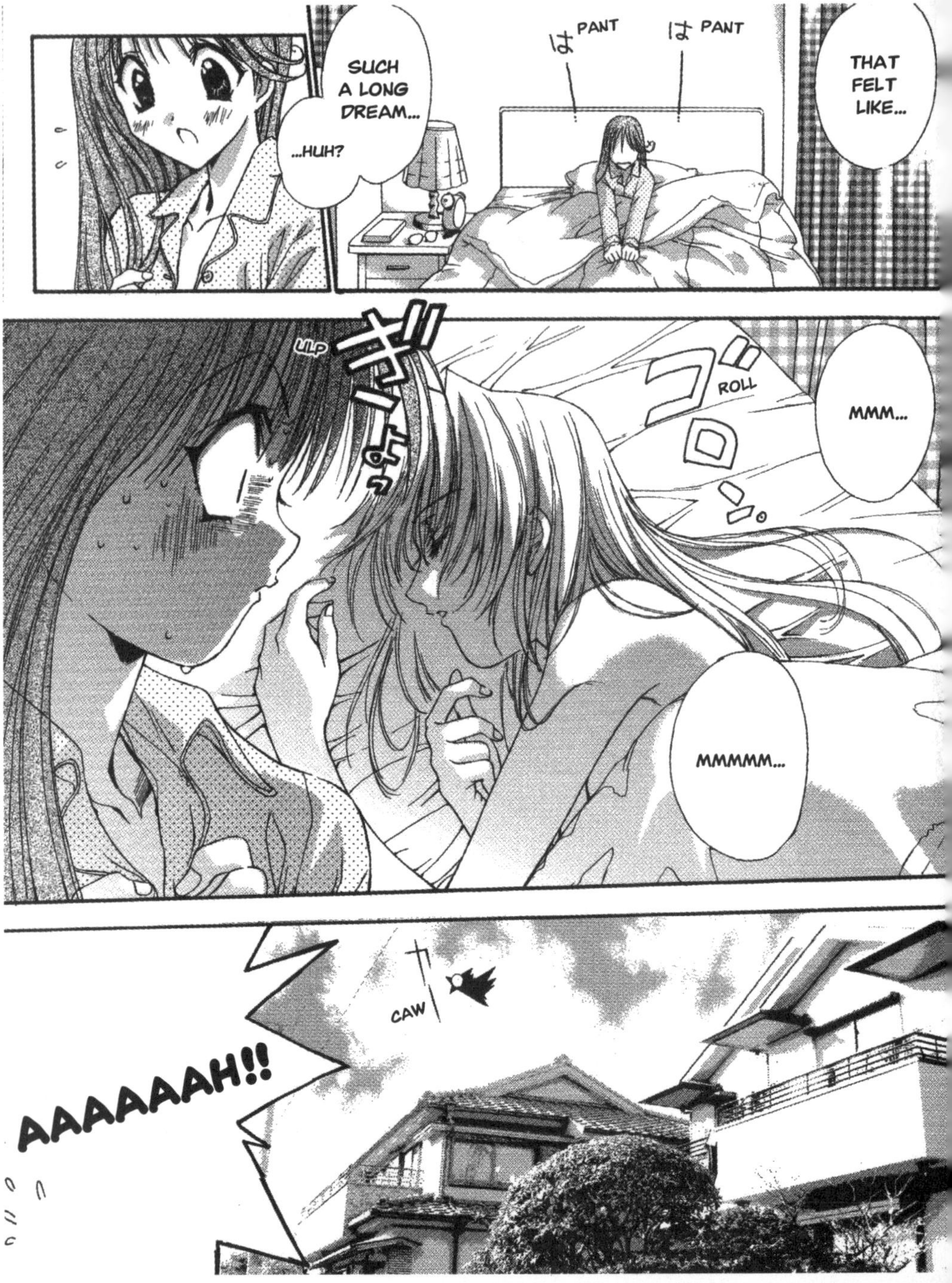
THAT FELT LIKE...
は PANT
は PANT
SUCH A LONG DREAM...
...HUH?
MMM...
ゴロ
ROLL
ギョッ
ULP
MMMMM...
CAW
AAAAAAH!!

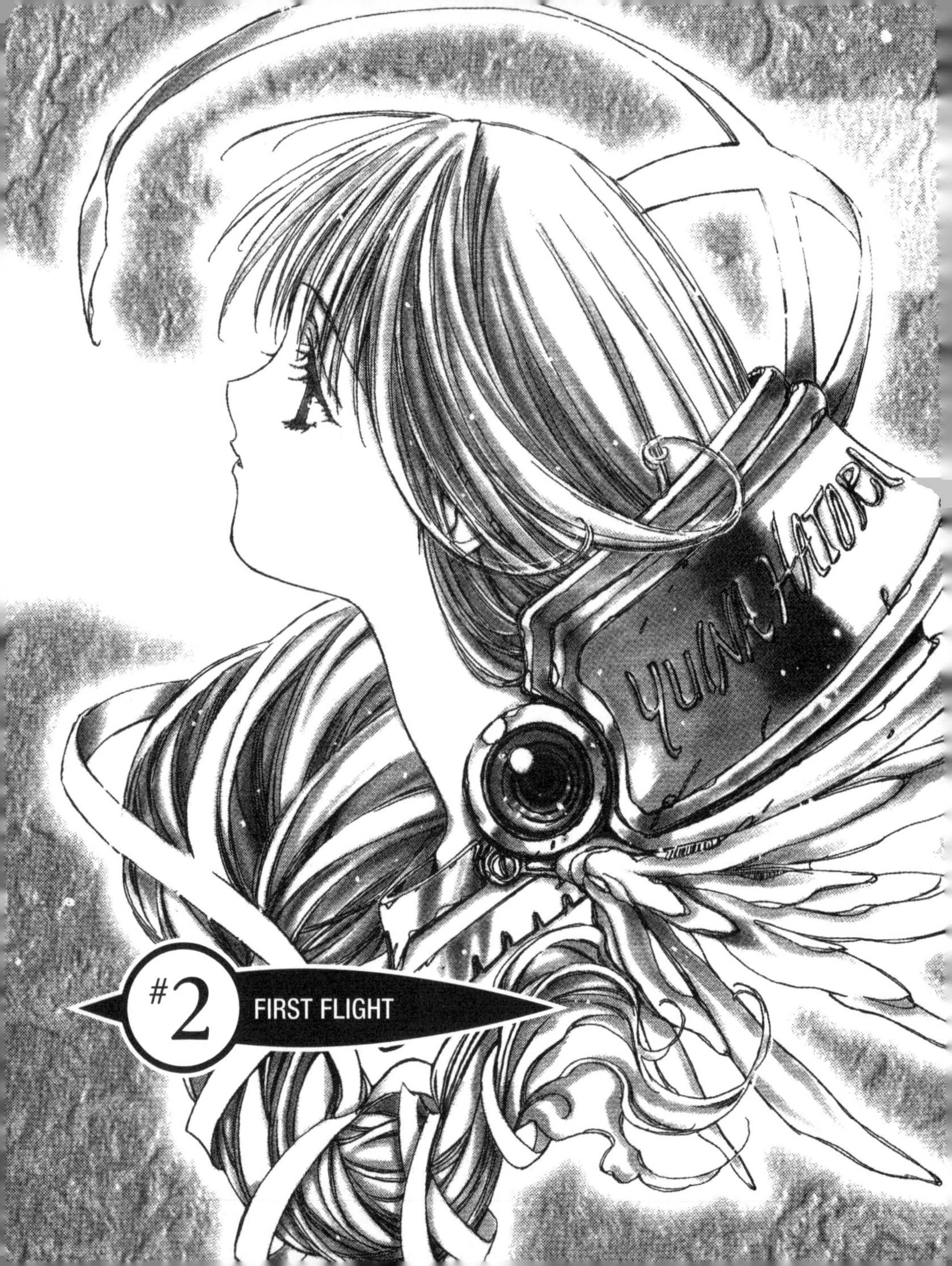
YUNA HATTORI
#2
FIRST FLIGHT

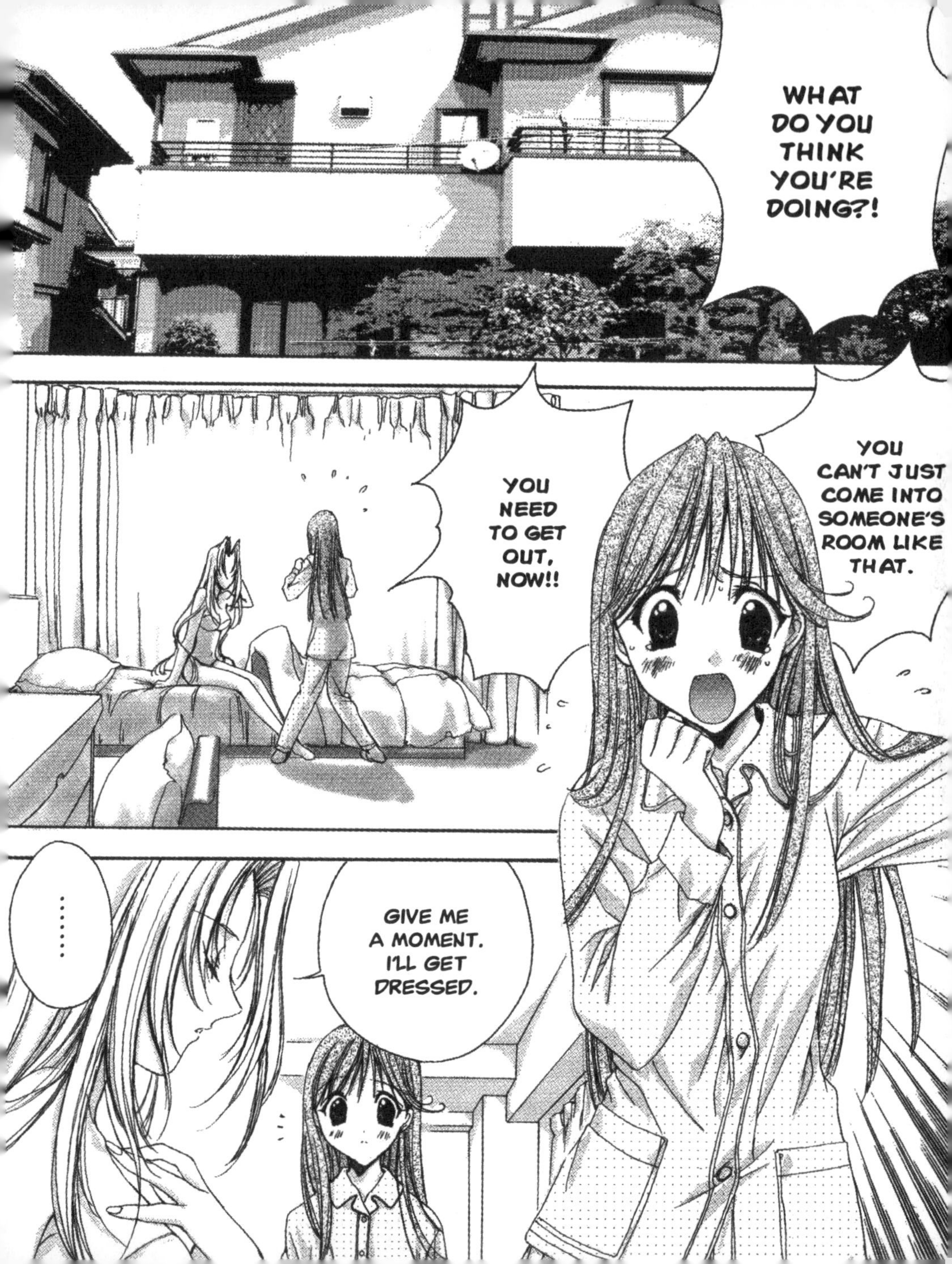
WHAT DO YOU THINK YOU'RE DOING?!
YOU CAN'T JUST COME INTO SOMEONE'S ROOM LIKE THAT.
YOU NEED TO GET OUT, NOW!!
GIVE ME A MOMENT. I'LL GET DRESSED.
......

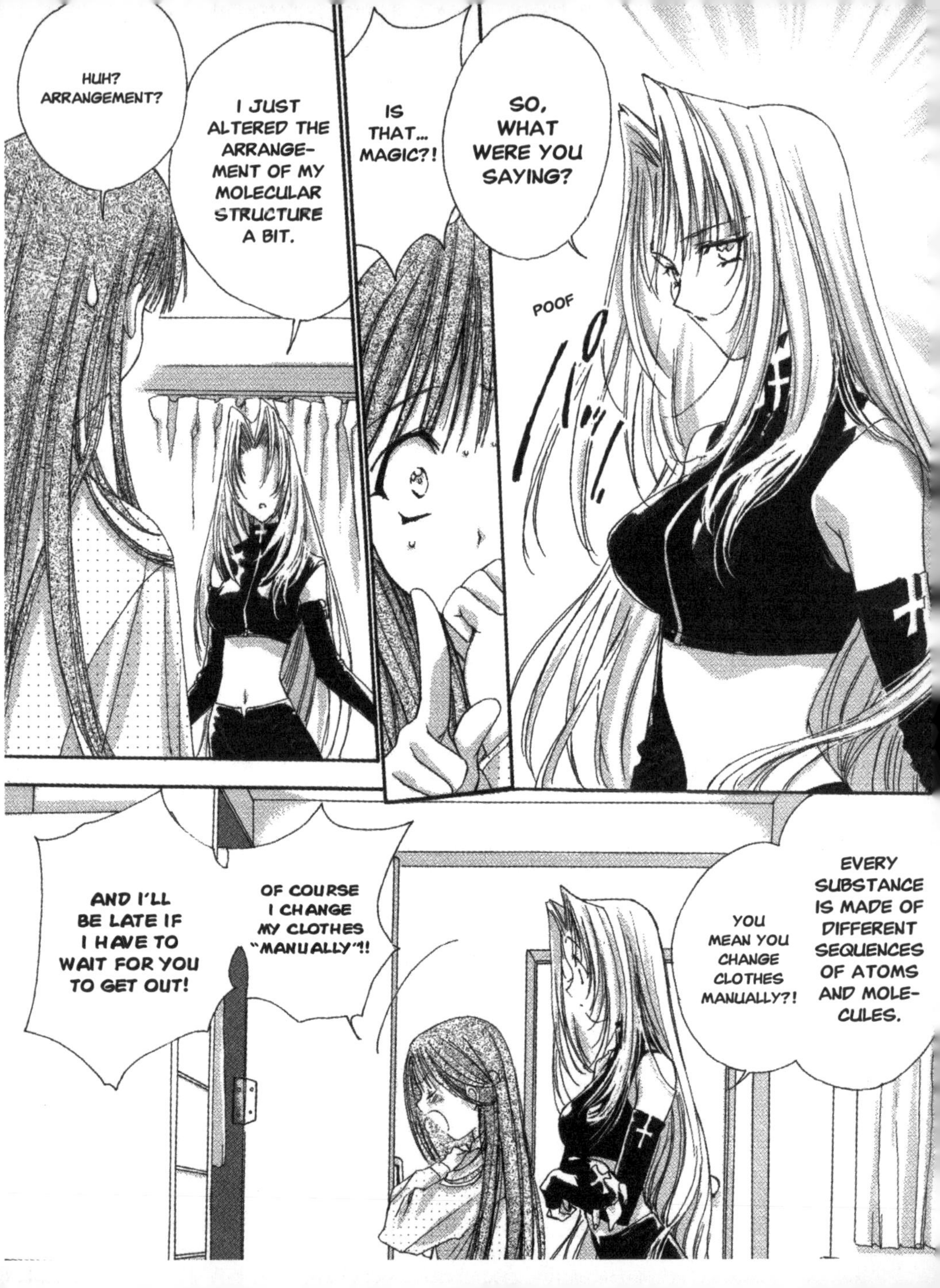
SO, WHAT WERE YOU SAYING?
POOF
IS THAT... MAGIC?!
I JUST ALTERED THE ARRANGEMENT OF MY MOLECULAR STRUCTURE A BIT.
HUH? ARRANGEMENT?
EVERY SUBSTANCE IS MADE OF DIFFERENT SEQUENCES OF ATOMS AND MOLECULES.
YOU MEAN YOU CHANGE CLOTHES MANUALLY?!
OF COURSE I CHANGE MY CLOTHES "MANUALLY"!!
AND I'LL BE LATE IF I HAVE TO WAIT FOR YOU TO GET OUT!

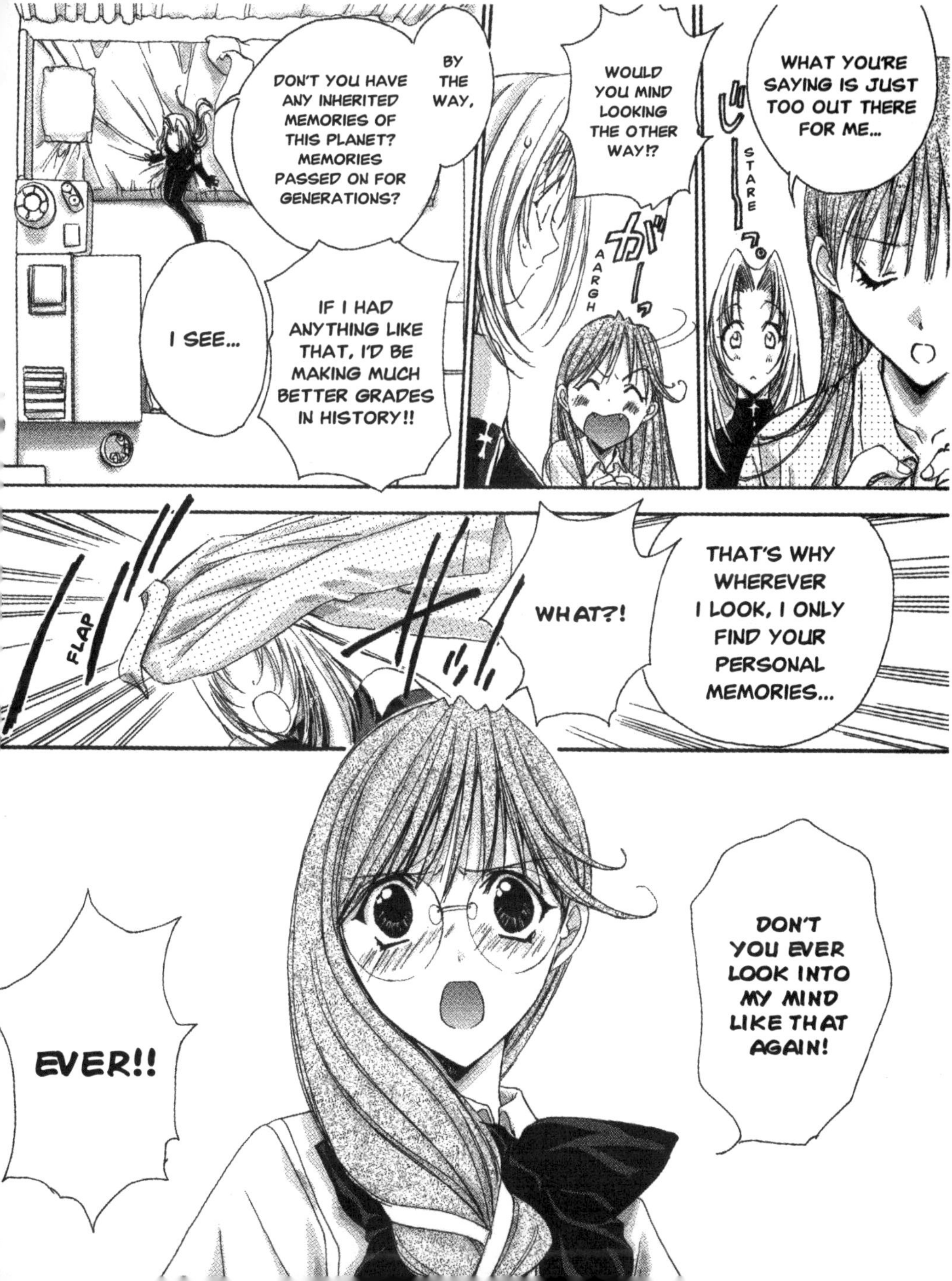
WHAT YOU'RE SAYING IS JUST TOO OUT THERE FOR ME...
STARE
WOULD YOU MIND LOOKING THE OTHER WAY!?
AARGH
BY THE WAY,
DON'T YOU HAVE ANY INHERITED MEMORIES OF THIS PLANET? MEMORIES PASSED ON FOR GENERATIONS?
IF I HAD ANYTHING LIKE THAT, I'D BE MAKING MUCH BETTER GRADES IN HISTORY!!
I SEE...
THAT'S WHY WHEREVER I LOOK, I ONLY FIND YOUR PERSONAL MEMORIES...
WHAT?!
FLAP
DON'T YOU EVER LOOK INTO MY MIND LIKE THAT AGAIN!
EVER!!

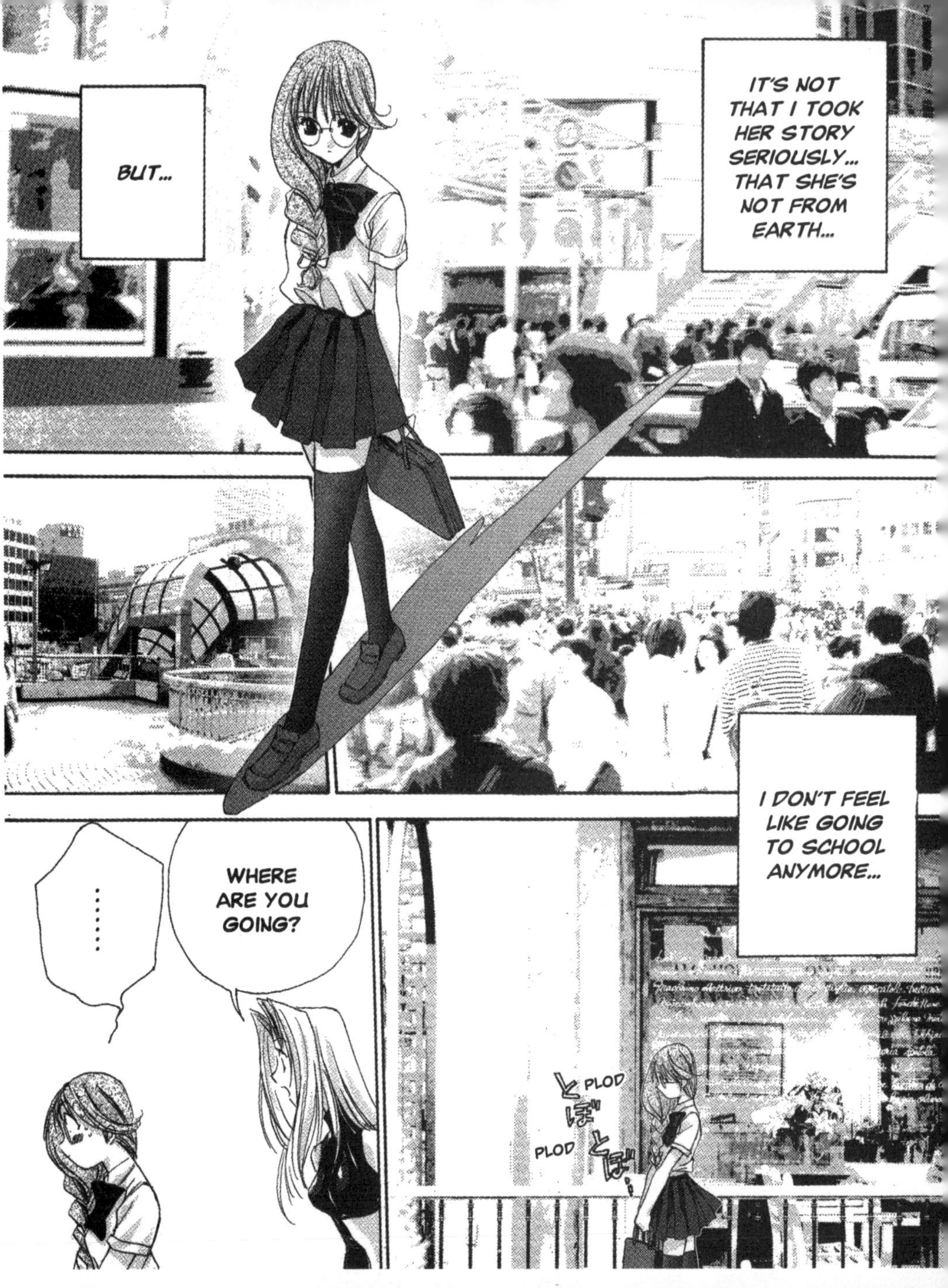
IT'S NOT THAT I TOOK HER STORY SERIOUSLY... THAT SHE'S NOT FROM EARTH...
BUT...
I DON'T FEEL LIKE GOING TO SCHOOL ANYMORE...
とぼ PLOD
とぼ PLOD
WHERE ARE YOU GOING?
.......

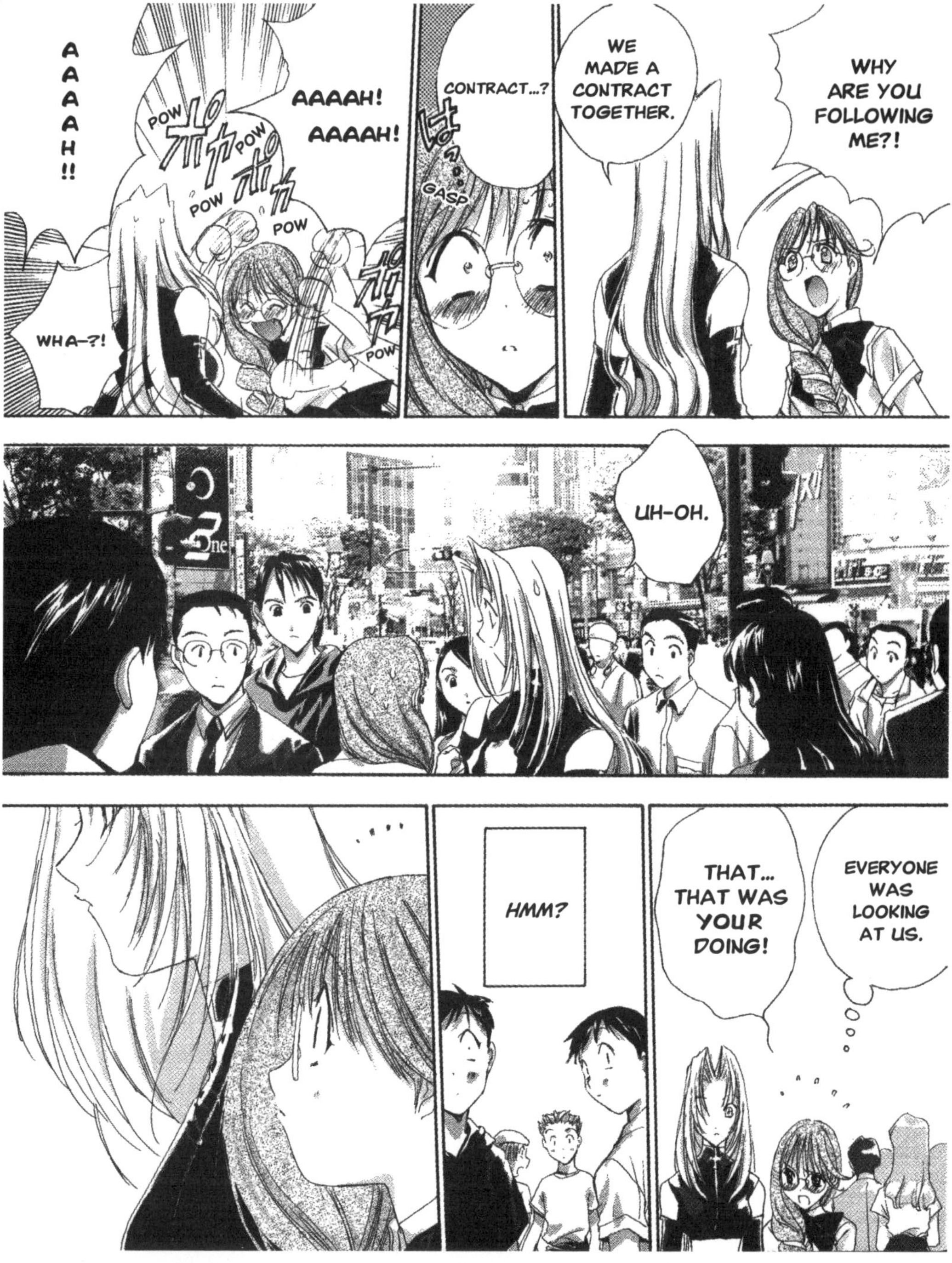
WHY ARE YOU FOLLOWING ME?!
WE MADE A CONTRACT TOGETHER.
CONTRACT...?
GASP
AAAAH! AAAAH!
AAAAAH!!
POW
POW
POW
POW
POW
WHA-?!
UH-OH.
EVERYONE WAS LOOKING AT US.
THAT... THAT WAS YOUR DOING!
HMM?
...

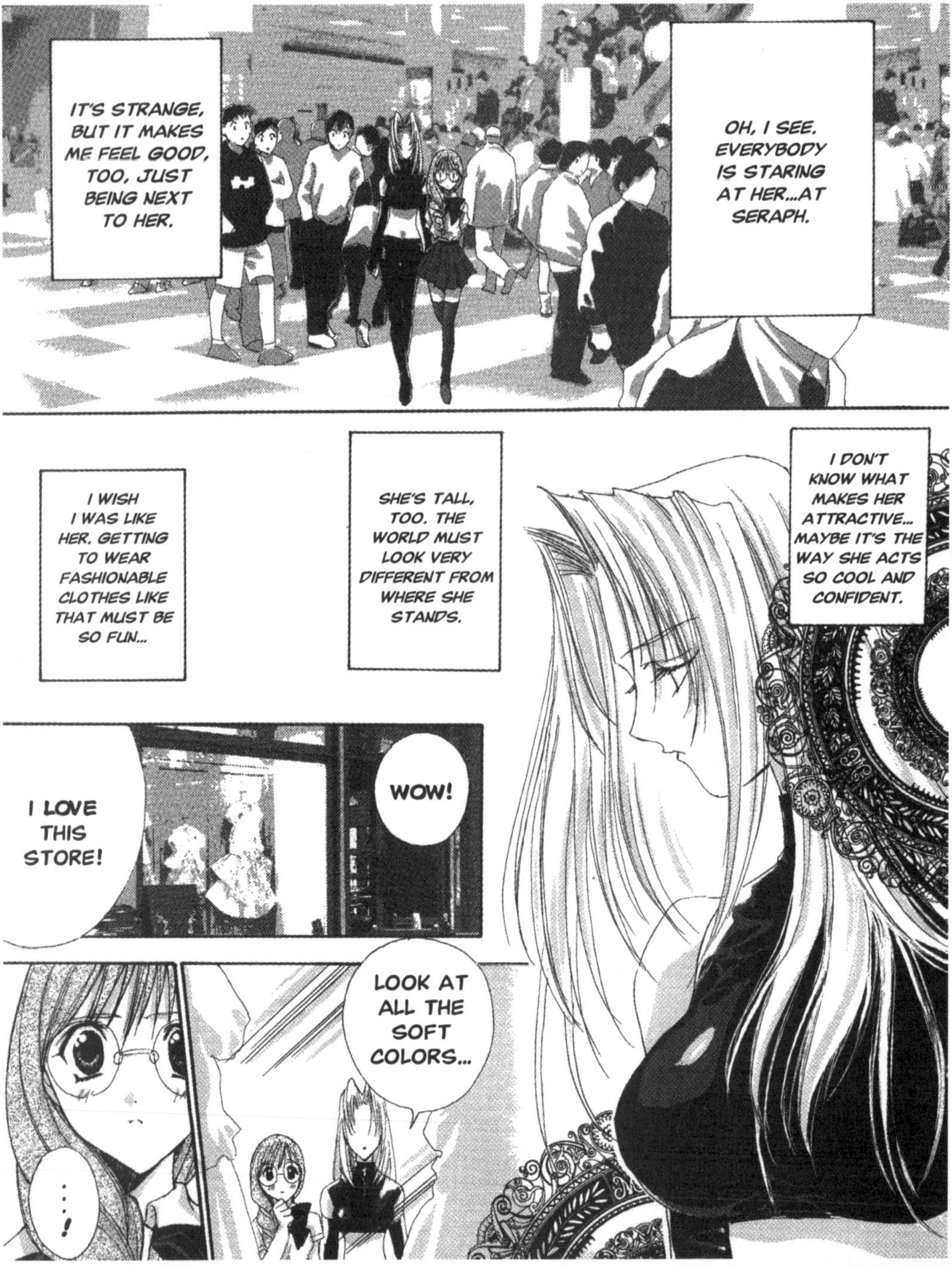
IT'S STRANGE, BUT IT MAKES ME FEEL GOOD, TOO, JUST BEING NEXT TO HER.
OH, I SEE. EVERYBODY IS STARING AT HER...AT SERAPH.
I WISH I WAS LIKE HER. GETTING TO WEAR FASHIONABLE CLOTHES LIKE THAT MUST BE SO FUN...
SHE'S TALL, TOO. THE WORLD MUST LOOK VERY DIFFERENT FROM WHERE SHE STANDS.
I DON'T KNOW WHAT MAKES HER ATTRACTIVE... MAYBE IT'S THE WAY SHE ACTS SO COOL AND CONFIDENT.
I LOVE THIS STORE!
WOW!
LOOK AT ALL THE SOFT COLORS...
...!

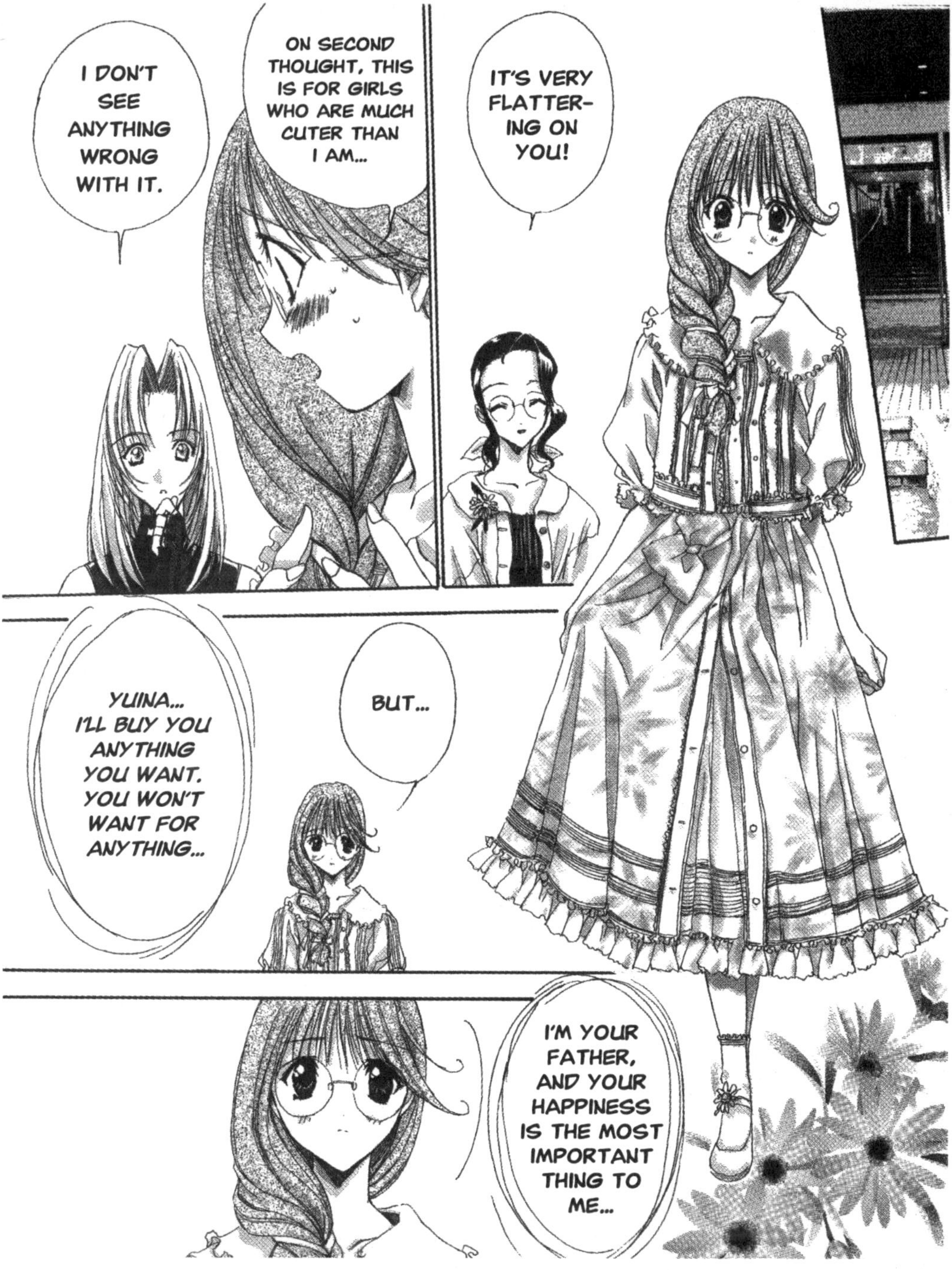
IT'S VERY FLATTER-ING ON YOU!
ON SECOND THOUGHT, THIS IS FOR GIRLS WHO ARE MUCH CUTER THAN I AM...
I DON'T SEE ANYTHING WRONG WITH IT.
BUT...
YUINA... I'LL BUY YOU ANYTHING YOU WANT. YOU WON'T WANT FOR ANYTHING...
I'M YOUR FATHER, AND YOUR HAPPINESS IS THE MOST IMPORTANT THING TO ME...

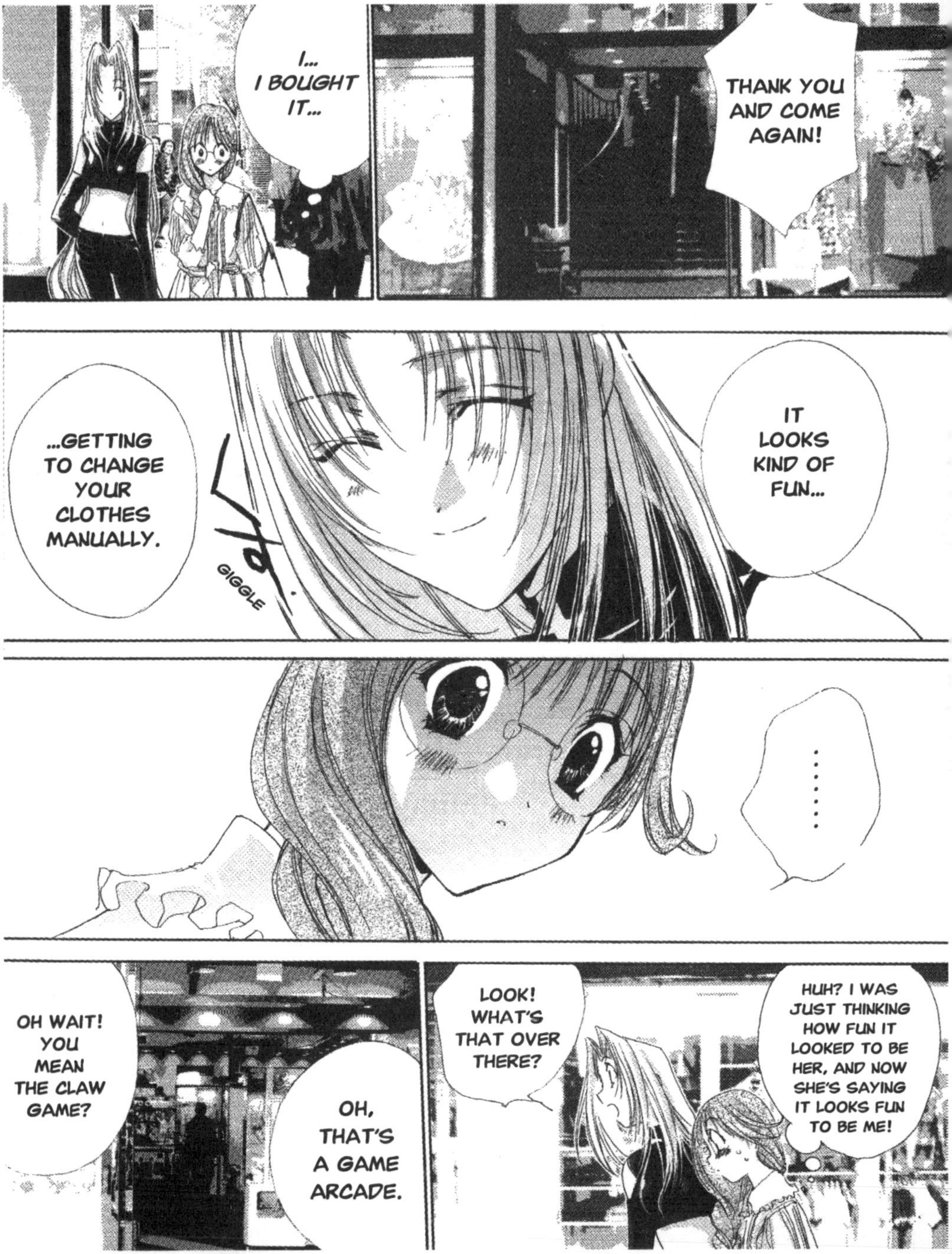
THANK YOU AND COME AGAIN!
I... I BOUGHT IT...
IT LOOKS KIND OF FUN...
...GETTING TO CHANGE YOUR CLOTHES MANUALLY.
GIGGLE
........
HUH? I WAS JUST THINKING HOW FUN IT LOOKED TO BE HER, AND NOW SHE'S SAYING IT LOOKS FUN TO BE ME!
LOOK! WHAT'S THAT OVER THERE?
OH, THAT'S A GAME ARCADE.
OH WAIT! YOU MEAN THE CLAW GAME?

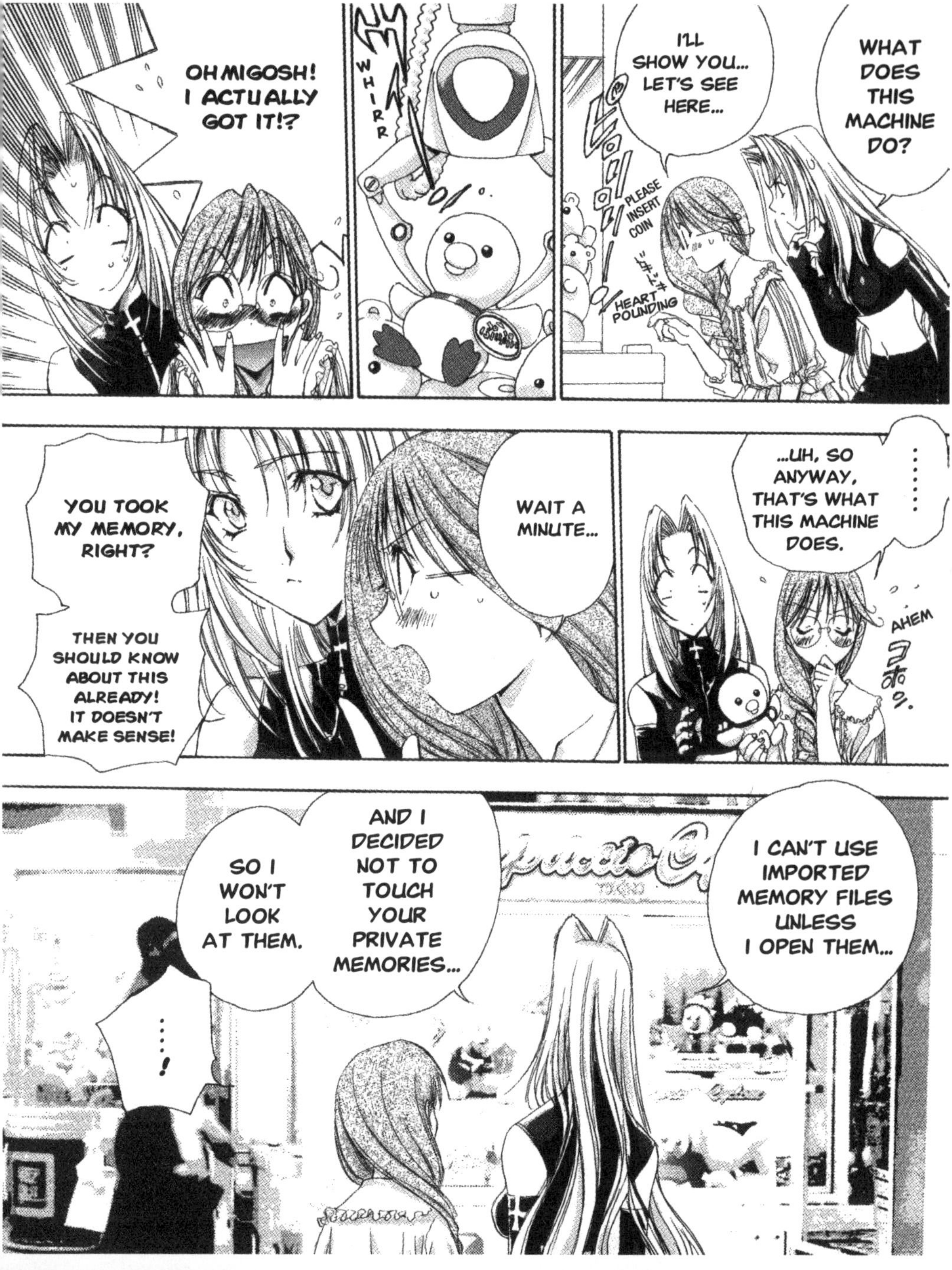

WHAT DOES THIS MACHINE DO?
I'LL SHOW YOU... LET'S SEE HERE...
PLEASE INSERT COIN
HEART POUNDING
WHIRR
OHMIGOSH! I ACTUALLY GOT IT!?
......
...UH, SO ANYWAY, THAT'S WHAT THIS MACHINE DOES.
AHEM
WAIT A MINUTE...
YOU TOOK MY MEMORY, RIGHT?
THEN YOU SHOULD KNOW ABOUT THIS ALREADY! IT DOESN'T MAKE SENSE!
I CAN'T USE IMPORTED MEMORY FILES UNLESS I OPEN THEM...
AND I DECIDED NOT TO TOUCH YOUR PRIVATE MEMORIES...
SO I WON'T LOOK AT THEM.
....!

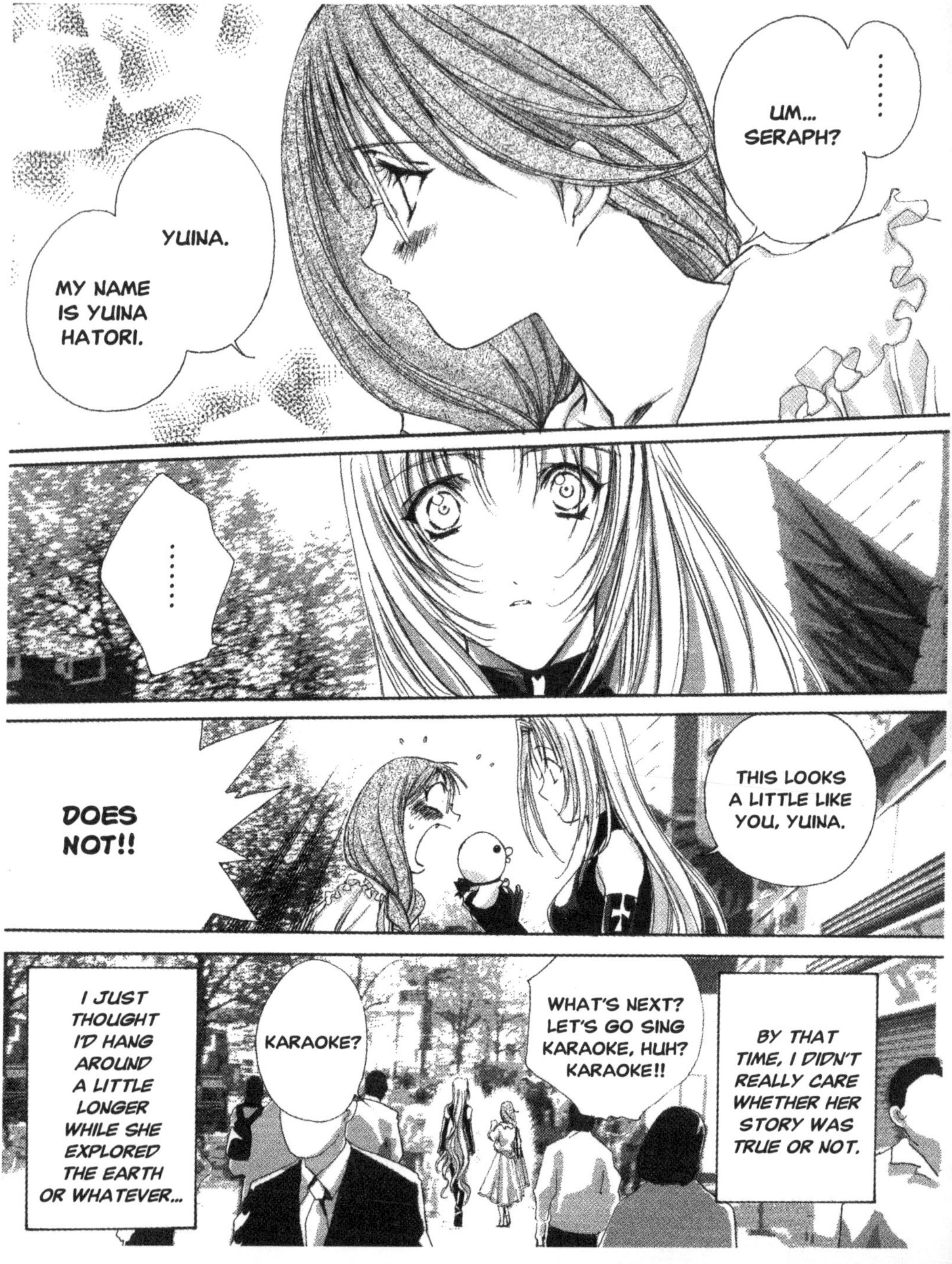

......
UM... SERAPH?
YUINA.
MY NAME IS YUINA HATORI.
......
THIS LOOKS A LITTLE LIKE YOU, YUINA.
DOES NOT!!
BY THAT TIME, I DIDN'T REALLY CARE WHETHER HER STORY WAS TRUE OR NOT.
WHAT'S NEXT? LET'S GO SING KARAOKE, HUH? KARAOKE!!
KARAOKE?
I JUST THOUGHT I'D HANG AROUND A LITTLE LONGER WHILE SHE EXPLORED THE EARTH OR WHATEVER...

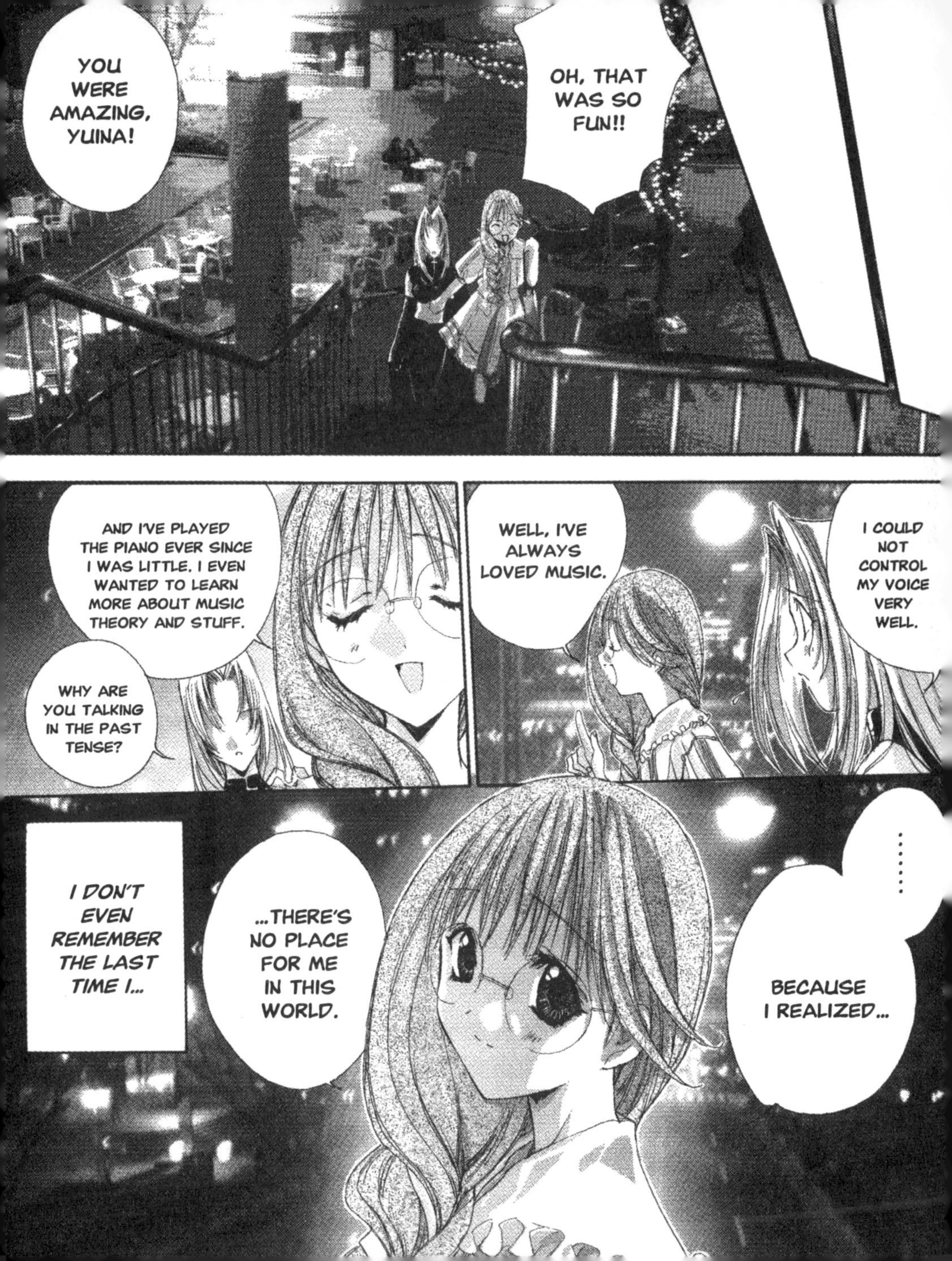
OH, THAT WAS SO FUN!!
YOU WERE AMAZING, YUINA!
I COULD NOT CONTROL MY VOICE VERY WELL.
WELL, I'VE ALWAYS LOVED MUSIC.
AND I'VE PLAYED THE PIANO EVER SINCE I WAS LITTLE. I EVEN WANTED TO LEARN MORE ABOUT MUSIC THEORY AND STUFF.
WHY ARE YOU TALKING IN THE PAST TENSE?
......
BECAUSE I REALIZED...
...THERE'S NO PLACE FOR ME IN THIS WORLD.
I DON'T EVEN REMEMBER THE LAST TIME I...

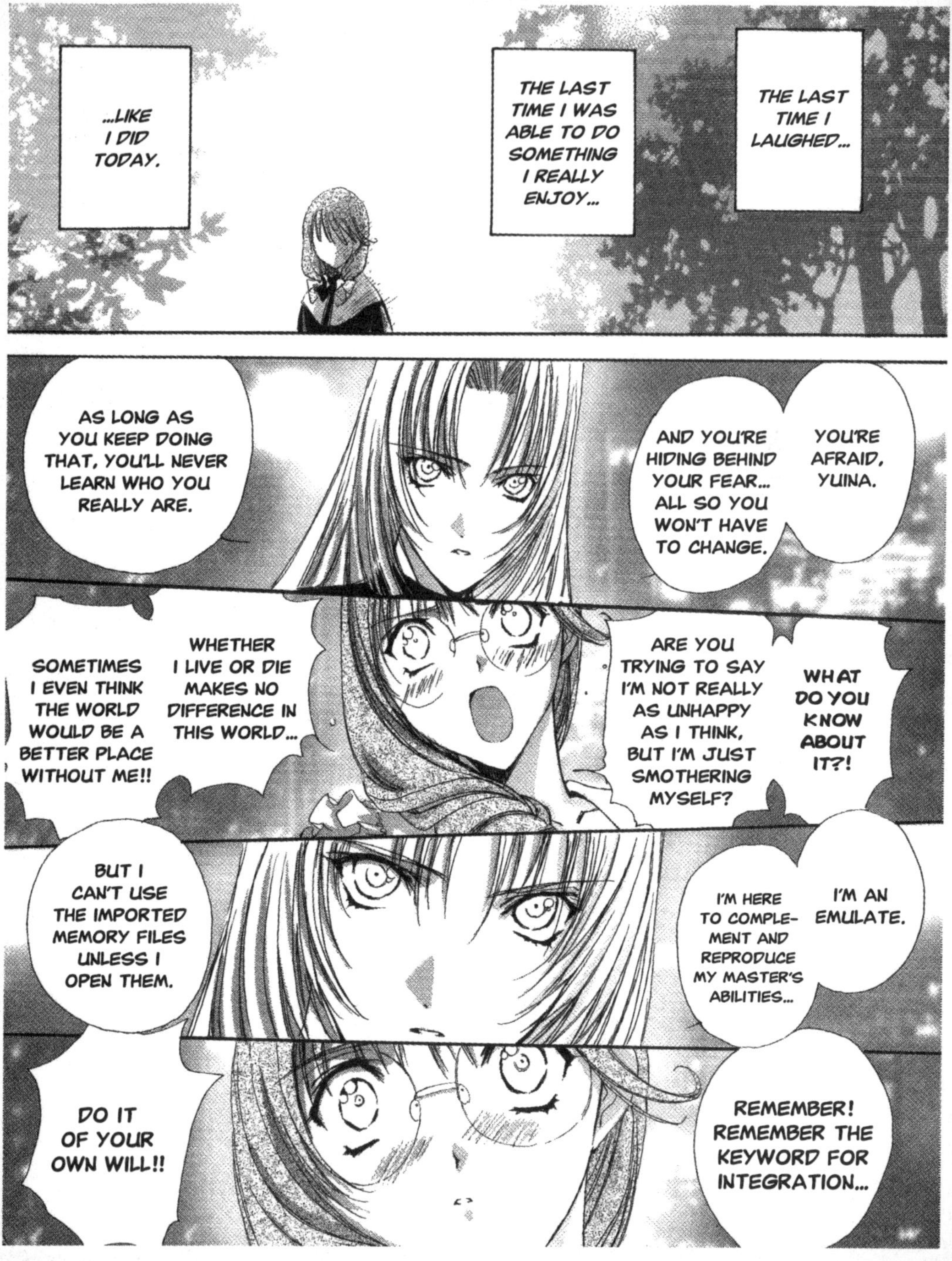
THE LAST TIME I LAUGHED...
THE LAST TIME I WAS ABLE TO DO SOMETHING I REALLY ENJOY...
...LIKE I DID TODAY.
YOU'RE AFRAID, YUINA.
AND YOU'RE HIDING BEHIND YOUR FEAR... ALL SO YOU WON'T HAVE TO CHANGE.
AS LONG AS YOU KEEP DOING THAT, YOU'LL NEVER LEARN WHO YOU REALLY ARE.
WHAT DO YOU KNOW ABOUT IT?!
ARE YOU TRYING TO SAY I'M NOT REALLY AS UNHAPPY AS I THINK, BUT I'M JUST SMOTHERING MYSELF?
WHETHER I LIVE OR DIE MAKES NO DIFFERENCE IN THIS WORLD...
SOMETIMES I EVEN THINK THE WORLD WOULD BE A BETTER PLACE WITHOUT ME!!
I'M AN EMULATE.
I'M HERE TO COMPLE-MENT AND REPRODUCE MY MASTER'S ABILITIES...
BUT I CAN'T USE THE IMPORTED MEMORY FILES UNLESS I OPEN THEM.
REMEMBER! REMEMBER THE KEYWORD FOR INTEGRATION...
DO IT OF YOUR OWN WILL!!

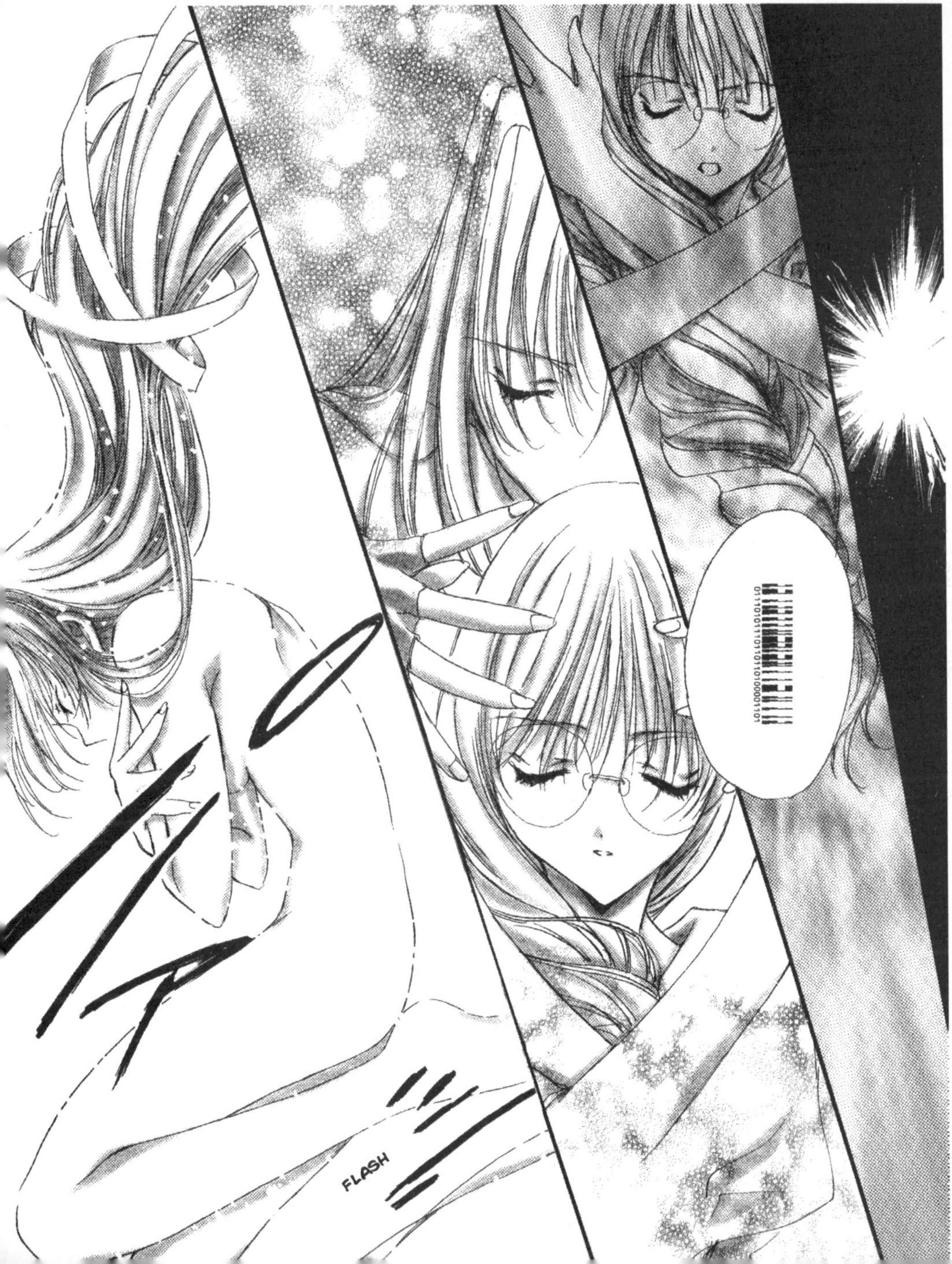
0111010111011010100001101
FLASH

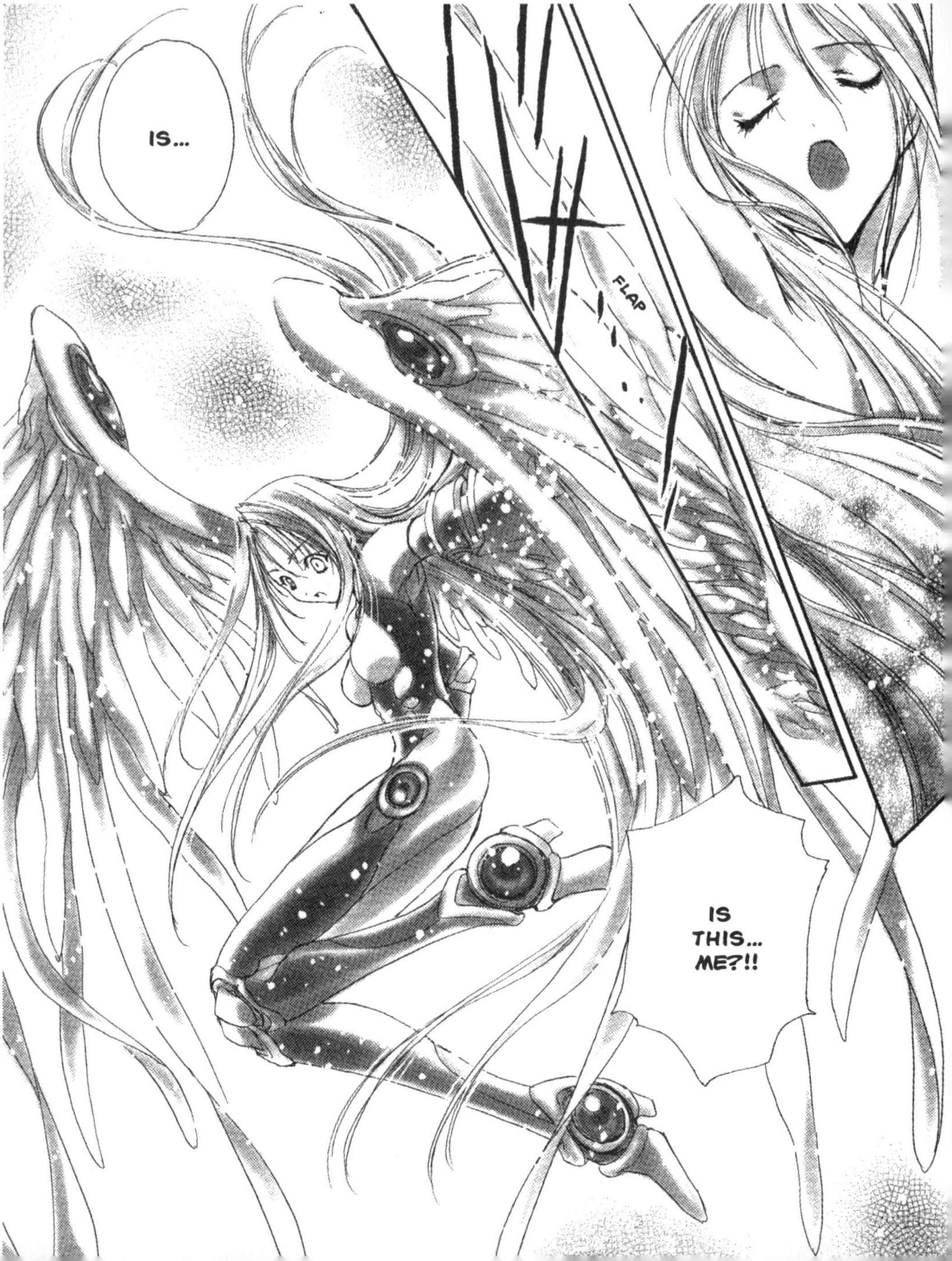
FLAP
IS...
IS THIS... ME?!!

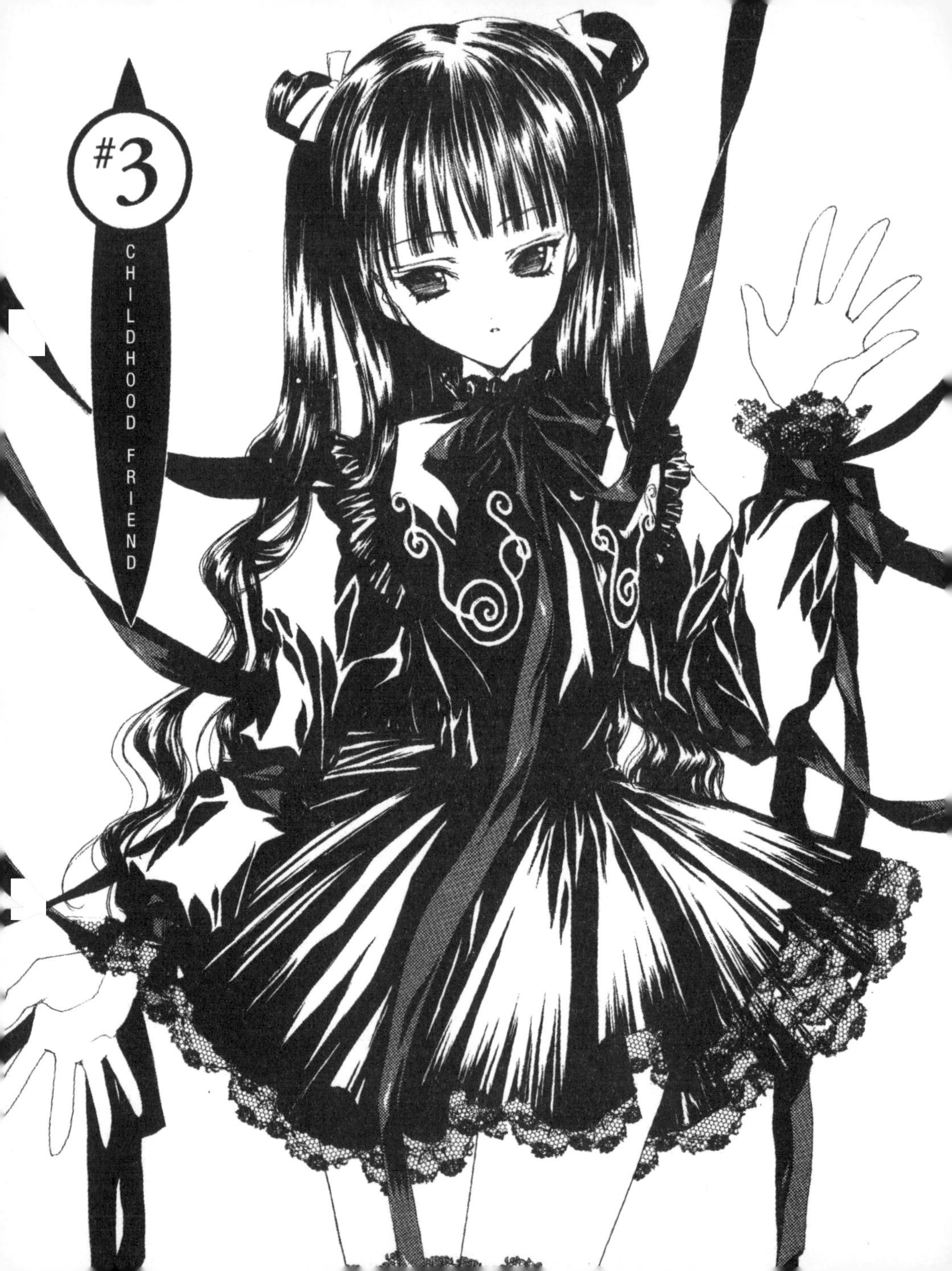
#3
CHILDHOOD FRIEND

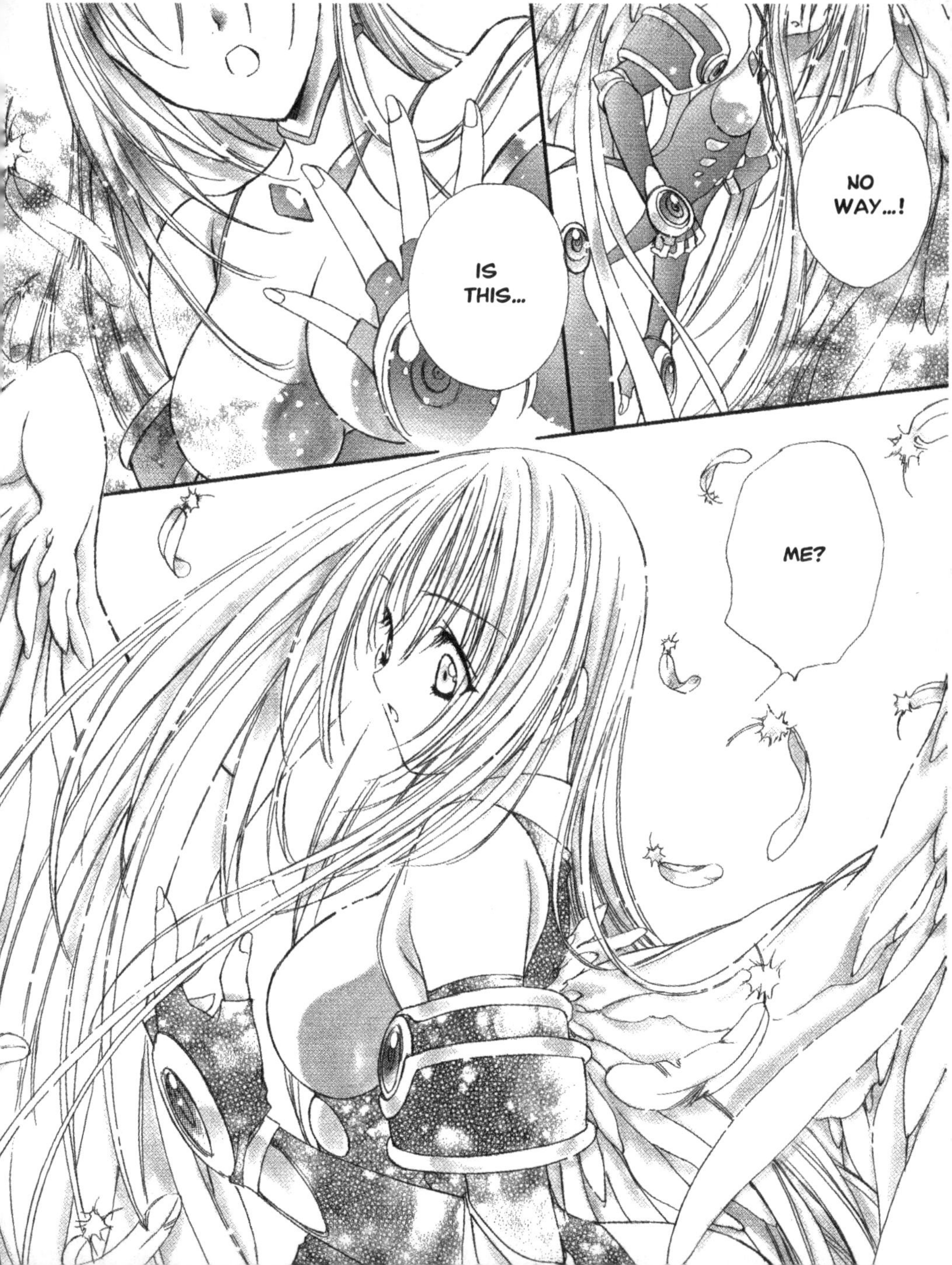
NO WAY...!
IS THIS...
ME?

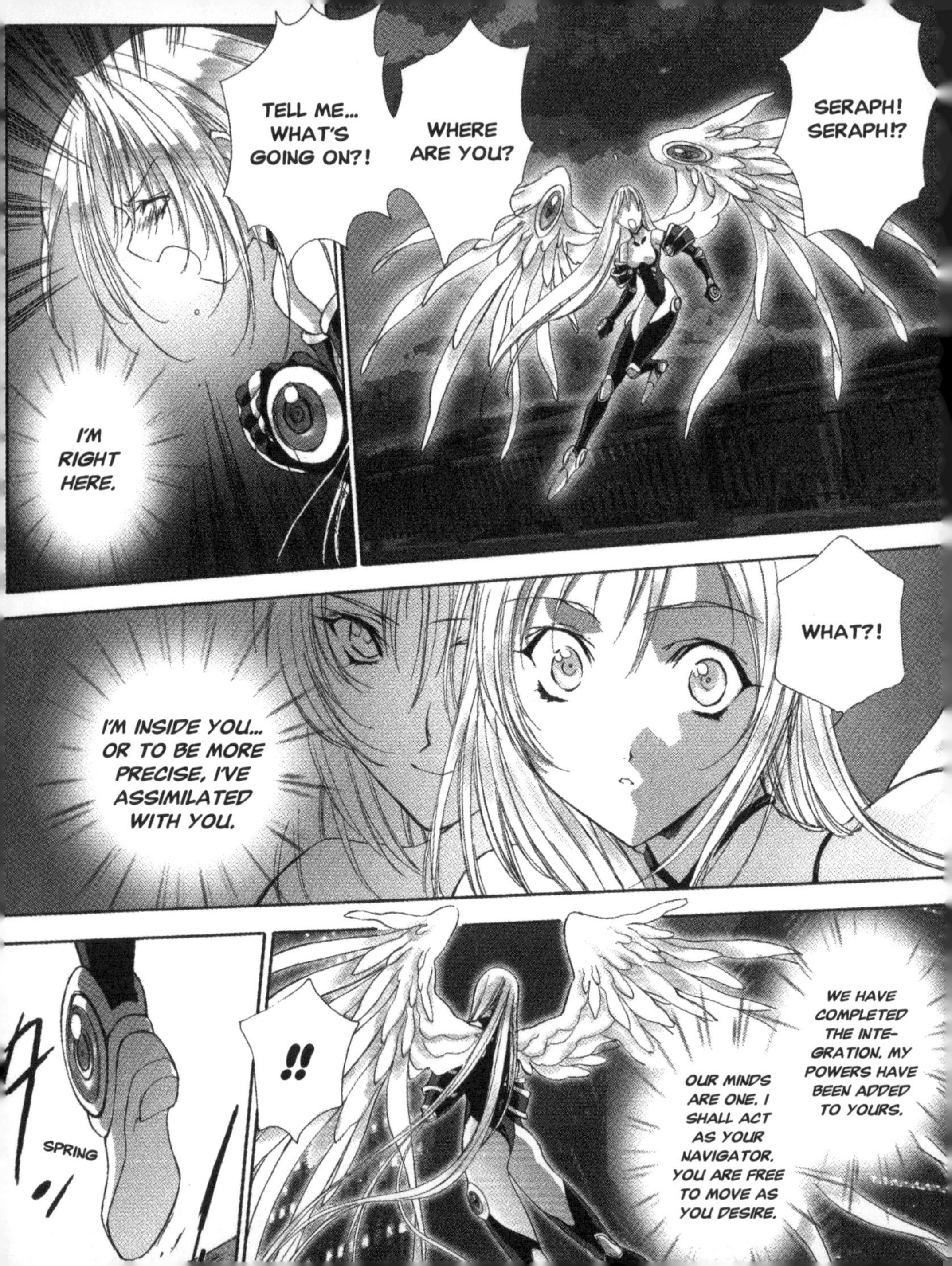
SERAPH! SERAPH!?
WHERE ARE YOU?
TELL ME... WHAT'S GOING ON?!
I'M RIGHT HERE.
WHAT?!
I'M INSIDE YOU... OR TO BE MORE PRECISE, I'VE ASSIMILATED WITH YOU.
WE HAVE COMPLETED THE INTE-GRATION. MY POWERS HAVE BEEN ADDED TO YOURS.
OUR MINDS ARE ONE. I SHALL ACT AS YOUR NAVIGATOR. YOU ARE FREE TO MOVE AS YOU DESIRE.
!!
SPRING

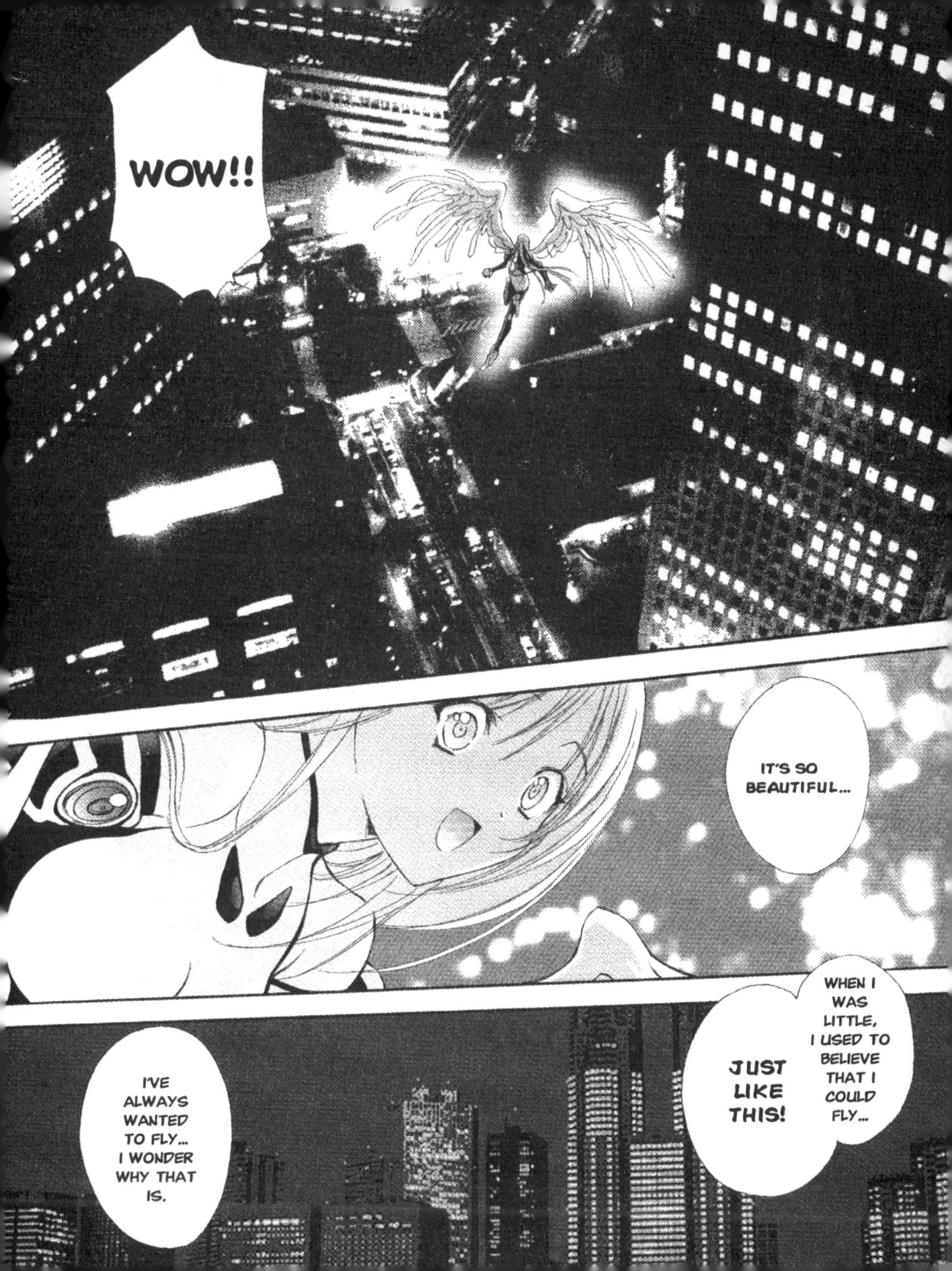
WOW!!
IT'S SO BEAUTIFUL...
WHEN I WAS LITTLE, I USED TO BELIEVE THAT I COULD FLY...
JUST LIKE THIS!
I'VE ALWAYS WANTED TO FLY... I WONDER WHY THAT IS.

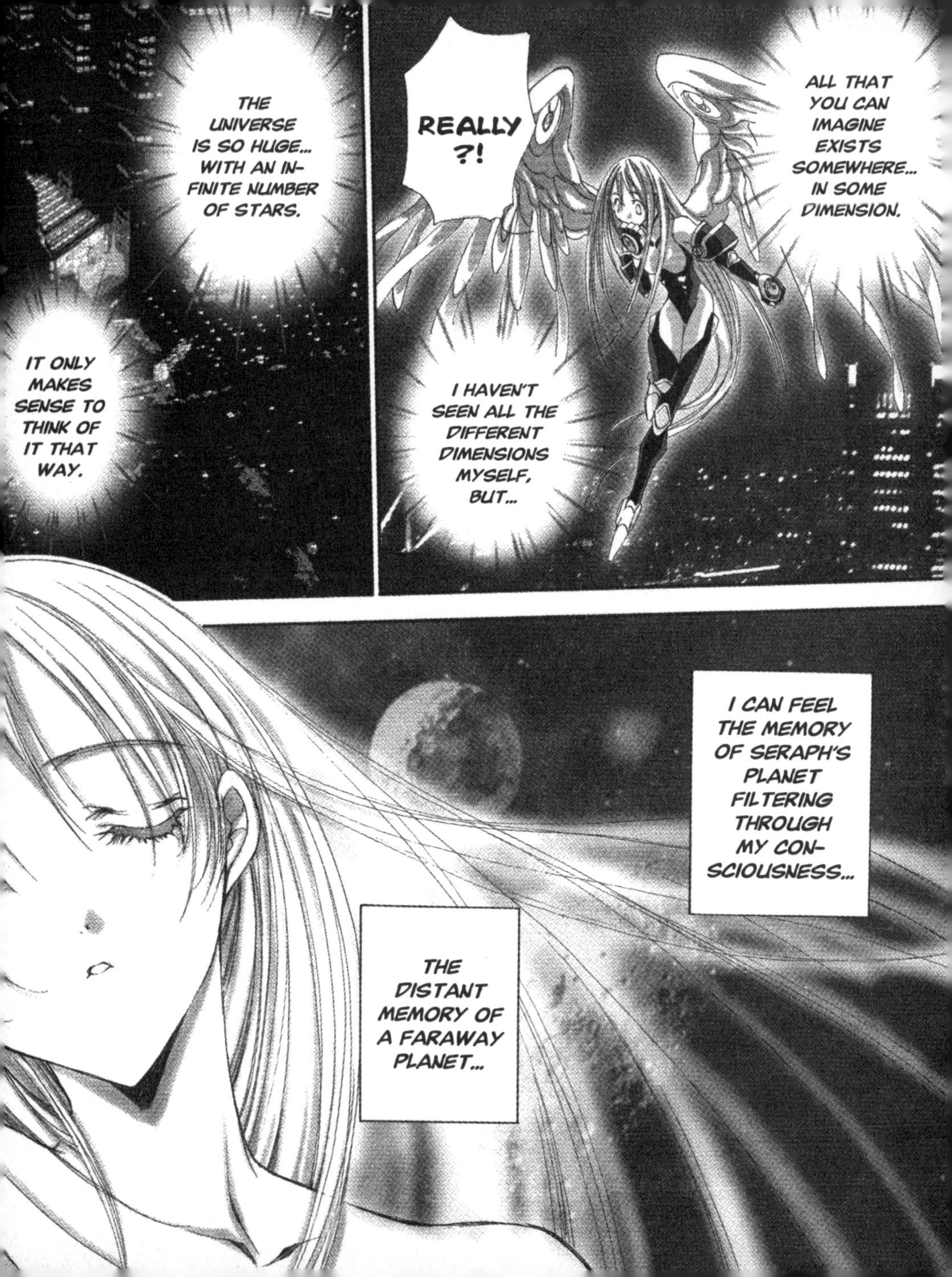
ALL THAT YOU CAN IMAGINE EXISTS SOMEWHERE... IN SOME DIMENSION.
REALLY ?!
I HAVEN'T SEEN ALL THE DIFFERENT DIMENSIONS MYSELF, BUT...
THE UNIVERSE IS SO HUGE... WITH AN IN-FINITE NUMBER OF STARS.
IT ONLY MAKES SENSE TO THINK OF IT THAT WAY.
I CAN FEEL THE MEMORY OF SERAPH'S PLANET FILTERING THROUGH MY CON-SCIOUSNESS...
THE DISTANT MEMORY OF A FARAWAY PLANET...

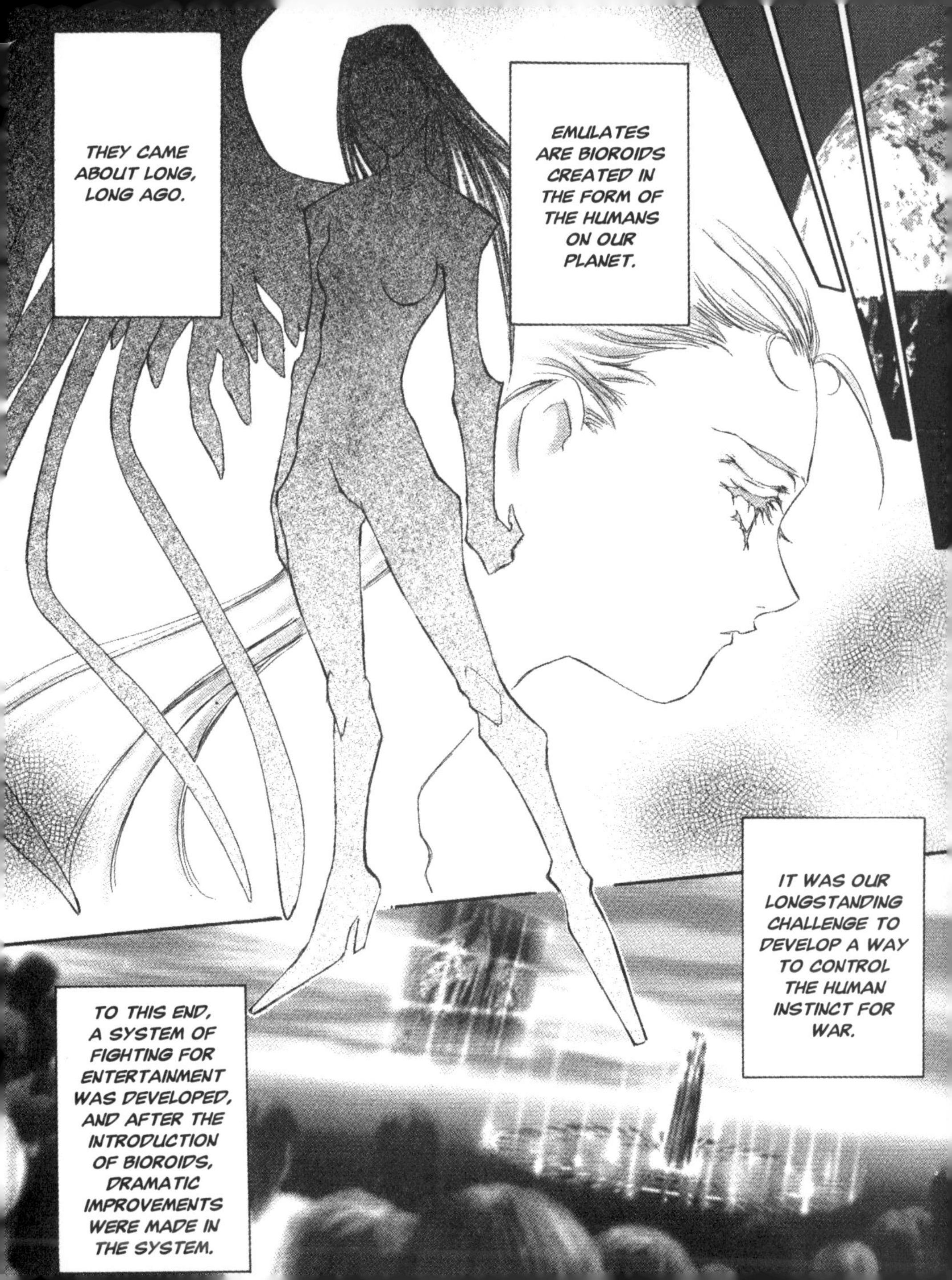
THEY CAME ABOUT LONG, LONG AGO.
EMULATES ARE BIOROIDS CREATED IN THE FORM OF THE HUMANS ON OUR PLANET.
IT WAS OUR LONGSTANDING CHALLENGE TO DEVELOP A WAY TO CONTROL THE HUMAN INSTINCT FOR WAR.
TO THIS END, A SYSTEM OF FIGHTING FOR ENTERTAINMENT WAS DEVELOPED, AND AFTER THE INTRODUCTION OF BIOROIDS, DRAMATIC IMPROVEMENTS WERE MADE IN THE SYSTEM.

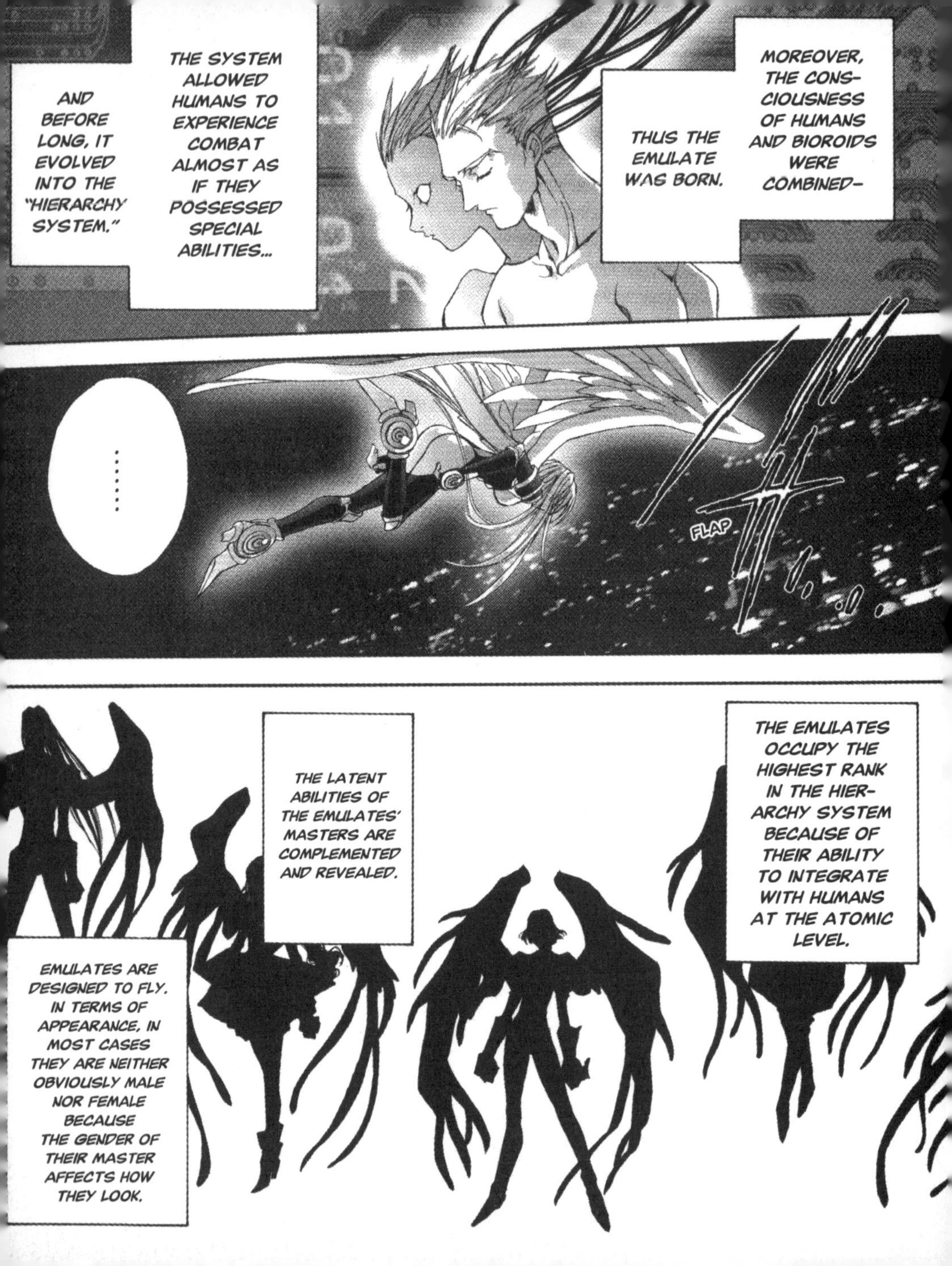
MOREOVER, THE CONSCIOUSNESS OF HUMANS AND BIOROIDS WERE COMBINED–
THUS THE EMULATE WAS BORN.
THE SYSTEM ALLOWED HUMANS TO EXPERIENCE COMBAT ALMOST AS IF THEY POSSESSED SPECIAL ABILITIES...
AND BEFORE LONG, IT EVOLVED INTO THE "HIERARCHY SYSTEM."
......
FLAP
THE EMULATES OCCUPY THE HIGHEST RANK IN THE HIERARCHY SYSTEM BECAUSE OF THEIR ABILITY TO INTEGRATE WITH HUMANS AT THE ATOMIC LEVEL.
THE LATENT ABILITIES OF THE EMULATES' MASTERS ARE COMPLEMENTED AND REVEALED.
EMULATES ARE DESIGNED TO FLY. IN TERMS OF APPEARANCE, IN MOST CASES THEY ARE NEITHER OBVIOUSLY MALE NOR FEMALE BECAUSE THE GENDER OF THEIR MASTER AFFECTS HOW THEY LOOK.

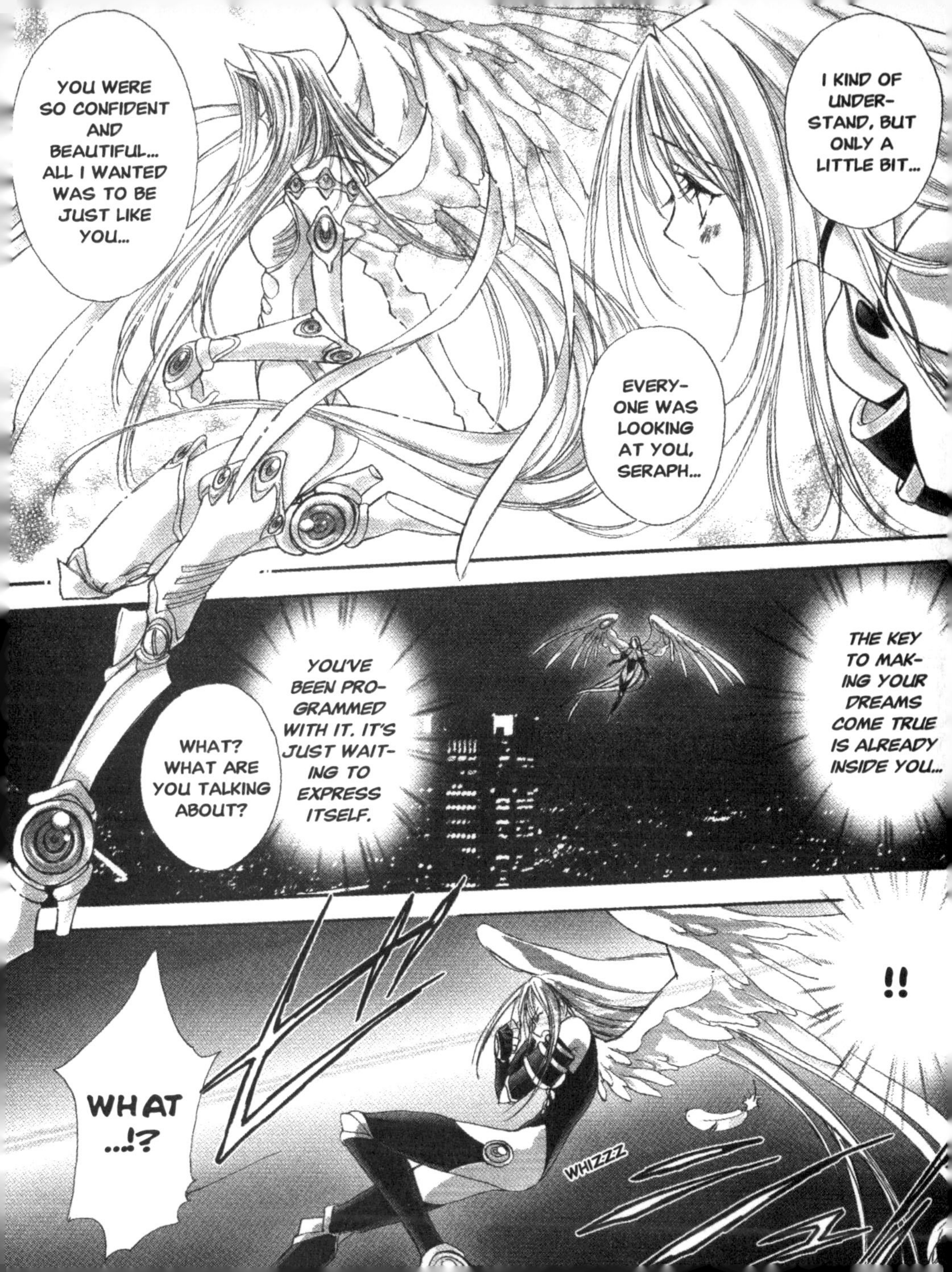
I KIND OF UNDER-STAND, BUT ONLY A LITTLE BIT...
YOU WERE SO CONFIDENT AND BEAUTIFUL... ALL I WANTED WAS TO BE JUST LIKE YOU...
EVERY-ONE WAS LOOKING AT YOU, SERAPH...
THE KEY TO MAK-ING YOUR DREAMS COME TRUE IS ALREADY INSIDE YOU...
YOU'VE BEEN PRO-GRAMMED WITH IT. IT'S JUST WAIT-ING TO EXPRESS ITSELF.
WHAT? WHAT ARE YOU TALKING ABOUT?
!!
WHIZZZ
WHAT ...!?

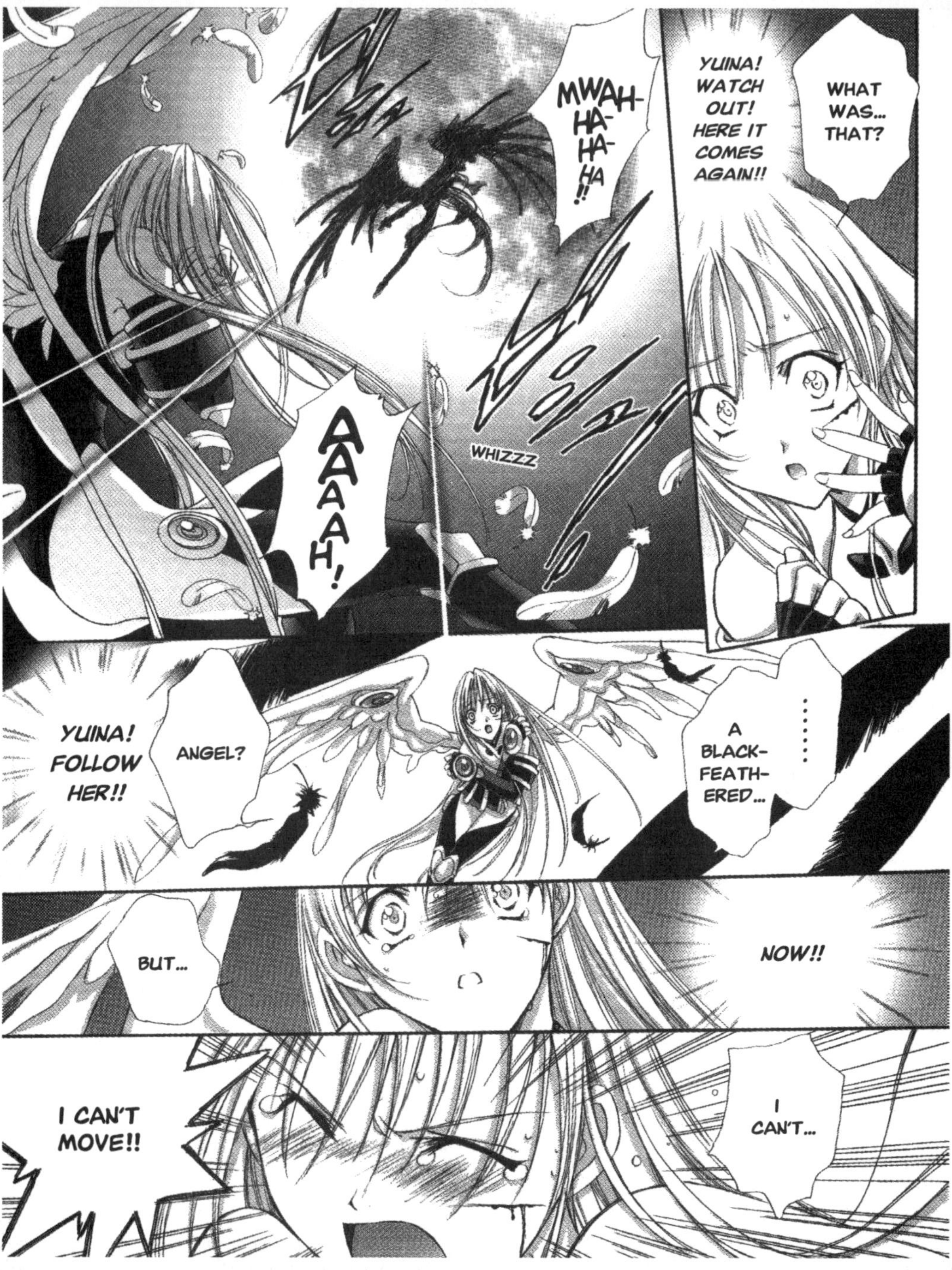
WHAT WAS... THAT?
YUINA! WATCH OUT! HERE IT COMES AGAIN!!
MWAH-HA-HA-HA!!
WHIZZZ
AAAAAH!
A BLACK-FEATHERED...
......
ANGEL?
YUINA! FOLLOW HER!!
NOW!!
BUT...
I CAN'T...
I CAN'T MOVE!!

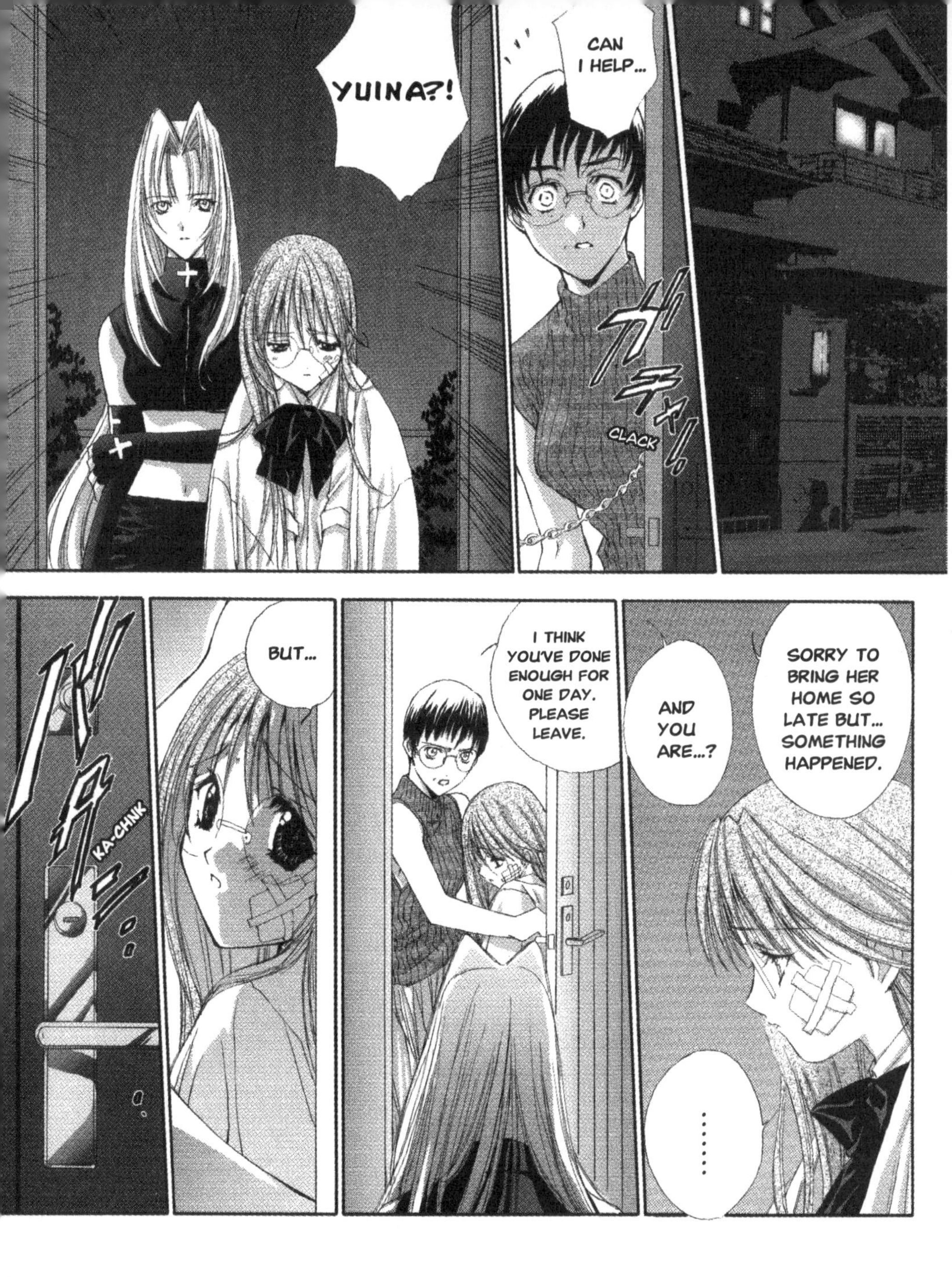
CAN I HELP...
CLACK
YUINA?!
SORRY TO BRING HER HOME SO LATE BUT... SOMETHING HAPPENED.
......
AND YOU ARE...?
I THINK YOU'VE DONE ENOUGH FOR ONE DAY. PLEASE LEAVE.
BUT...
KA-CHNK

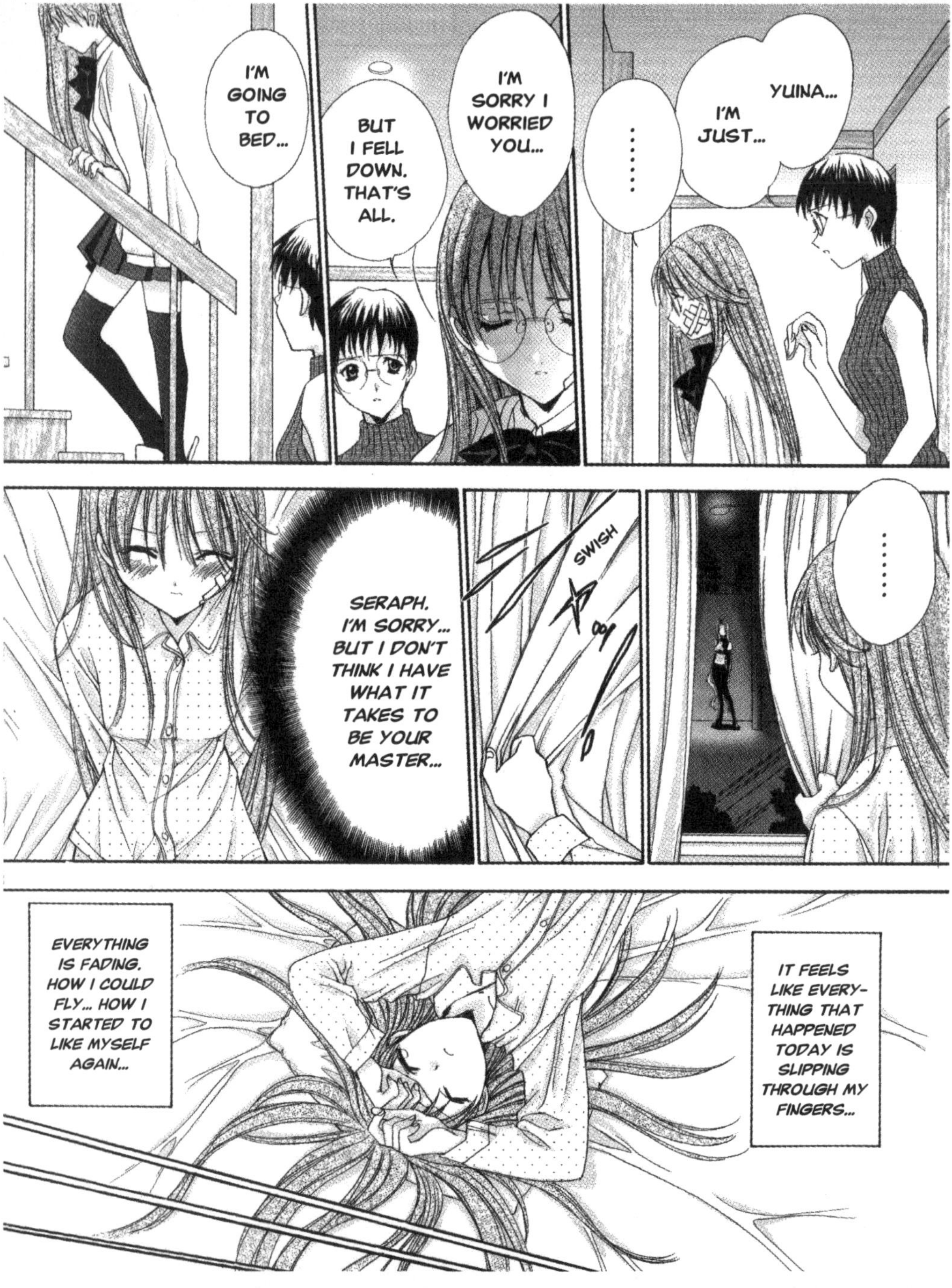
YUINA...
I'M JUST...
......
I'M SORRY I WORRIED YOU...
BUT I FELL DOWN. THAT'S ALL.
I'M GOING TO BED...
......
SWISH
SERAPH. I'M SORRY... BUT I DON'T THINK I HAVE WHAT IT TAKES TO BE YOUR MASTER...
IT FEELS LIKE EVERY-THING THAT HAPPENED TODAY IS SLIPPING THROUGH MY FINGERS...
EVERYTHING IS FADING. HOW I COULD FLY... HOW I STARTED TO LIKE MYSELF AGAIN...

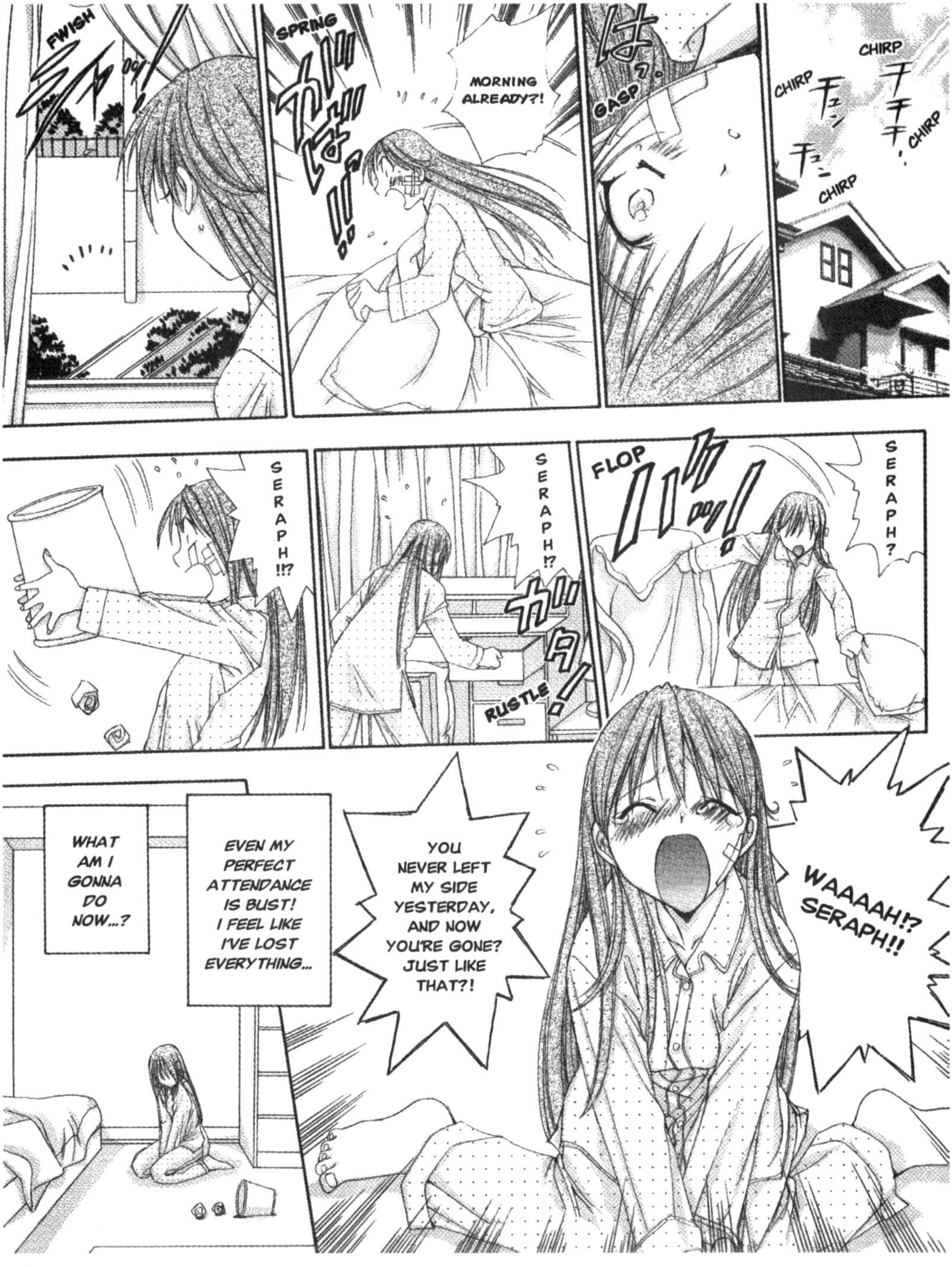

CHIRP
CHIRP
CHIRP
CHIRP
GASP
MORNING ALREADY?!
SPRING
FWISH
SERAPH?
FLOP
SERAPH!?
RUSTLE
SERAPH!!?
WAAAAH!? SERAPH!!
YOU NEVER LEFT MY SIDE YESTERDAY, AND NOW YOU'RE GONE? JUST LIKE THAT?!
EVEN MY PERFECT ATTENDANCE IS BUST! I FEEL LIKE I'VE LOST EVERYTHING...
WHAT AM I GONNA DO NOW...?

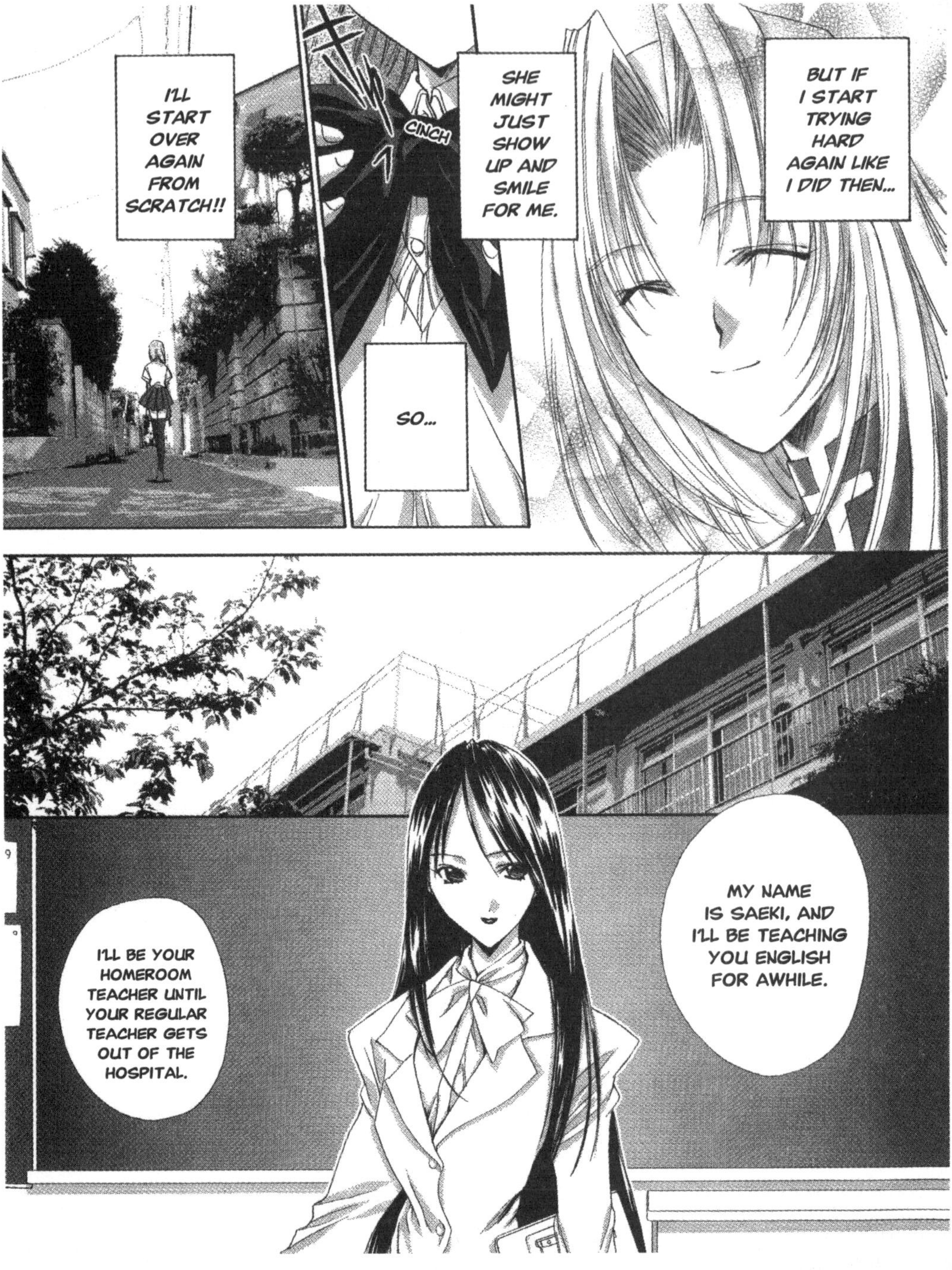
BUT IF I START TRYING HARD AGAIN LIKE I DID THEN...
SHE MIGHT JUST SHOW UP AND SMILE FOR ME.
CINCH
SO...
I'LL START OVER AGAIN FROM SCRATCH!!
MY NAME IS SAEKI, AND I'LL BE TEACHING YOU ENGLISH FOR AWHILE.
I'LL BE YOUR HOMEROOM TEACHER UNTIL YOUR REGULAR TEACHER GETS OUT OF THE HOSPITAL.

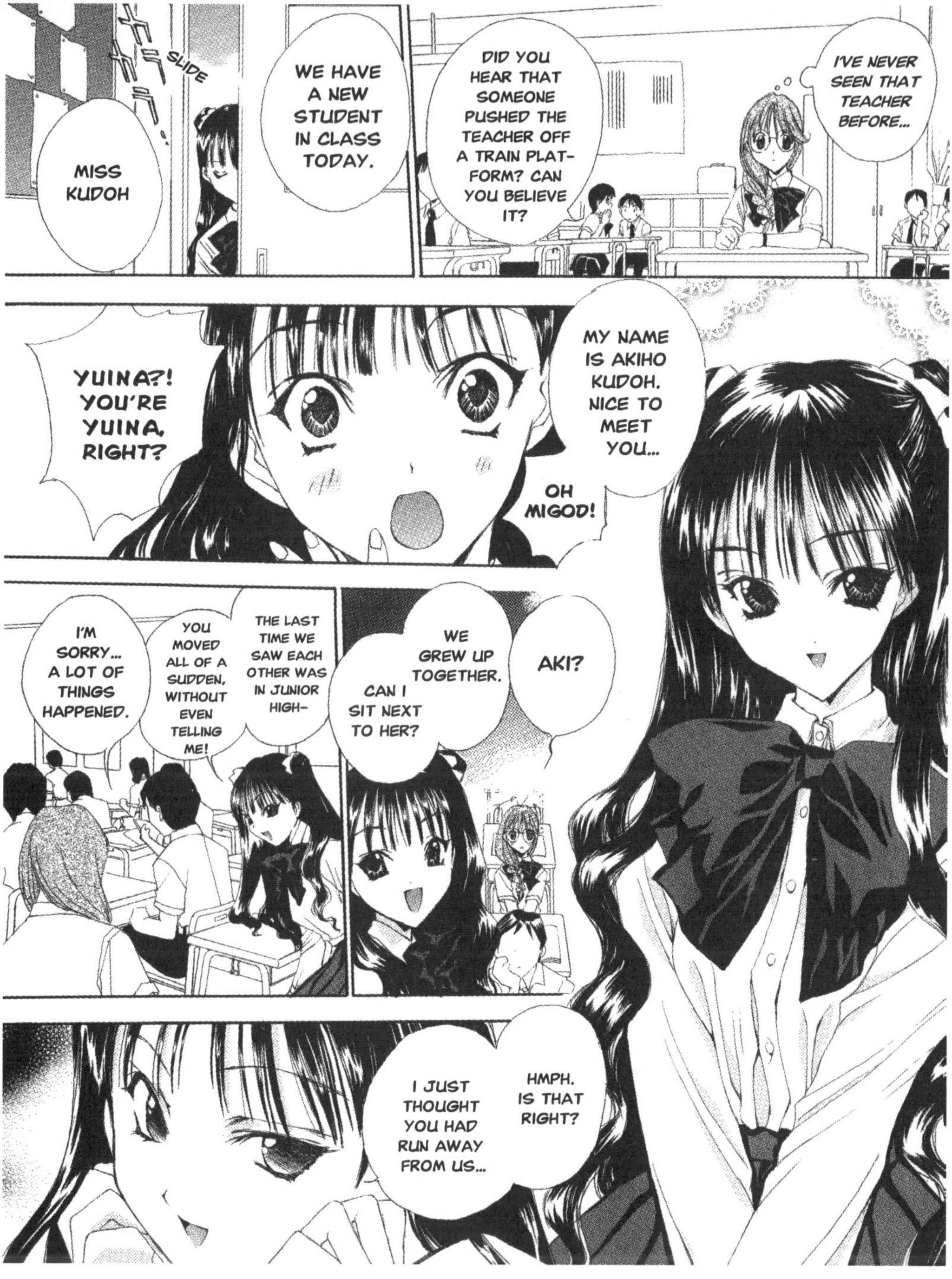
WE HAVE A NEW STUDENT IN CLASS TODAY.
MISS KUDOH
SLIDE
DID YOU HEAR THAT SOMEONE PUSHED THE TEACHER OFF A TRAIN PLAT-FORM? CAN YOU BELIEVE IT?
I'VE NEVER SEEN THAT TEACHER BEFORE...
MY NAME IS AKIHO KUDOH. NICE TO MEET YOU...
OH MIGOD!
YUINA?! YOU'RE YUINA, RIGHT?
AKI?
WE GREW UP TOGETHER.
CAN I SIT NEXT TO HER?
THE LAST TIME WE SAW EACH OTHER WAS IN JUNIOR HIGH-
YOU MOVED ALL OF A SUDDEN, WITHOUT EVEN TELLING ME!
I'M SORRY... A LOT OF THINGS HAPPENED.
HMPH. IS THAT RIGHT?
I JUST THOUGHT YOU HAD RUN AWAY FROM US...

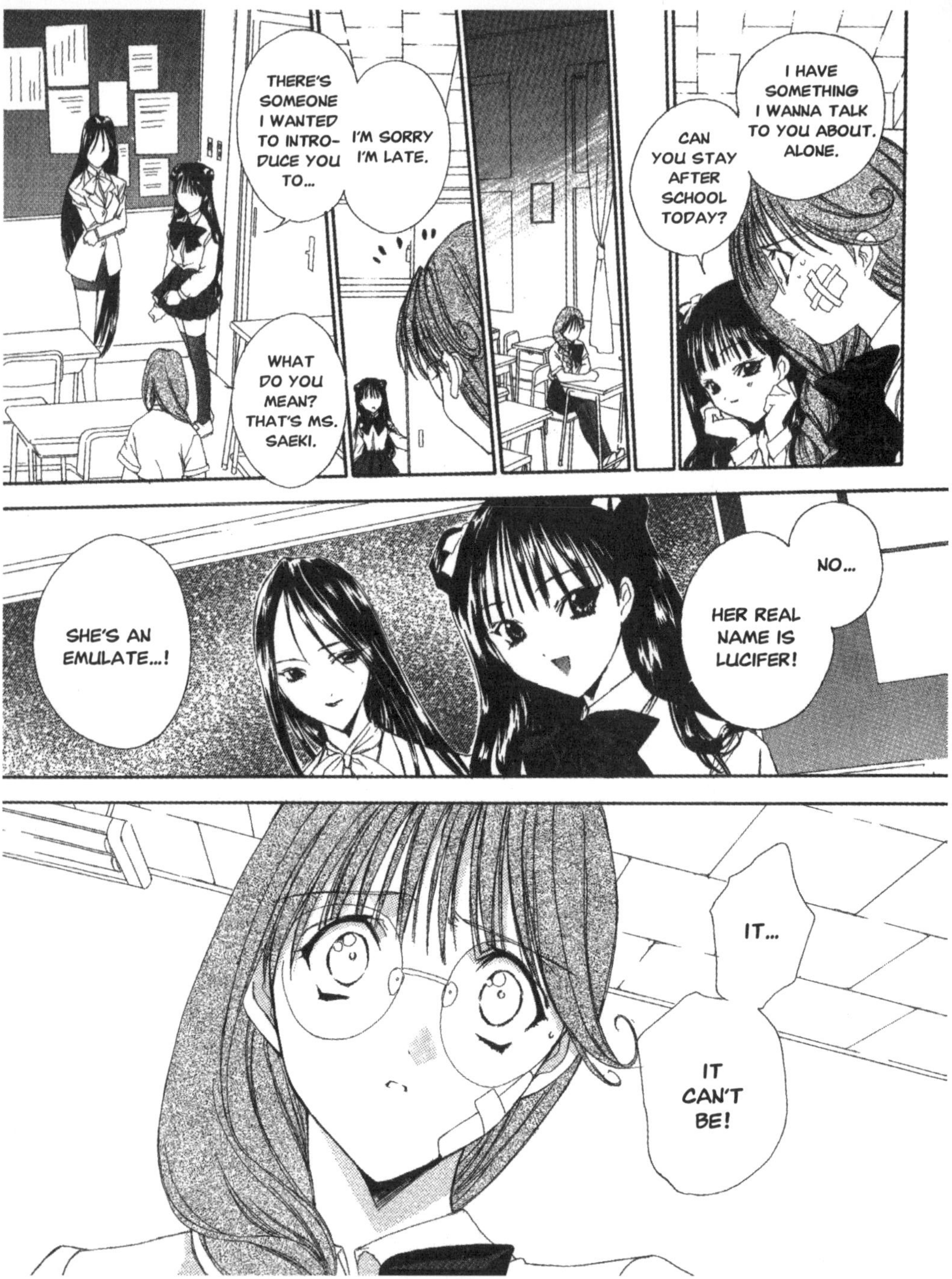
I HAVE SOMETHING I WANNA TALK TO YOU ABOUT. ALONE.
CAN YOU STAY AFTER SCHOOL TODAY?
I'M SORRY I'M LATE.
THERE'S SOMEONE I WANTED TO INTRO-DUCE YOU TO...
WHAT DO YOU MEAN? THAT'S MS. SAEKI.
NO...
HER REAL NAME IS LUCIFER!
SHE'S AN EMULATE...!
IT...
IT CAN'T BE!

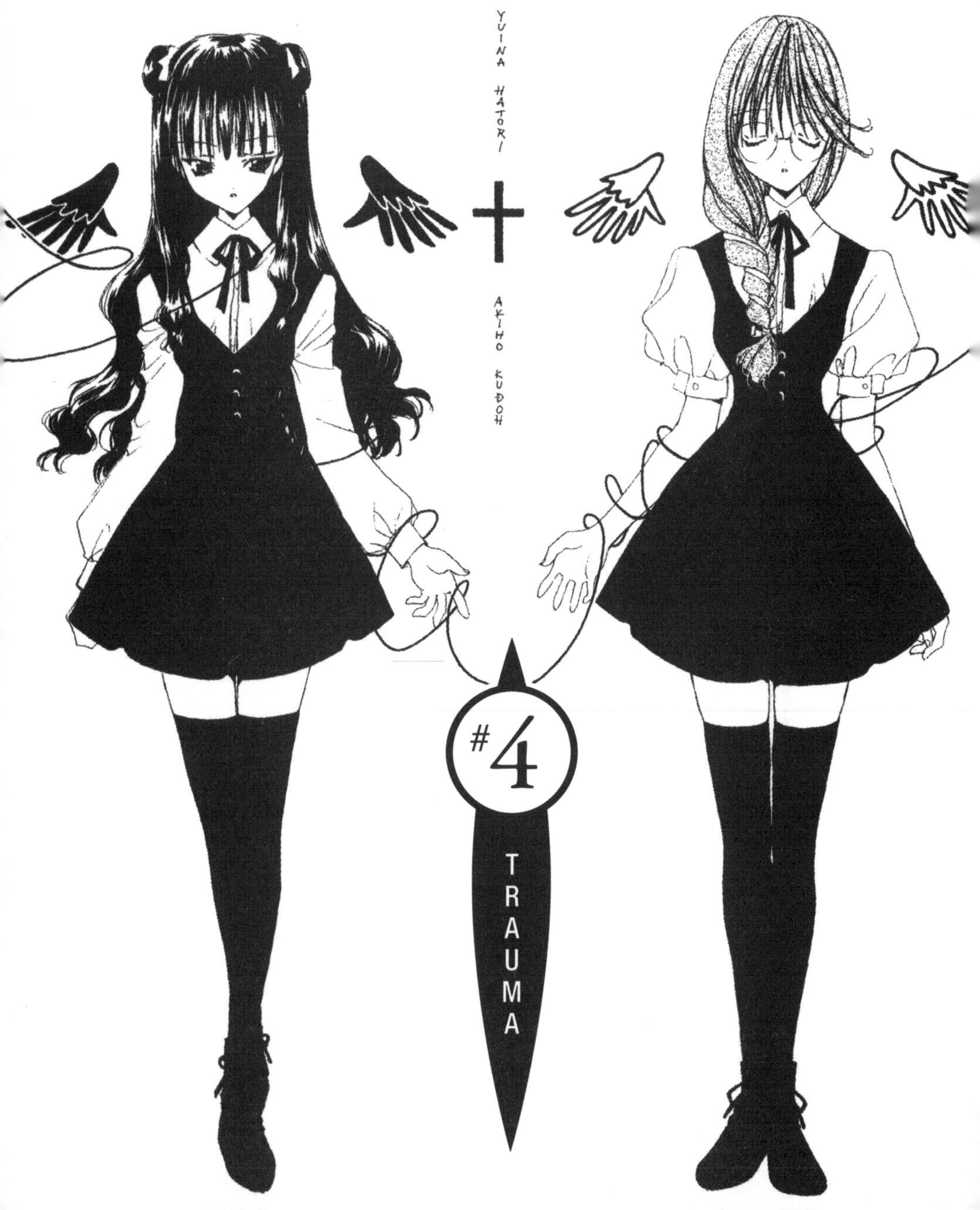
YUINA HATORI
+
AKIHO KUDOH
#4
TRAUMA

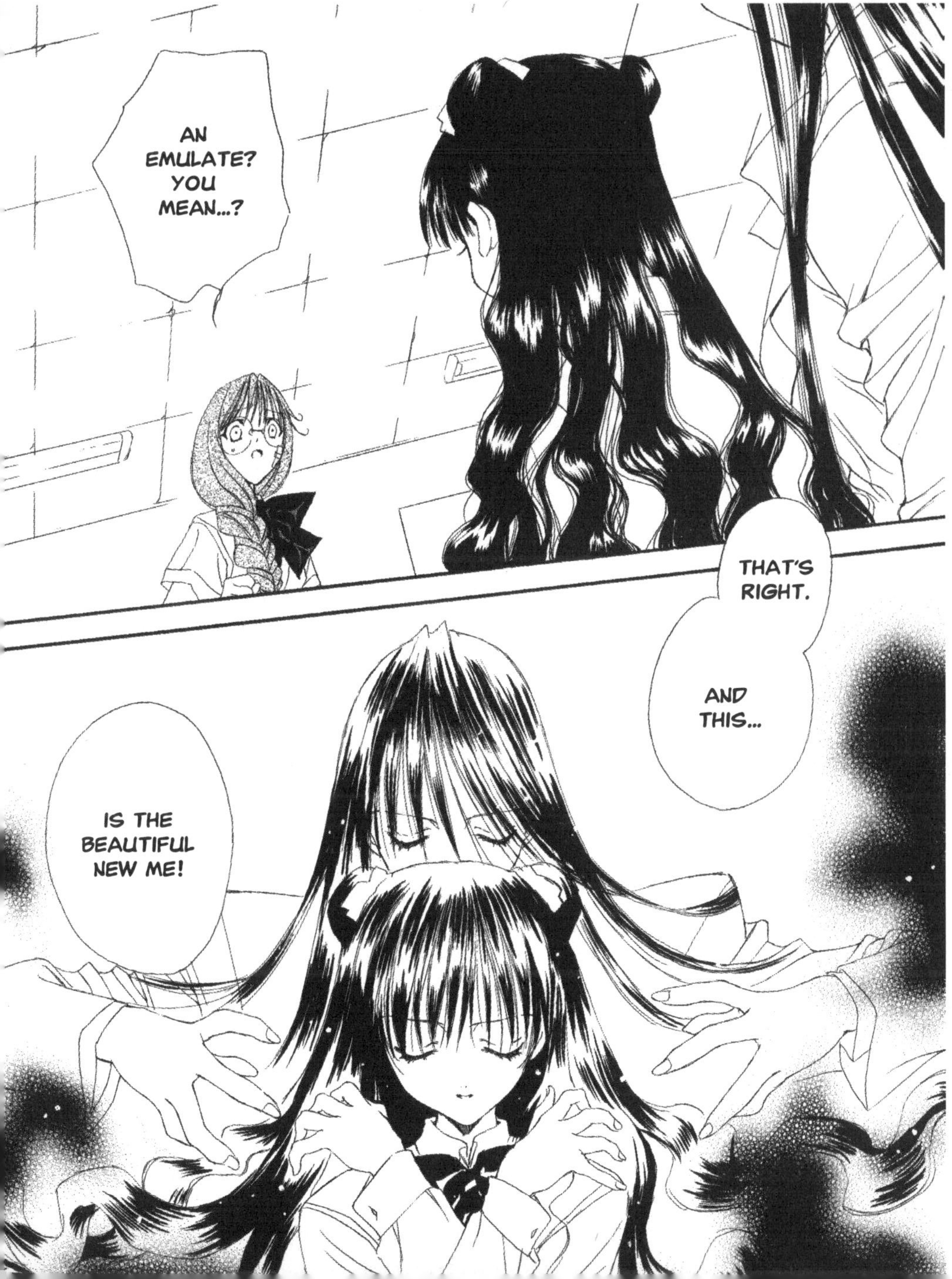
AN EMULATE? YOU MEAN...?
THAT'S RIGHT.
AND THIS...
IS THE BEAUTIFUL NEW ME!

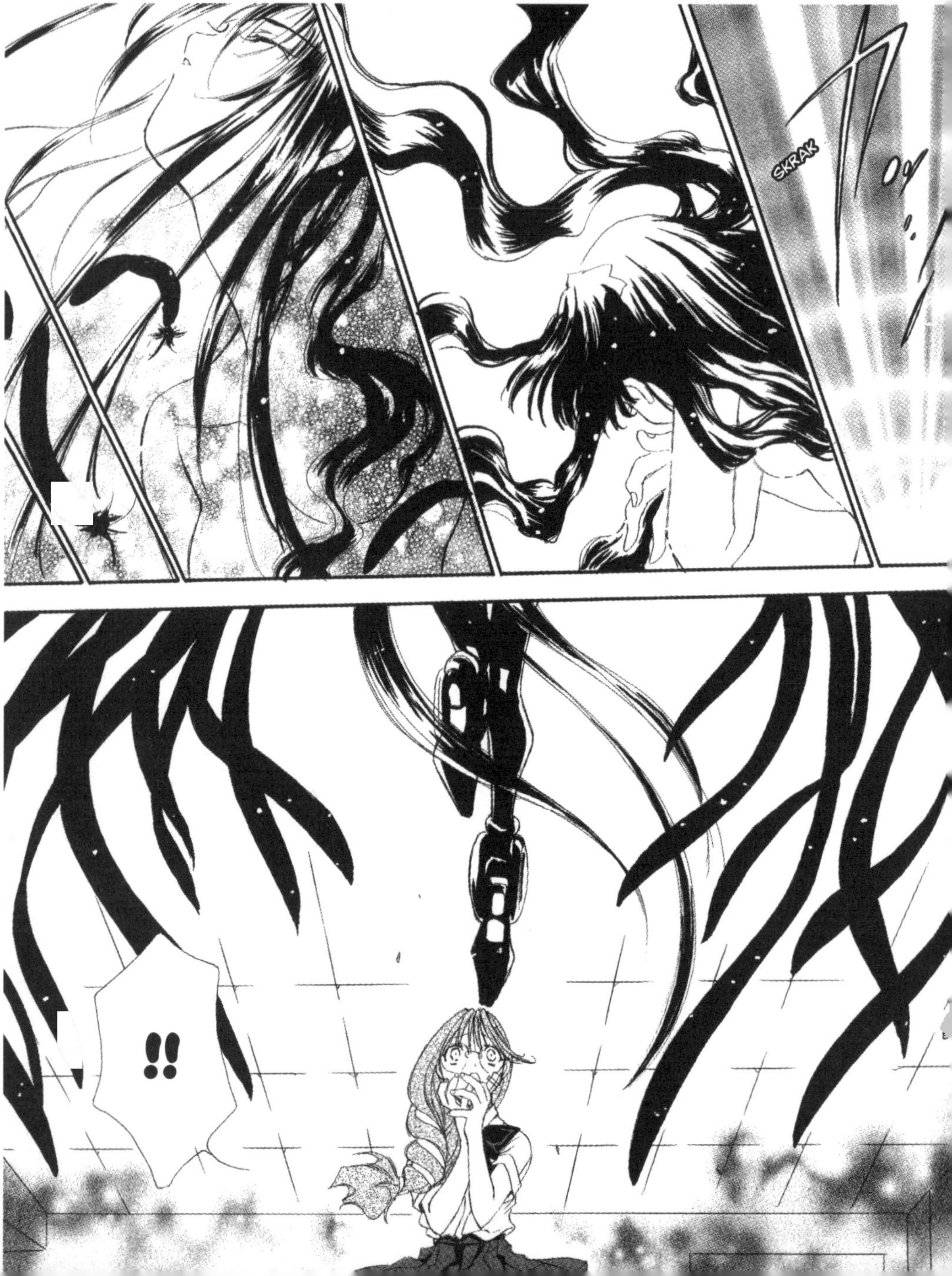
SKRAK
!!

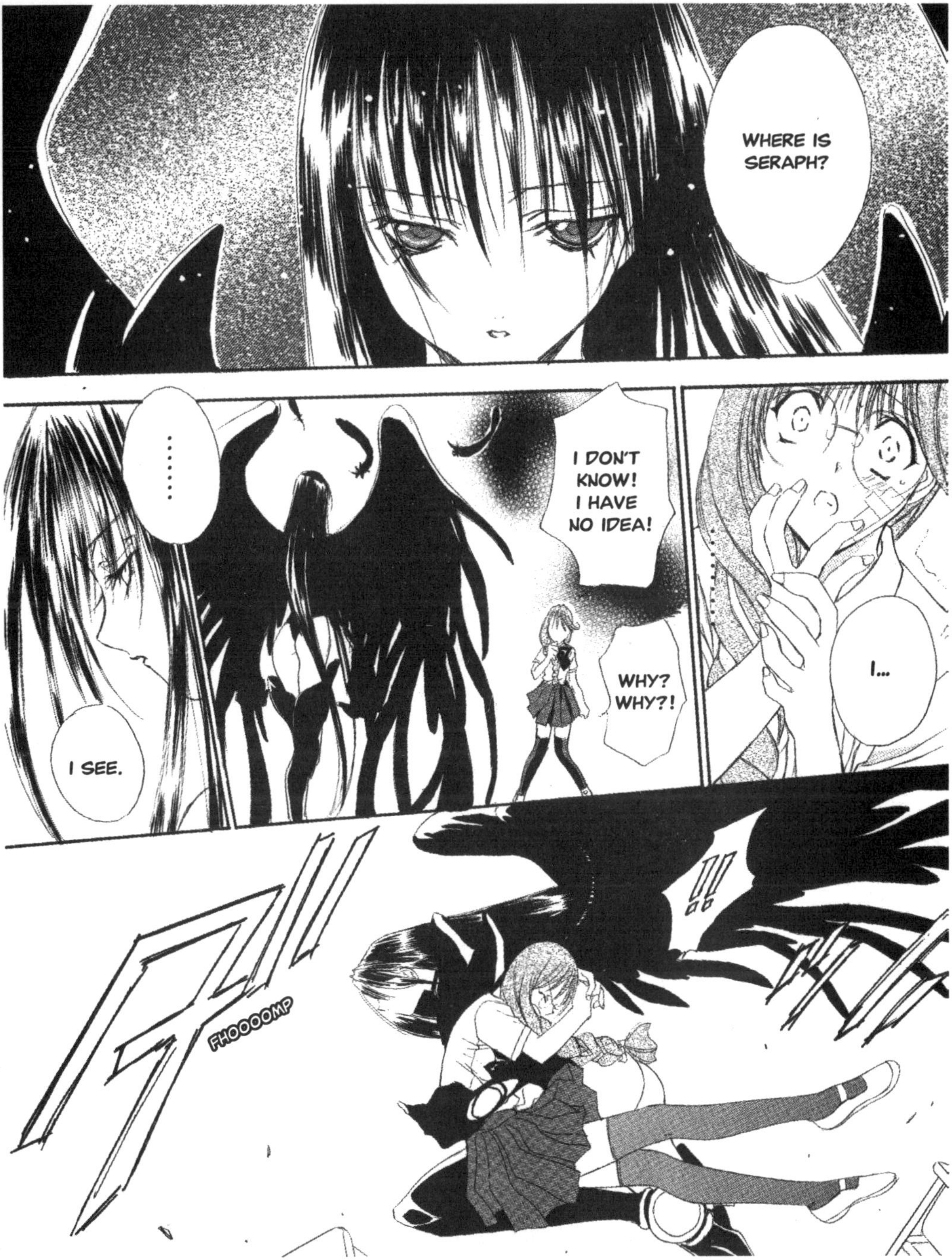
WHERE IS SERAPH?
I...
I DON'T KNOW! I HAVE NO IDEA!
WHY? WHY?!
......
I SEE.
!!
FHOOOOMP

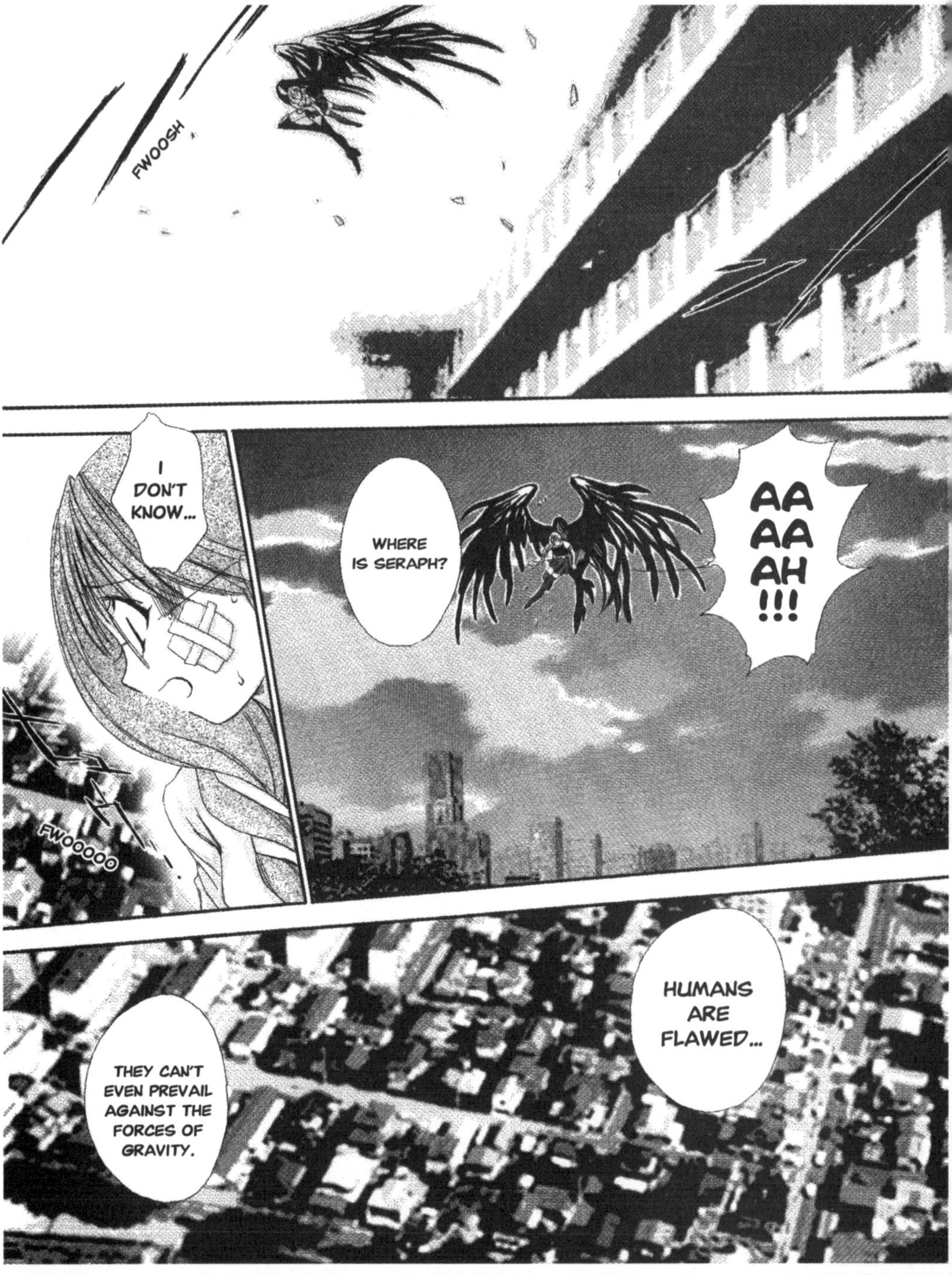
FWOOSH
AAAAAAH!!!
WHERE IS SERAPH?
I DON'T KNOW...
FWOOOOOO
HUMANS ARE FLAWED...
THEY CAN'T EVEN PREVAIL AGAINST THE FORCES OF GRAVITY.

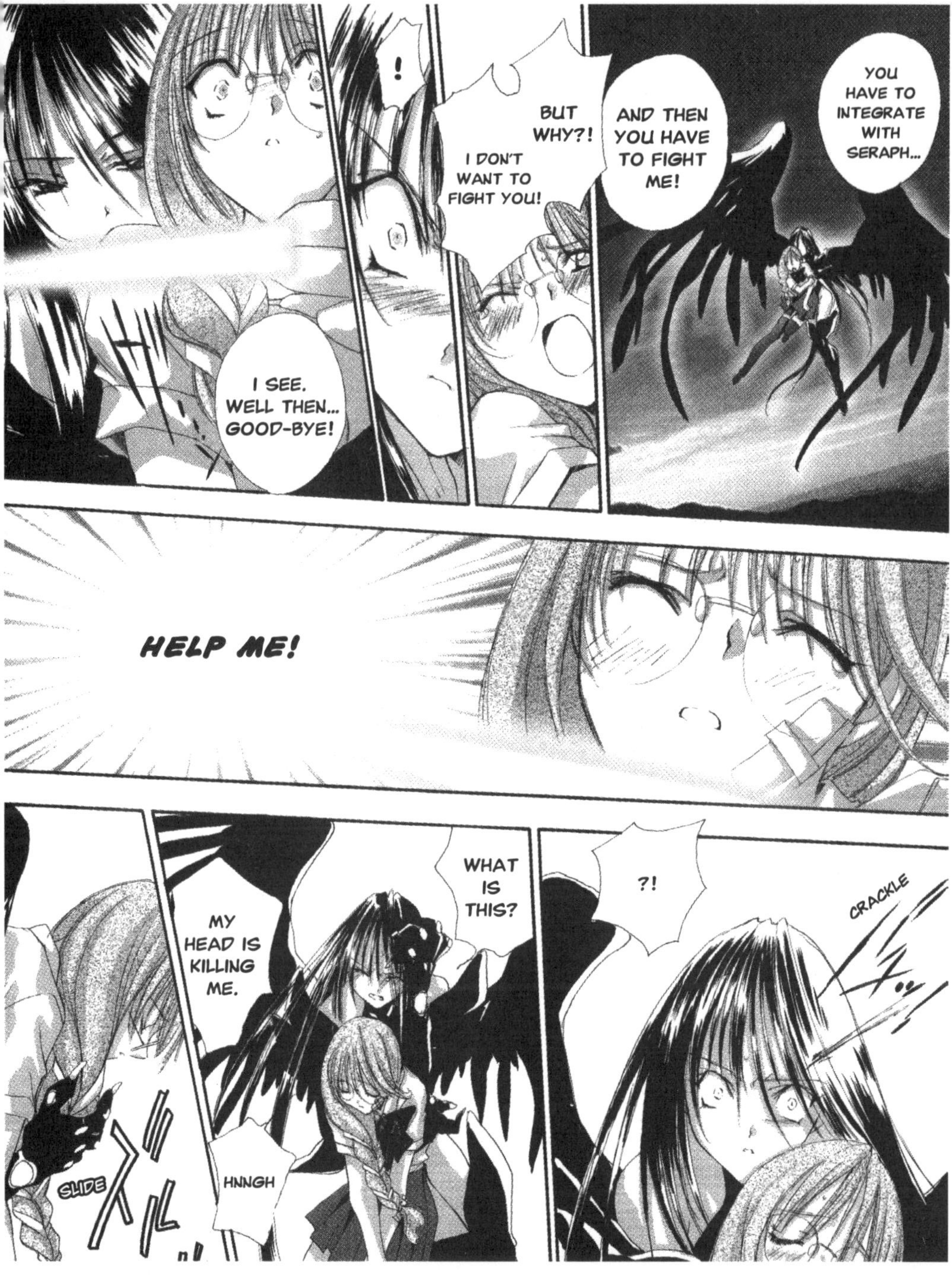
YOU HAVE TO INTEGRATE WITH SERAPH...
AND THEN YOU HAVE TO FIGHT ME!
BUT WHY?!
I DON'T WANT TO FIGHT YOU!
!
I SEE. WELL THEN... GOOD-BYE!
HELP ME!
CRACKLE
?!
WHAT IS THIS?
MY HEAD IS KILLING ME.
HNNGH
SLIDE

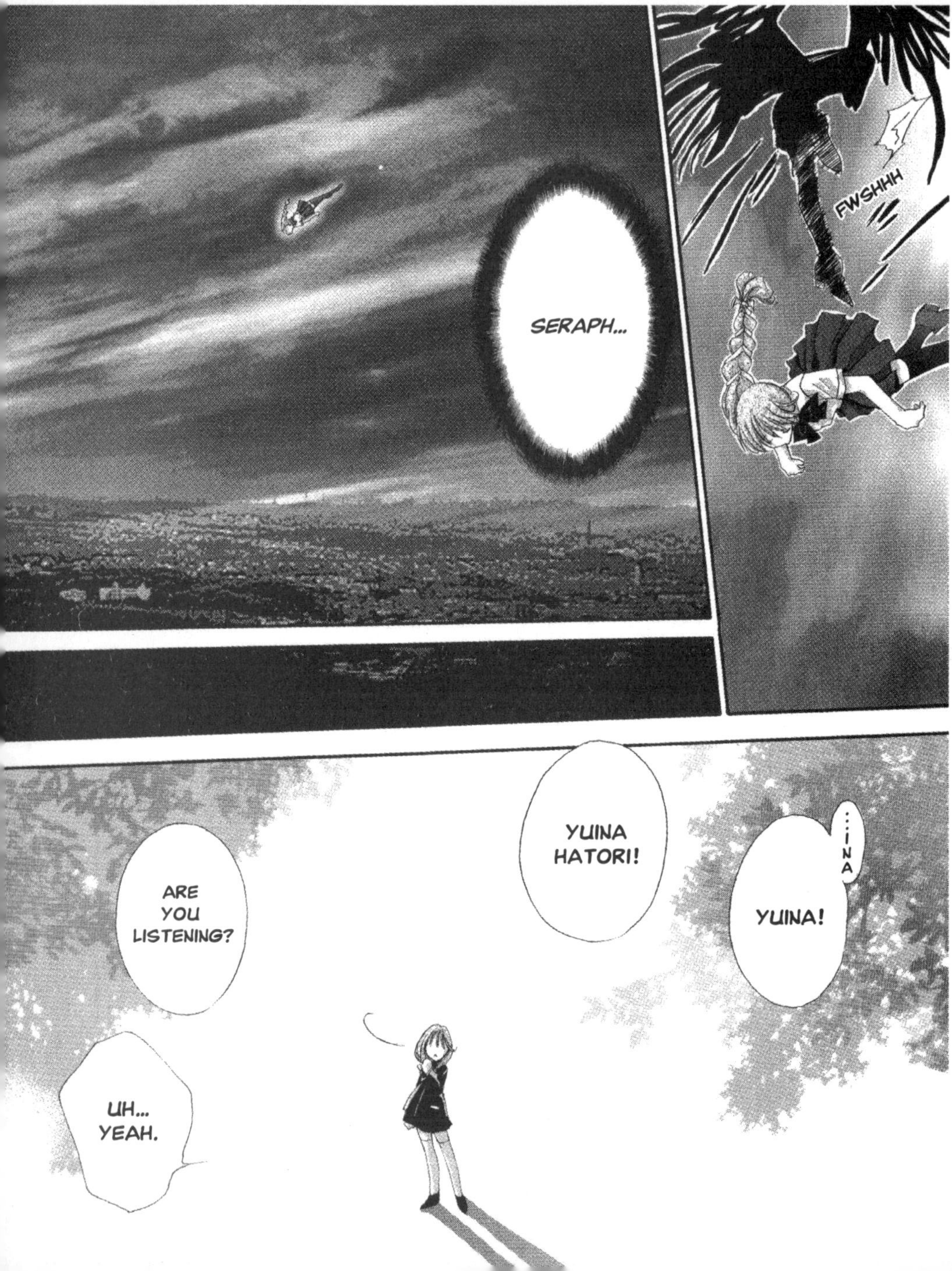
FWSHHH
SERAPH...
...INA
YUINA!
YUINA HATORI!
ARE YOU LISTENING?
UH... YEAH.

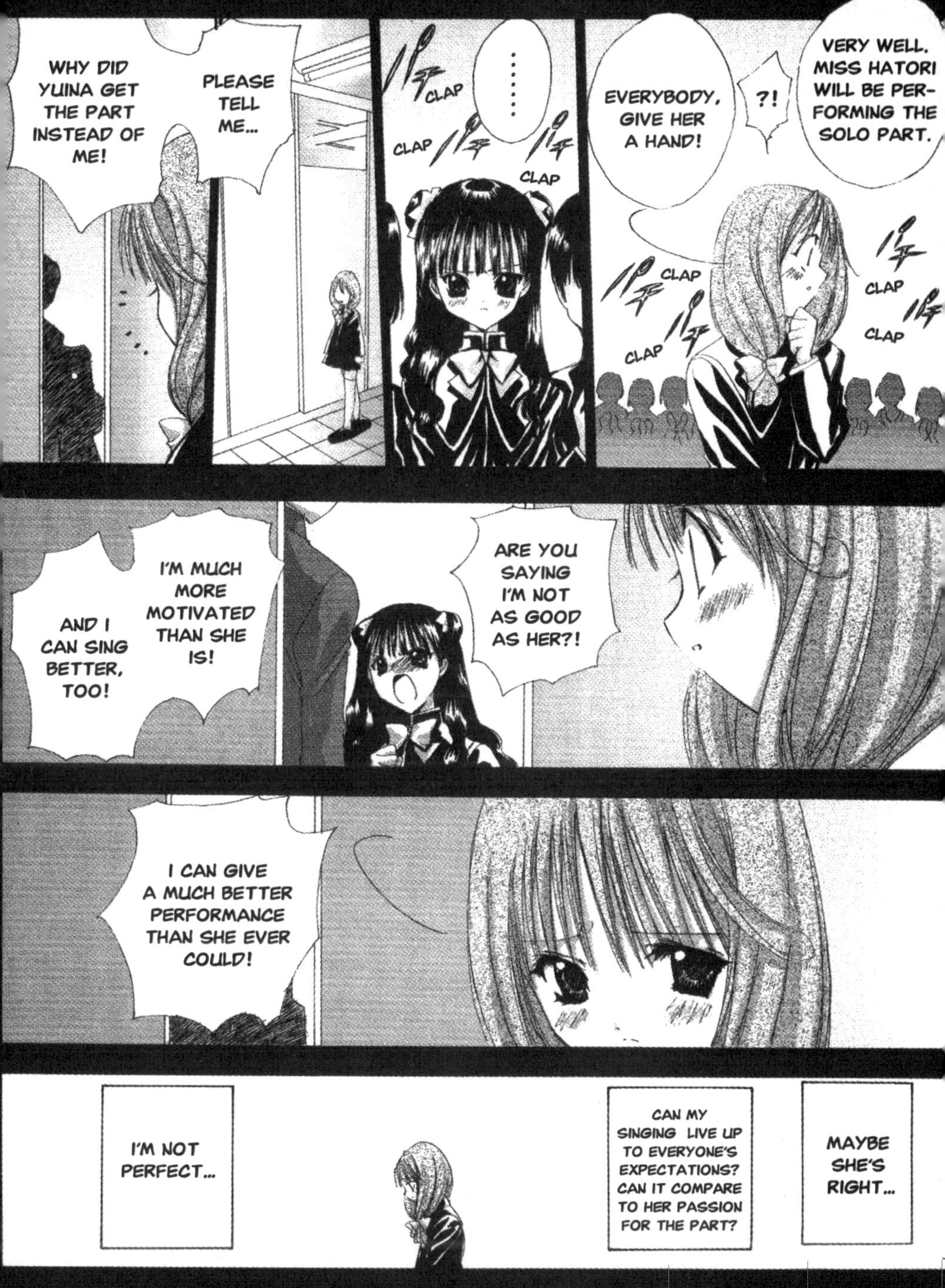
VERY WELL. MISS HATORI WILL BE PERFORMING THE SOLO PART.
?!
EVERYBODY, GIVE HER A HAND!
CLAP
CLAP
CLAP
CLAP
......
CLAP
CLAP
CLAP
PLEASE TELL ME...
WHY DID YUINA GET THE PART INSTEAD OF ME!
ARE YOU SAYING I'M NOT AS GOOD AS HER?!
I'M MUCH MORE MOTIVATED THAN SHE IS!
AND I CAN SING BETTER, TOO!
I CAN GIVE A MUCH BETTER PERFORMANCE THAN SHE EVER COULD!
MAYBE SHE'S RIGHT...
CAN MY SINGING LIVE UP TO EVERYONE'S EXPECTATIONS? CAN IT COMPARE TO HER PASSION FOR THE PART?
I'M NOT PERFECT...

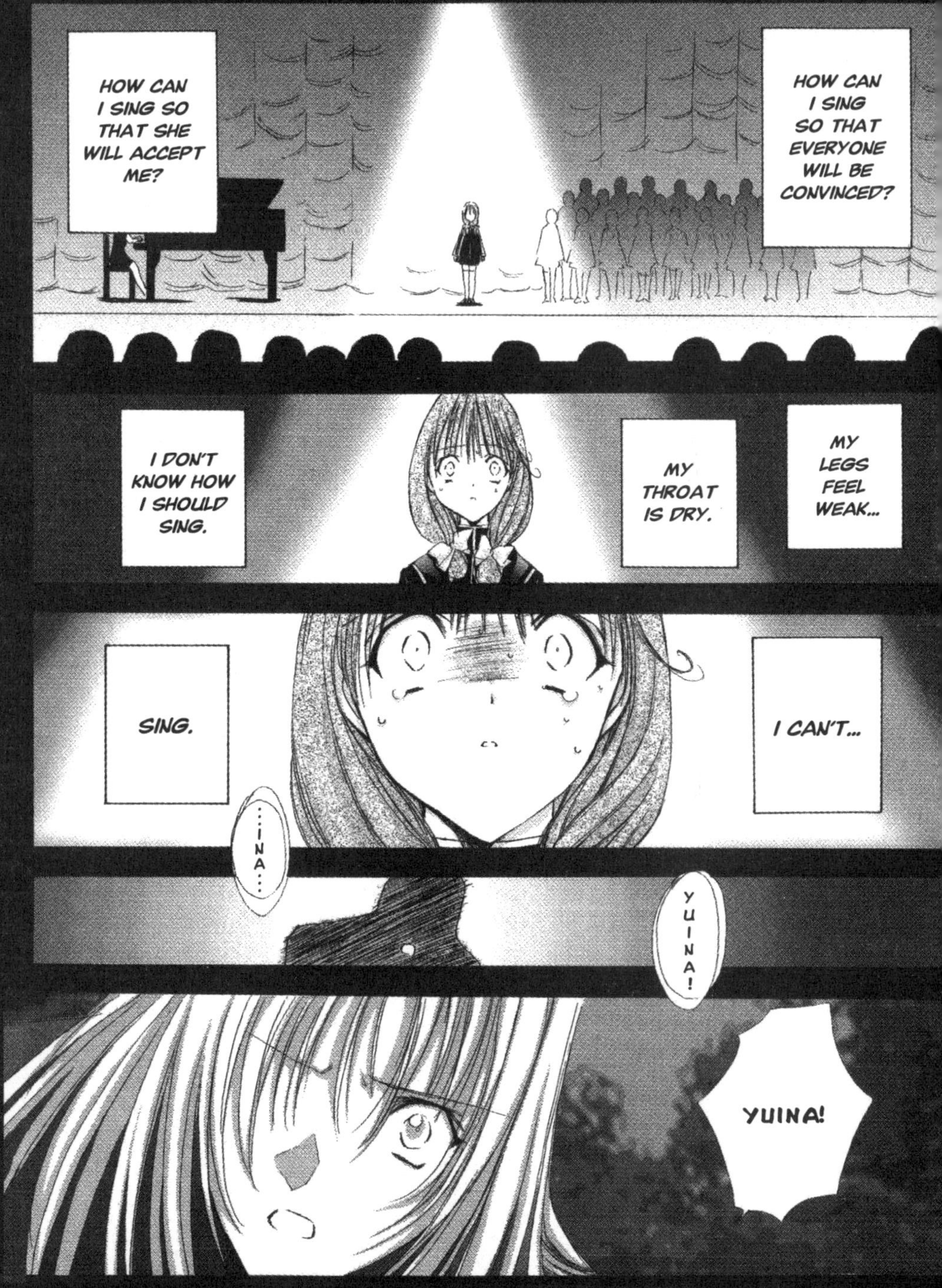
HOW CAN I SING SO THAT SHE WILL ACCEPT ME?
HOW CAN I SING SO THAT EVERYONE WILL BE CONVINCED?
I DON'T KNOW HOW I SHOULD SING.
MY THROAT IS DRY.
MY LEGS FEEL WEAK...
SING.
I CAN'T...
...INA...
YUINA!
YUINA!

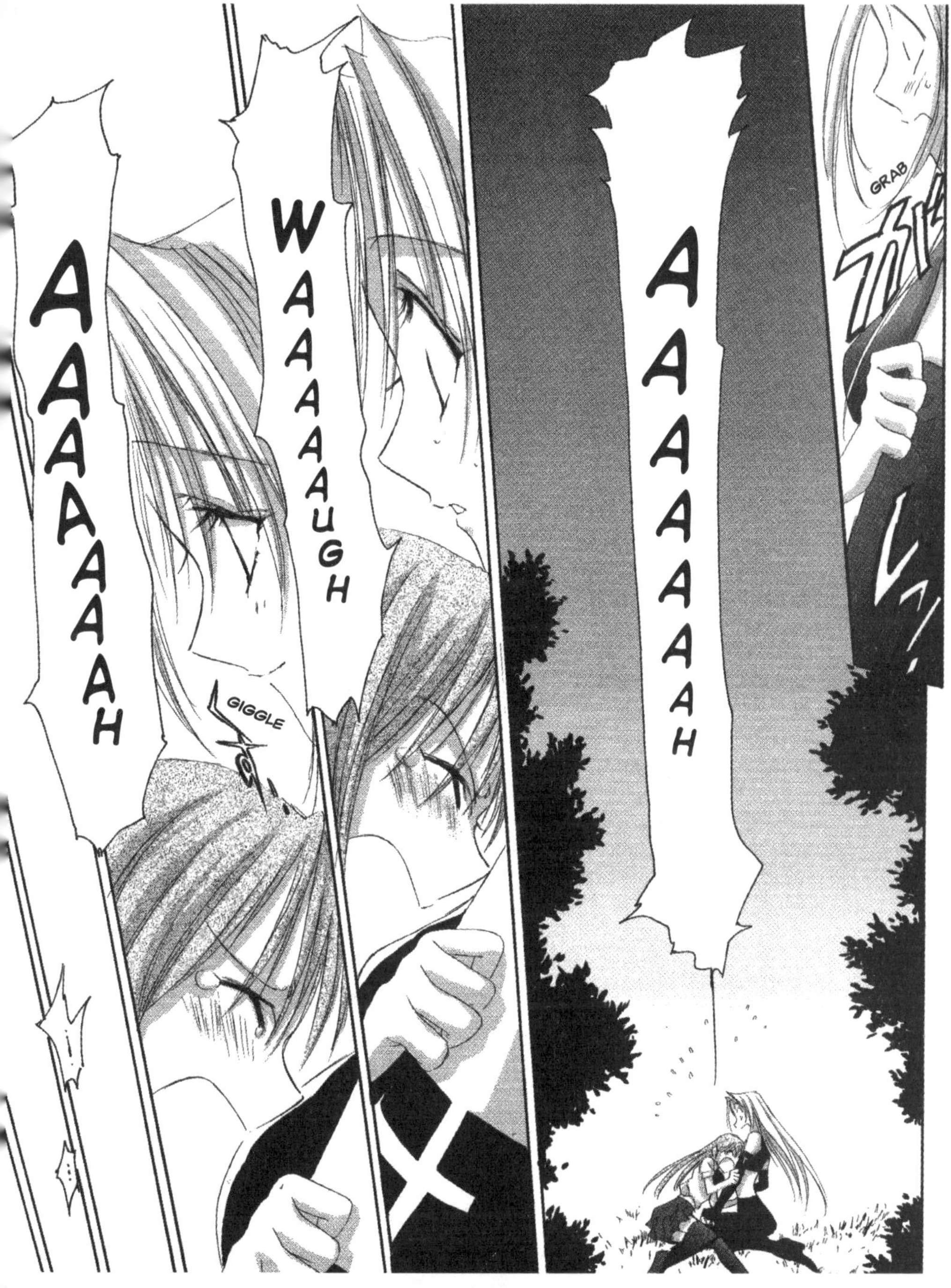
GRAB
AAAAAAAH
WAAAAAUGH
GIGGLE
AAAAAAAH
...!
...

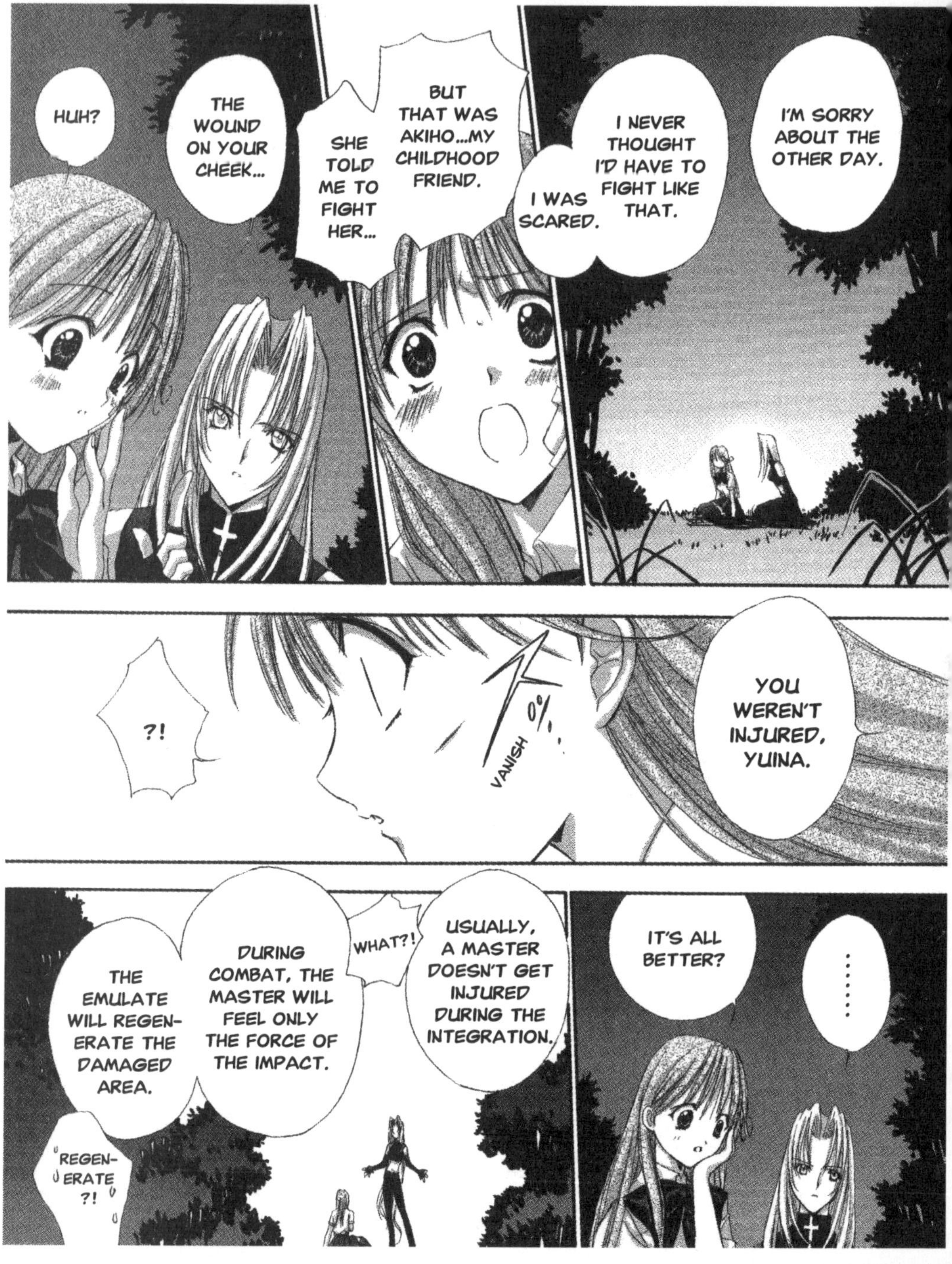
I'M SORRY ABOUT THE OTHER DAY.
I NEVER THOUGHT I'D HAVE TO FIGHT LIKE THAT.
I WAS SCARED.
BUT THAT WAS AKIHO...MY CHILDHOOD FRIEND.
SHE TOLD ME TO FIGHT HER...
THE WOUND ON YOUR CHEEK...
HUH?
YOU WEREN'T INJURED, YUINA.
VANISH
?!
.......
IT'S ALL BETTER?
USUALLY, A MASTER DOESN'T GET INJURED DURING THE INTEGRATION.
WHAT?!
DURING COMBAT, THE MASTER WILL FEEL ONLY THE FORCE OF THE IMPACT.
THE EMULATE WILL REGEN-ERATE THE DAMAGED AREA.
REGEN-ERATE ?!

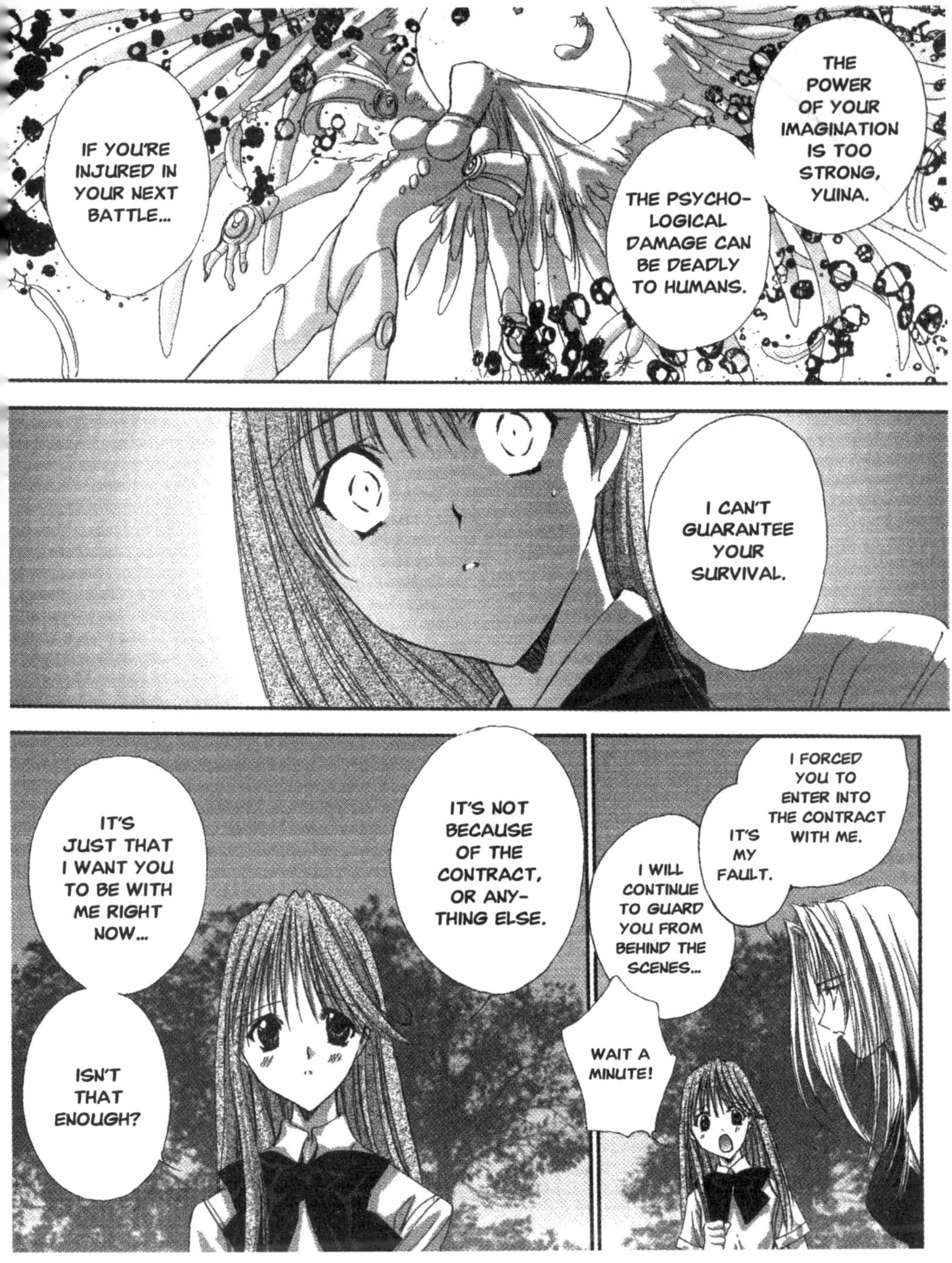
THE POWER OF YOUR IMAGINATION IS TOO STRONG, YUINA.
THE PSYCHOLOGICAL DAMAGE CAN BE DEADLY TO HUMANS.
IF YOU'RE INJURED IN YOUR NEXT BATTLE...
I CAN'T GUARANTEE YOUR SURVIVAL.
I FORCED YOU TO ENTER INTO THE CONTRACT WITH ME.
IT'S MY FAULT.
I WILL CONTINUE TO GUARD YOU FROM BEHIND THE SCENES...
WAIT A MINUTE!
IT'S NOT BECAUSE OF THE CONTRACT, OR ANYTHING ELSE.
IT'S JUST THAT I WANT YOU TO BE WITH ME RIGHT NOW...
ISN'T THAT ENOUGH?

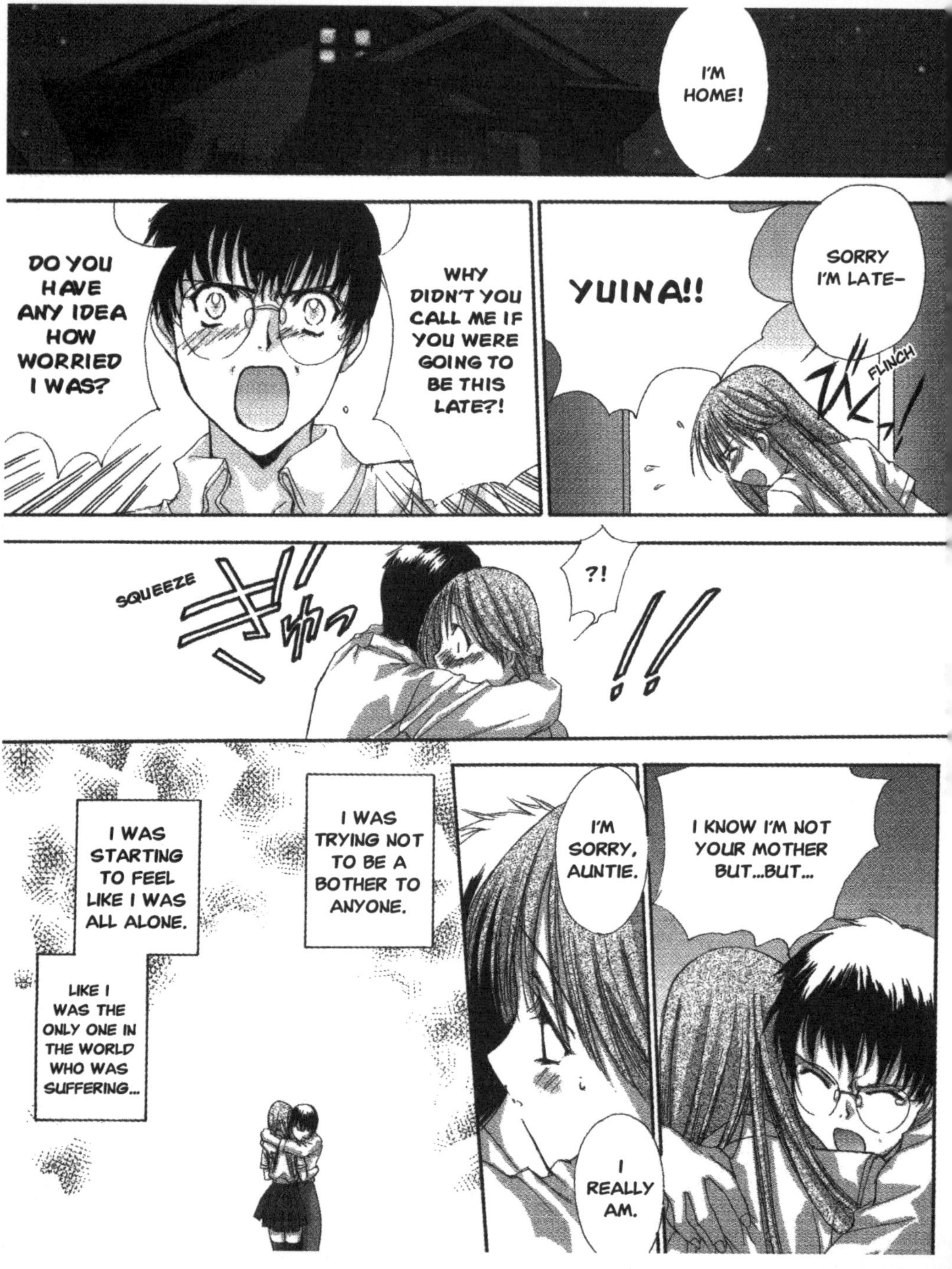
I'M HOME!
SORRY I'M LATE-
FLINCH
YUINA!!
WHY DIDN'T YOU CALL ME IF YOU WERE GOING TO BE THIS LATE?!
DO YOU HAVE ANY IDEA HOW WORRIED I WAS?
?!
SQUEEZE
I KNOW I'M NOT YOUR MOTHER BUT...BUT...
I'M SORRY, AUNTIE.
I REALLY AM.
I WAS TRYING NOT TO BE A BOTHER TO ANYONE.
I WAS STARTING TO FEEL LIKE I WAS ALL ALONE.
LIKE I WAS THE ONLY ONE IN THE WORLD WHO WAS SUFFERING...

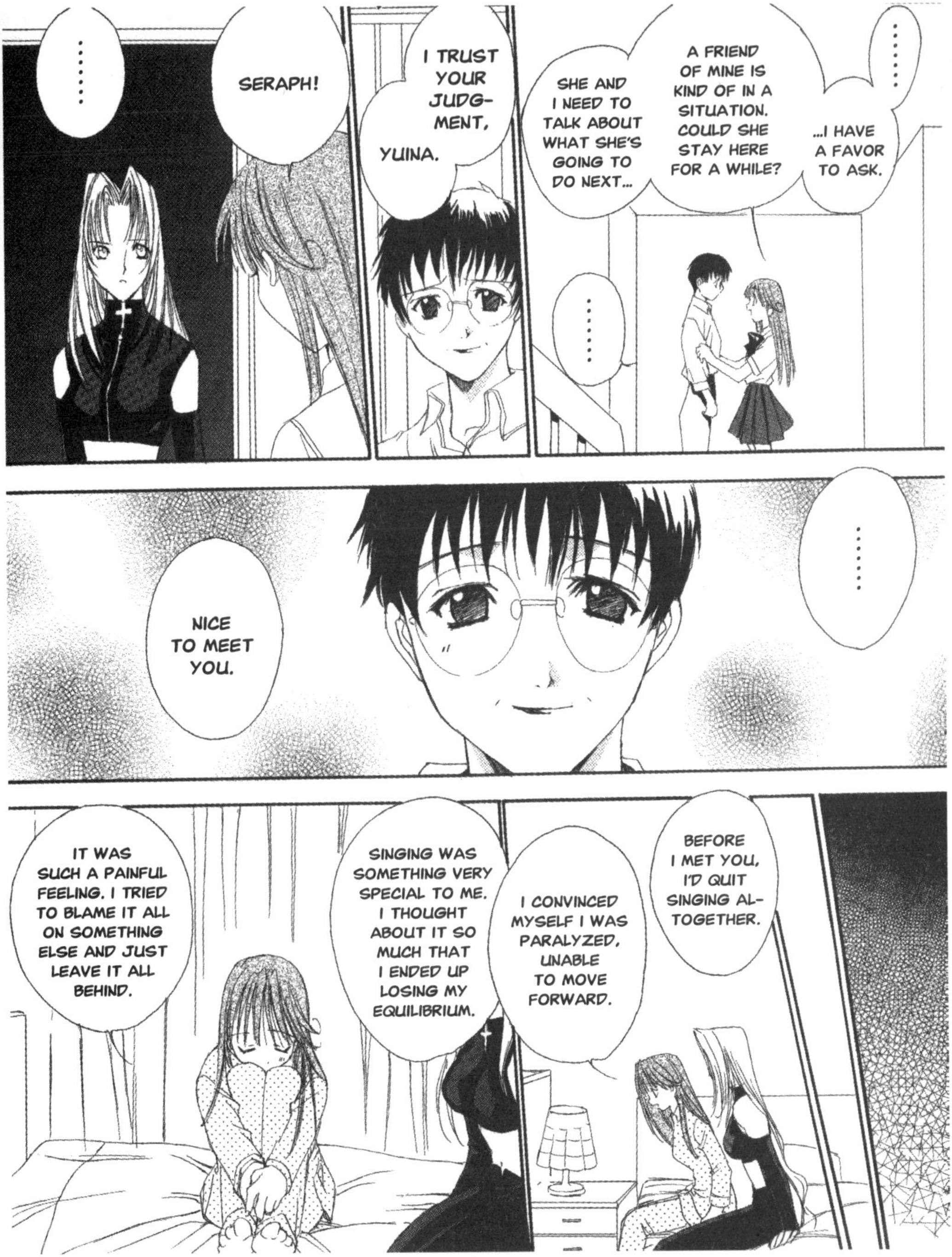
......
...I HAVE A FAVOR TO ASK.
A FRIEND OF MINE IS KIND OF IN A SITUATION. COULD SHE STAY HERE FOR A WHILE?
SHE AND I NEED TO TALK ABOUT WHAT SHE'S GOING TO DO NEXT...
......
I TRUST YOUR JUDG-MENT, YUINA.
SERAPH!
......
......
NICE TO MEET YOU.
BEFORE I MET YOU, I'D QUIT SINGING AL-TOGETHER.
I CONVINCED MYSELF I WAS PARALYZED, UNABLE TO MOVE FORWARD.
SINGING WAS SOMETHING VERY SPECIAL TO ME. I THOUGHT ABOUT IT SO MUCH THAT I ENDED UP LOSING MY EQUILIBRIUM.
IT WAS SUCH A PAINFUL FEELING. I TRIED TO BLAME IT ALL ON SOMETHING ELSE AND JUST LEAVE IT ALL BEHIND.

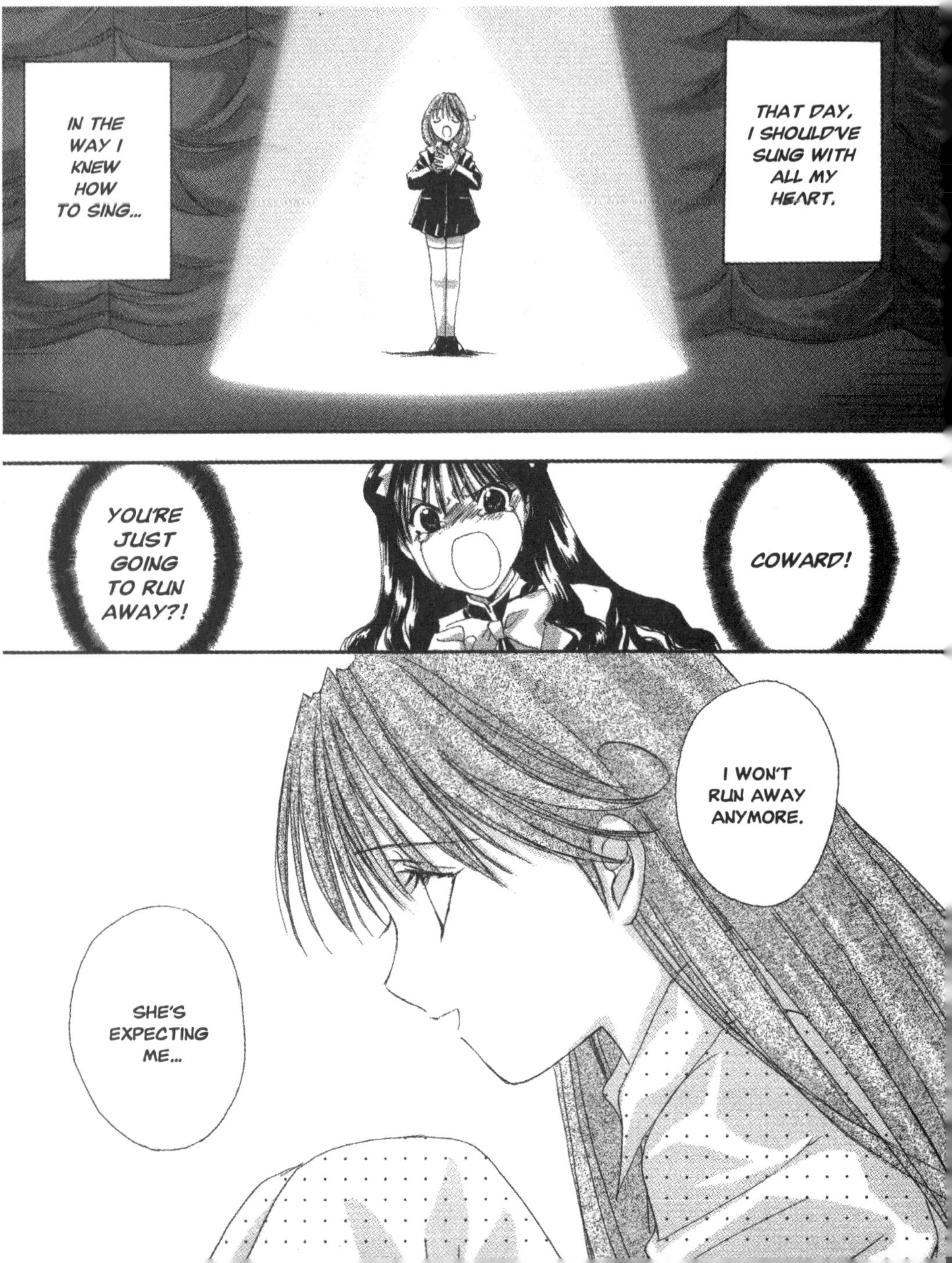
THAT DAY, I SHOULD'VE SUNG WITH ALL MY HEART.
IN THE WAY I KNEW HOW TO SING...
COWARD!
YOU'RE JUST GOING TO RUN AWAY?!
I WON'T RUN AWAY ANYMORE.
SHE'S EXPECTING ME...

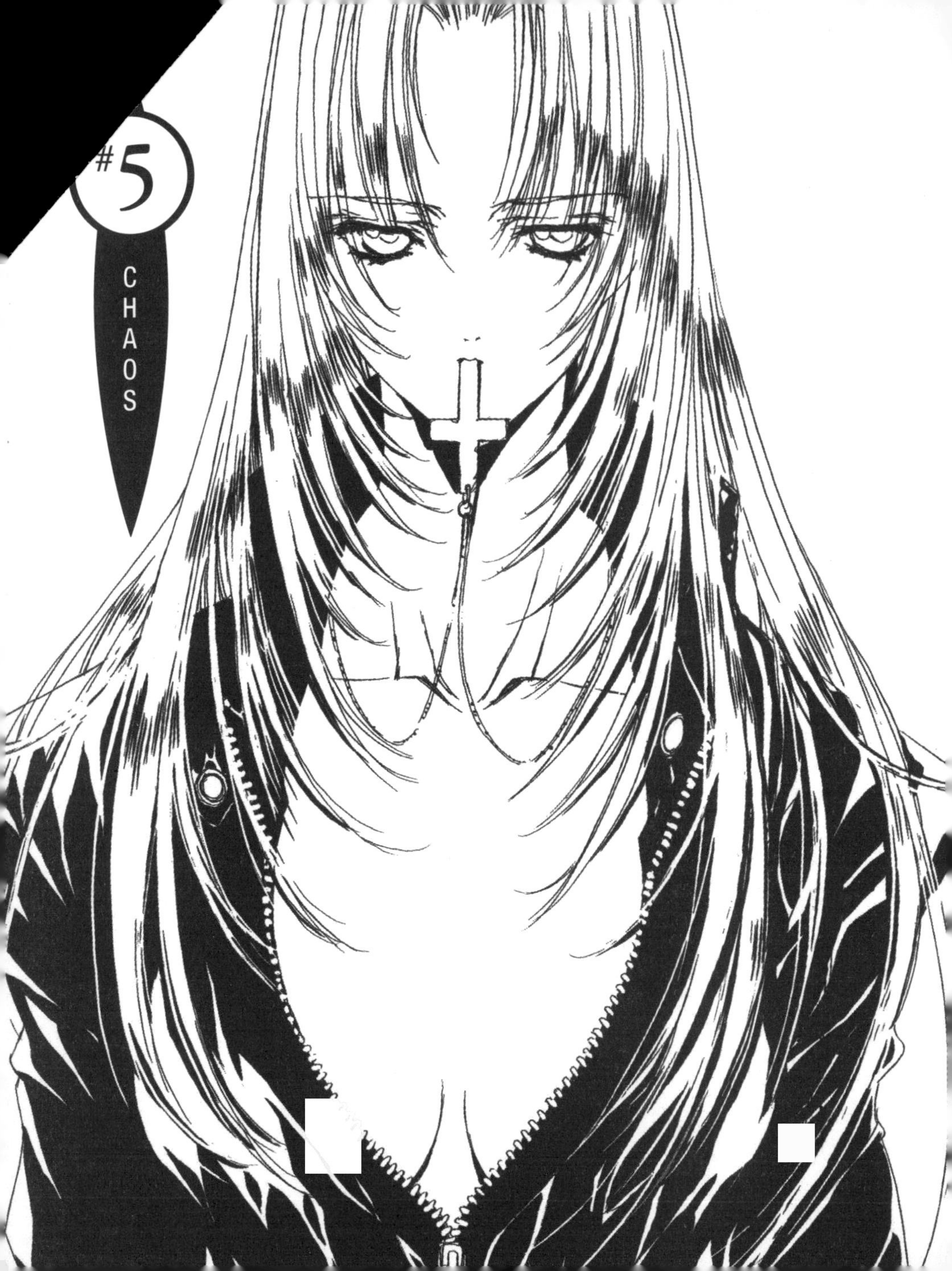
#5
CHAOS

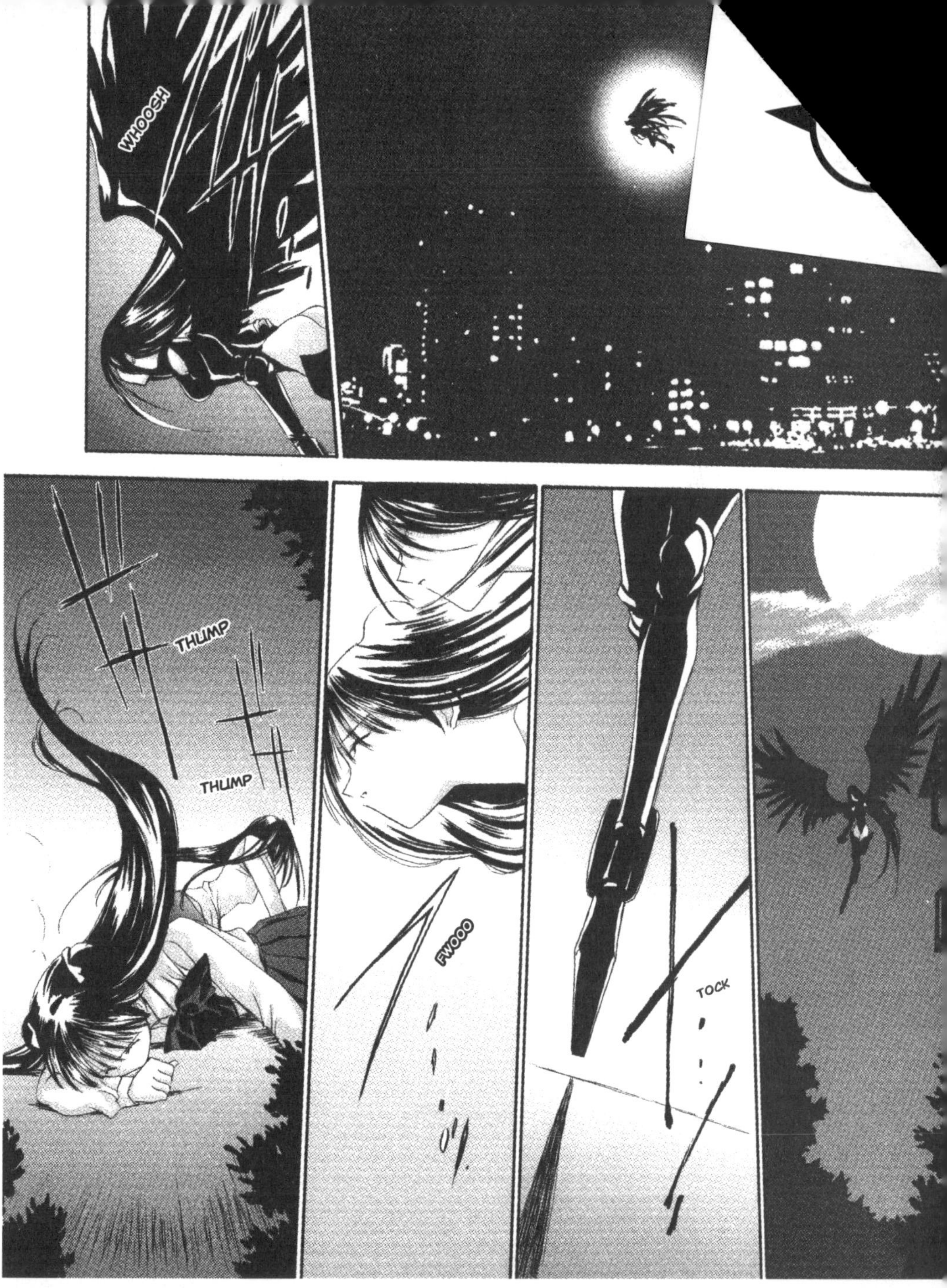
WHOOSH
TOCK
FWOOO
THUMP
THUMP

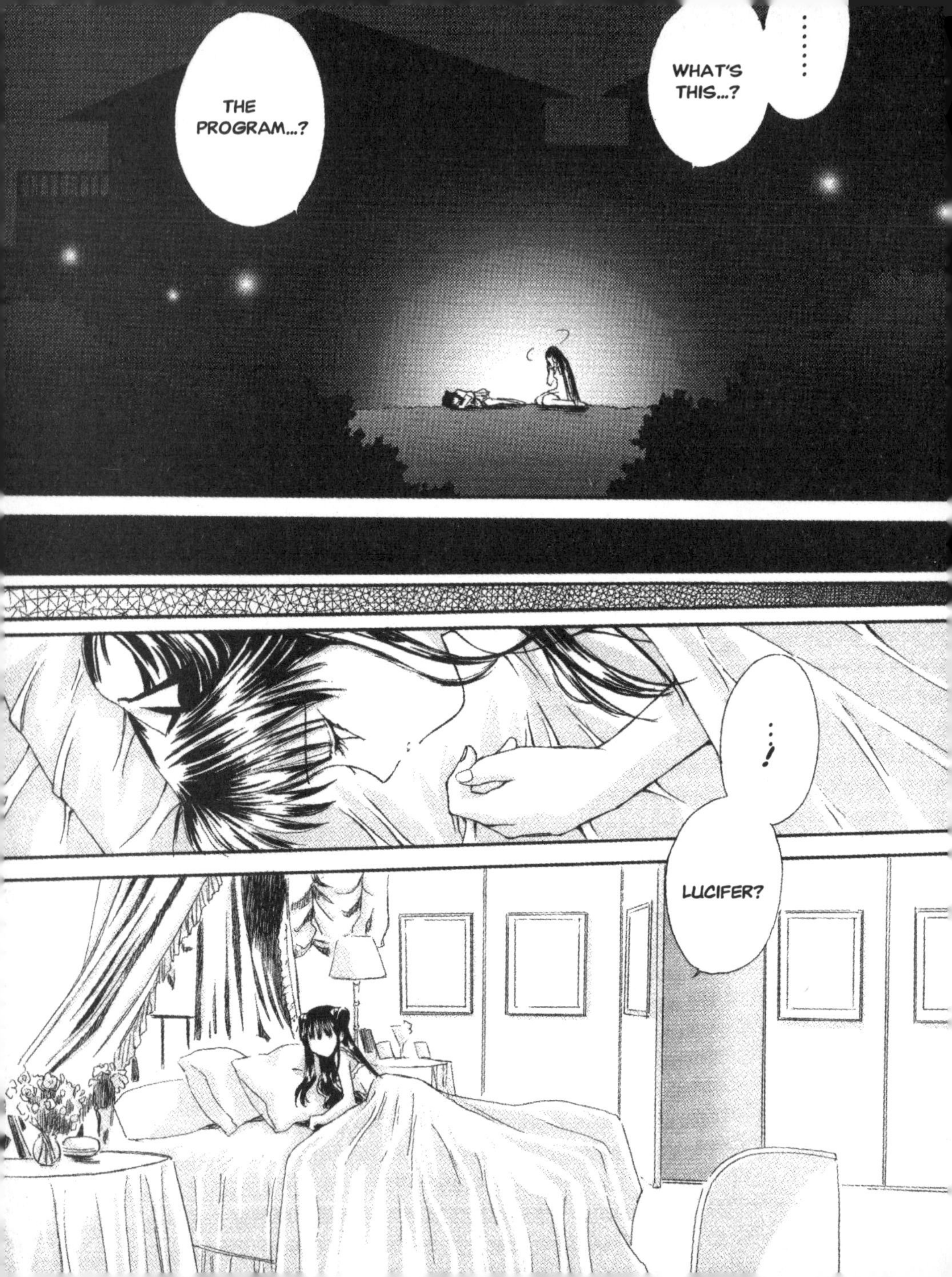
......
WHAT'S THIS...?
THE PROGRAM...?
...!
LUCIFER?

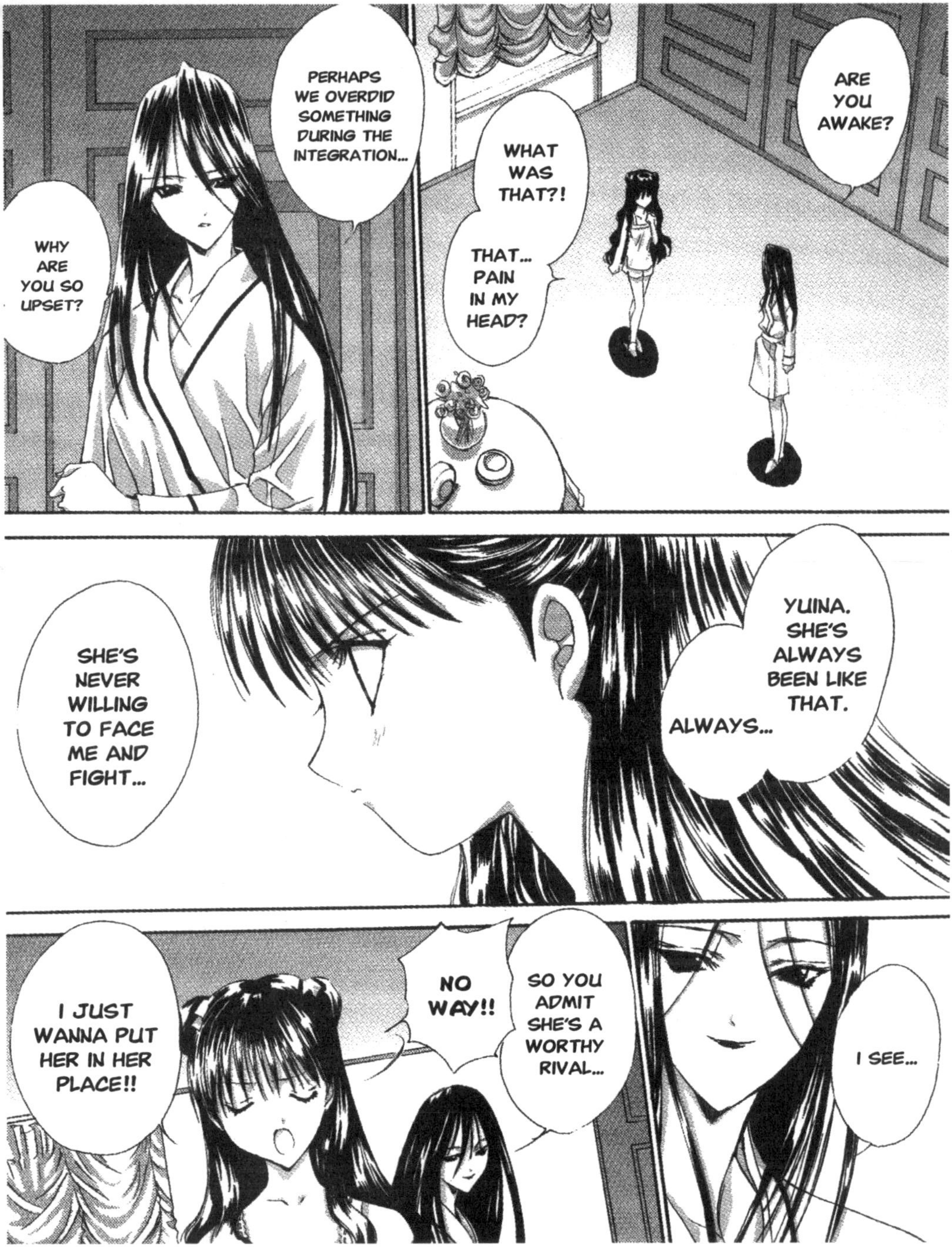
ARE YOU AWAKE?
WHAT WAS THAT?!
THAT... PAIN IN MY HEAD?
PERHAPS WE OVERDID SOMETHING DURING THE INTEGRATION...
WHY ARE YOU SO UPSET?
YUINA. SHE'S ALWAYS BEEN LIKE THAT.
ALWAYS...
SHE'S NEVER WILLING TO FACE ME AND FIGHT...
I SEE...
SO YOU ADMIT SHE'S A WORTHY RIVAL...
NO WAY!!
I JUST WANNA PUT HER IN HER PLACE!!

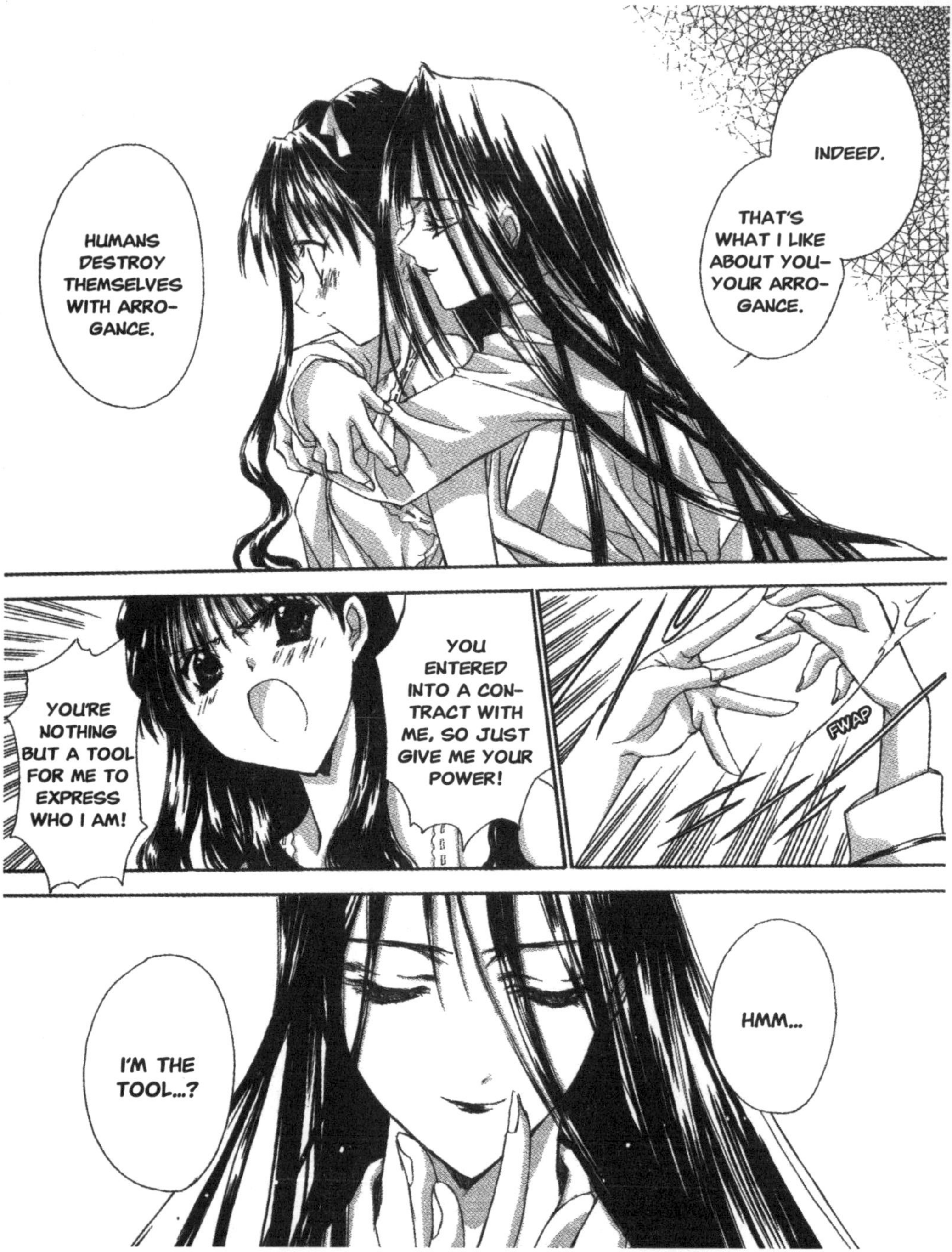
HUMANS DESTROY THEMSELVES WITH ARRO-GANCE.
INDEED.
THAT'S WHAT I LIKE ABOUT YOU— YOUR ARRO-GANCE.
YOU'RE NOTHING BUT A TOOL FOR ME TO EXPRESS WHO I AM!
YOU ENTERED INTO A CON-TRACT WITH ME, SO JUST GIVE ME YOUR POWER!
FWAP
I'M THE TOOL...?
HMM...

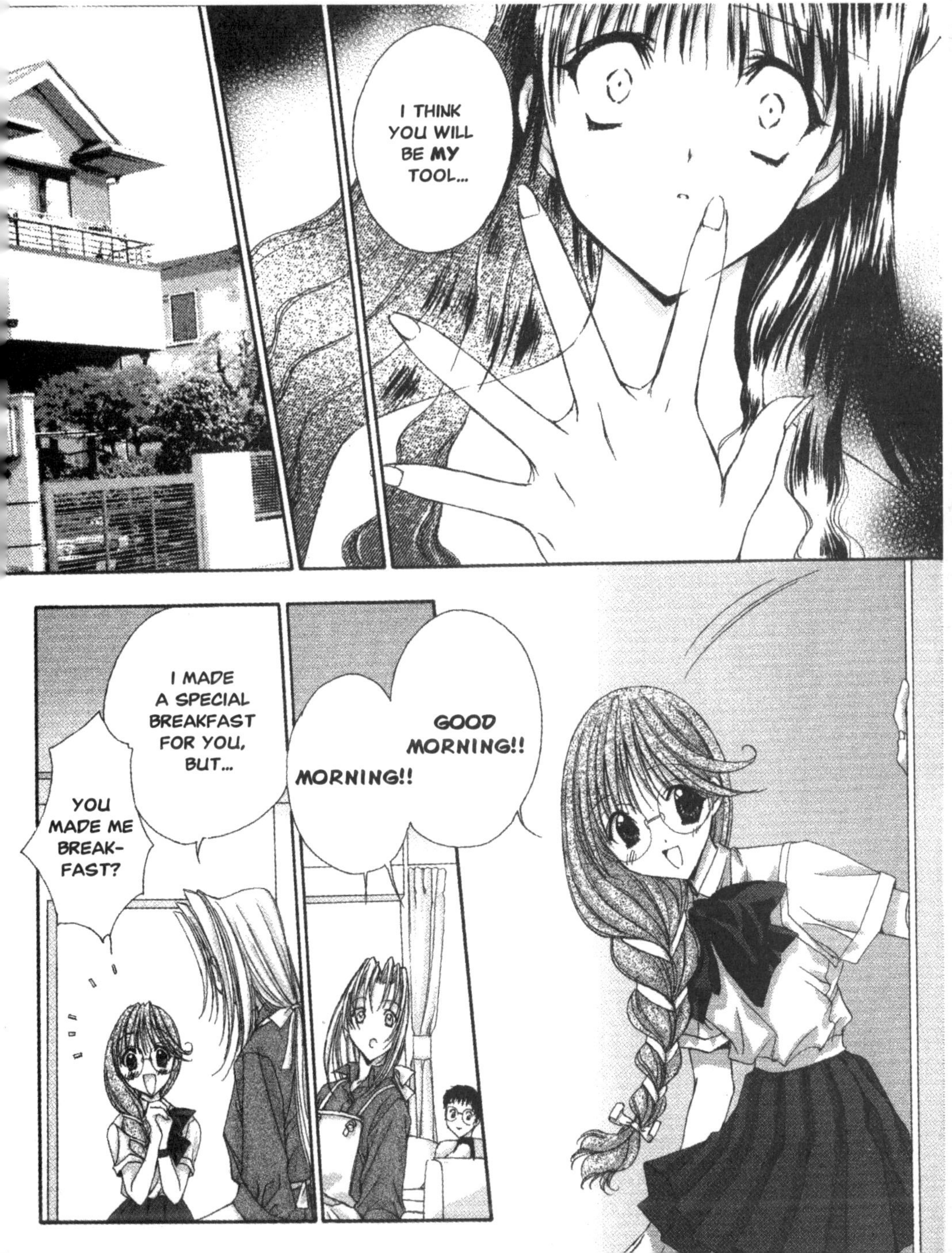
I THINK YOU WILL BE MY TOOL...
GOOD MORNING!!
MORNING!!
I MADE A SPECIAL BREAKFAST FOR YOU, BUT...
YOU MADE ME BREAK-FAST?

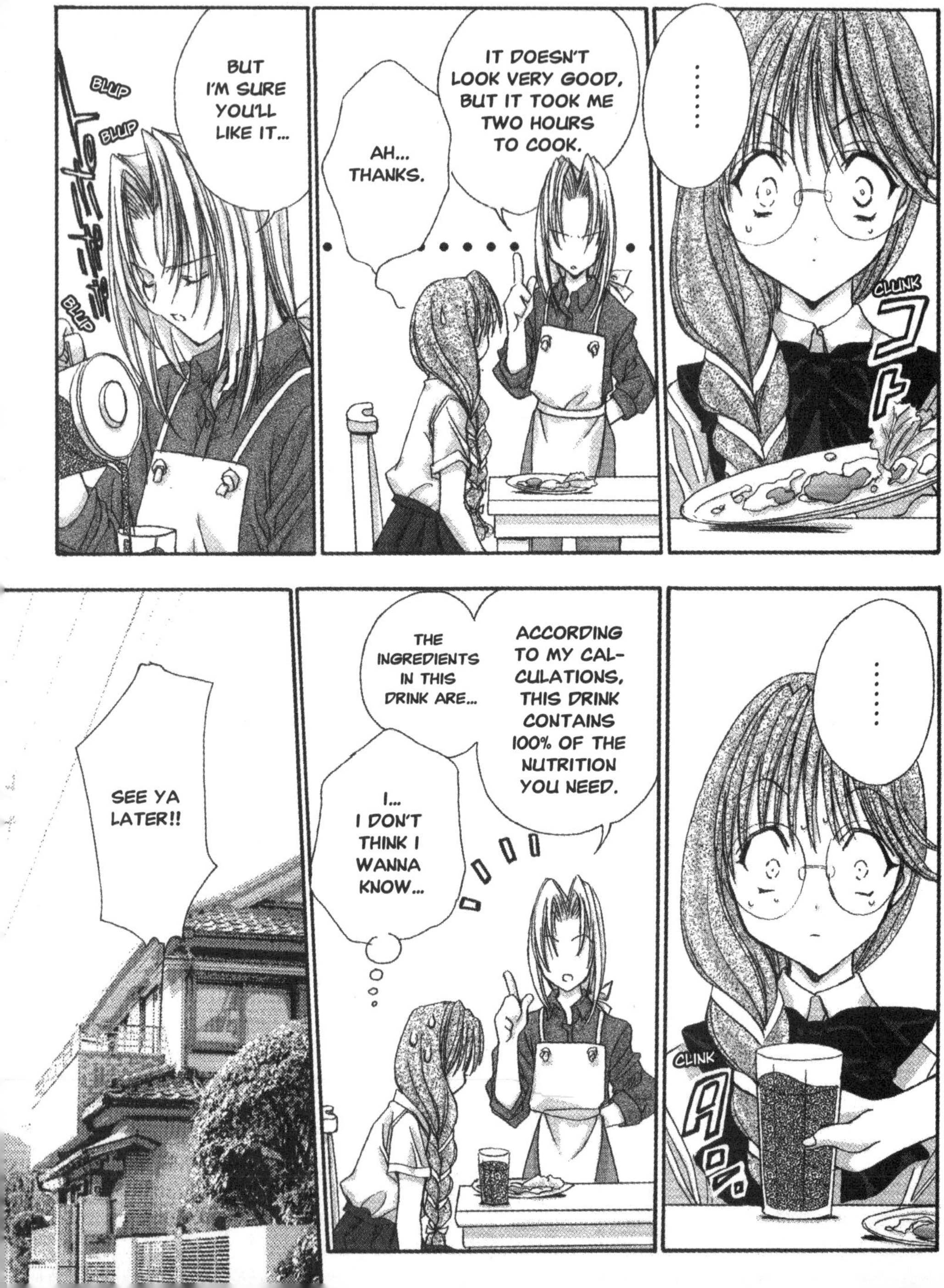
......
CLINK
IT DOESN'T LOOK VERY GOOD, BUT IT TOOK ME TWO HOURS TO COOK.
AH... THANKS.
BUT I'M SURE YOU'LL LIKE IT...
BLUP
BLUP
BLUP
......
CLINK
ACCORDING TO MY CAL- CULATIONS, THIS DRINK CONTAINS 100% OF THE NUTRITION YOU NEED.
THE INGREDIENTS IN THIS DRINK ARE...
I... I DON'T THINK I WANNA KNOW...
SEE YA LATER!!

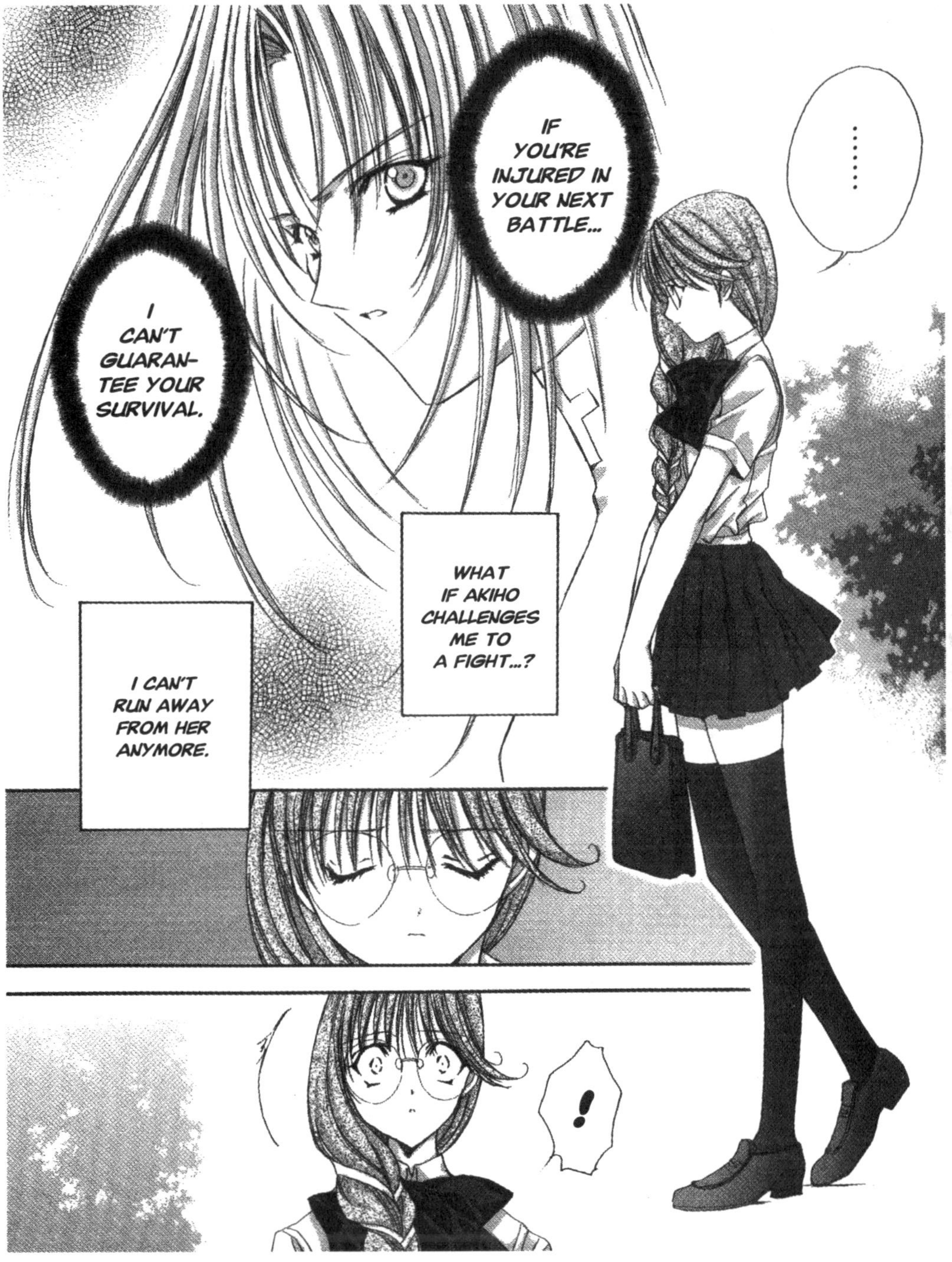

......
IF YOU'RE INJURED IN YOUR NEXT BATTLE...
I CAN'T GUARANTEE YOUR SURVIVAL.
WHAT IF AKIHO CHALLENGES ME TO A FIGHT...?
I CAN'T RUN AWAY FROM HER ANYMORE.
!

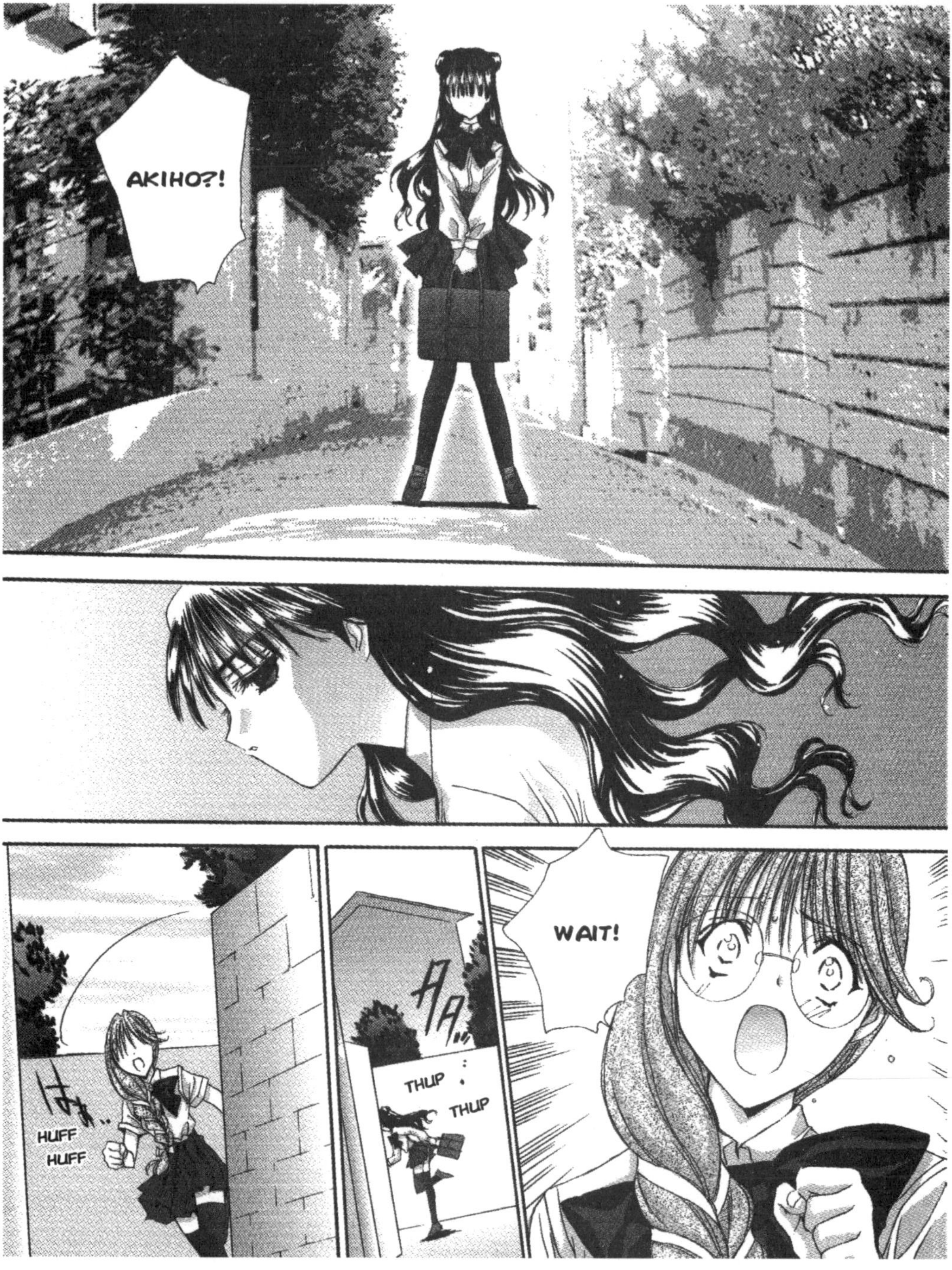
AKIHO?!
WAIT!
THUP
THUP
HUFF
HUFF

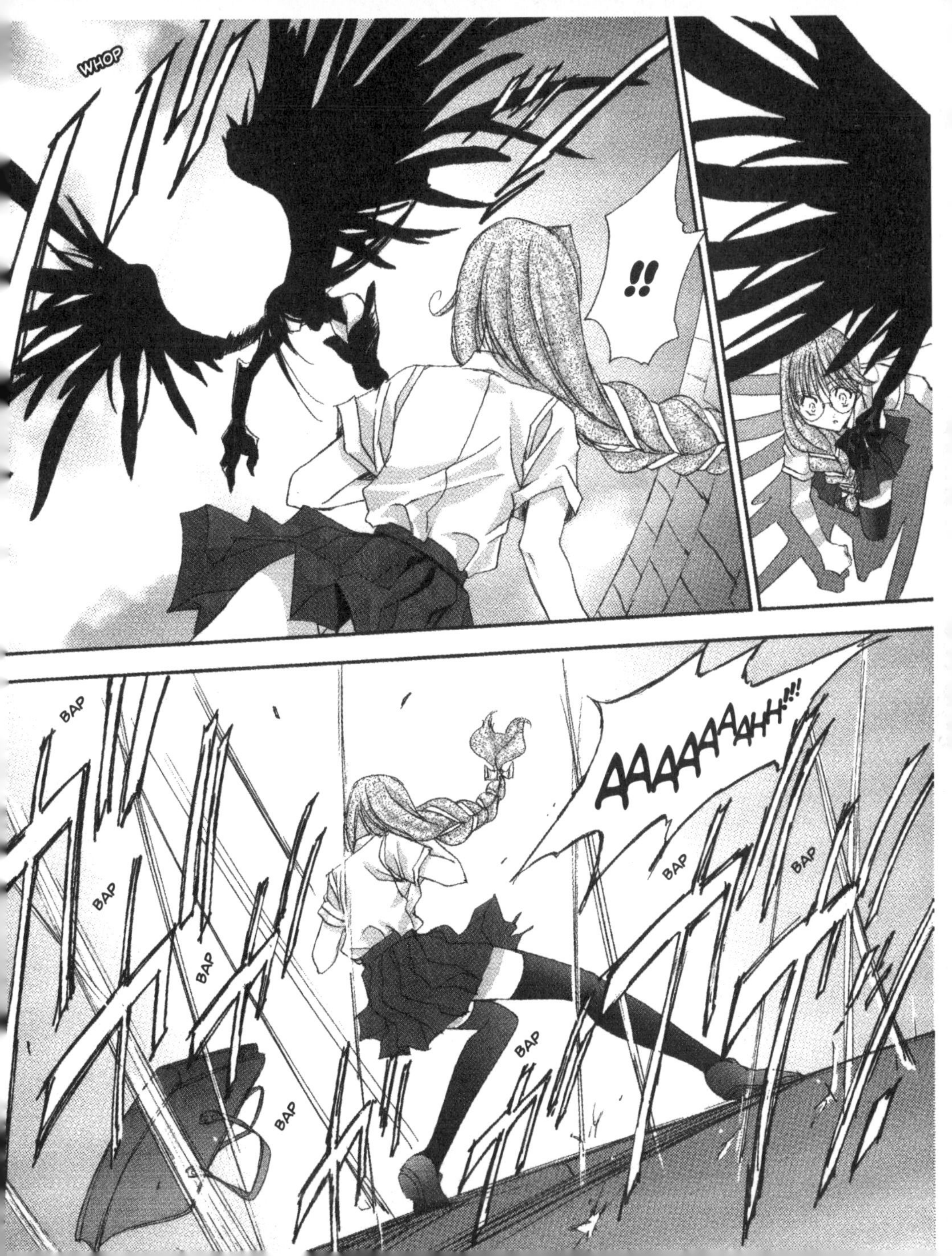
!!
WHOP
AAAAAAAHH!!!
BAP
BAP
BAP
BAP
BAP
BAP
BAP

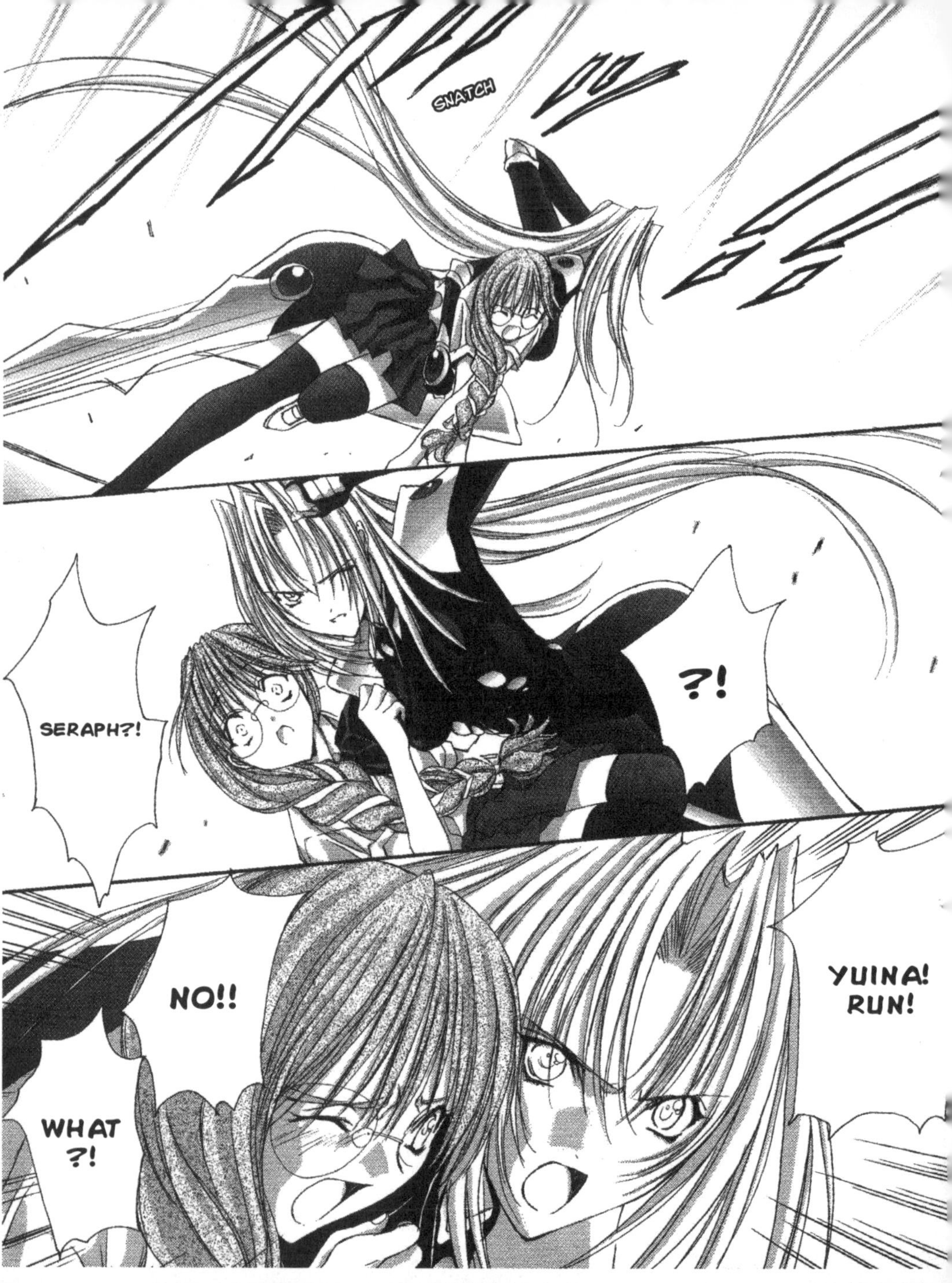
SNATCH
?!
SERAPH?!
YUINA! RUN!
NO!!
WHAT ?!

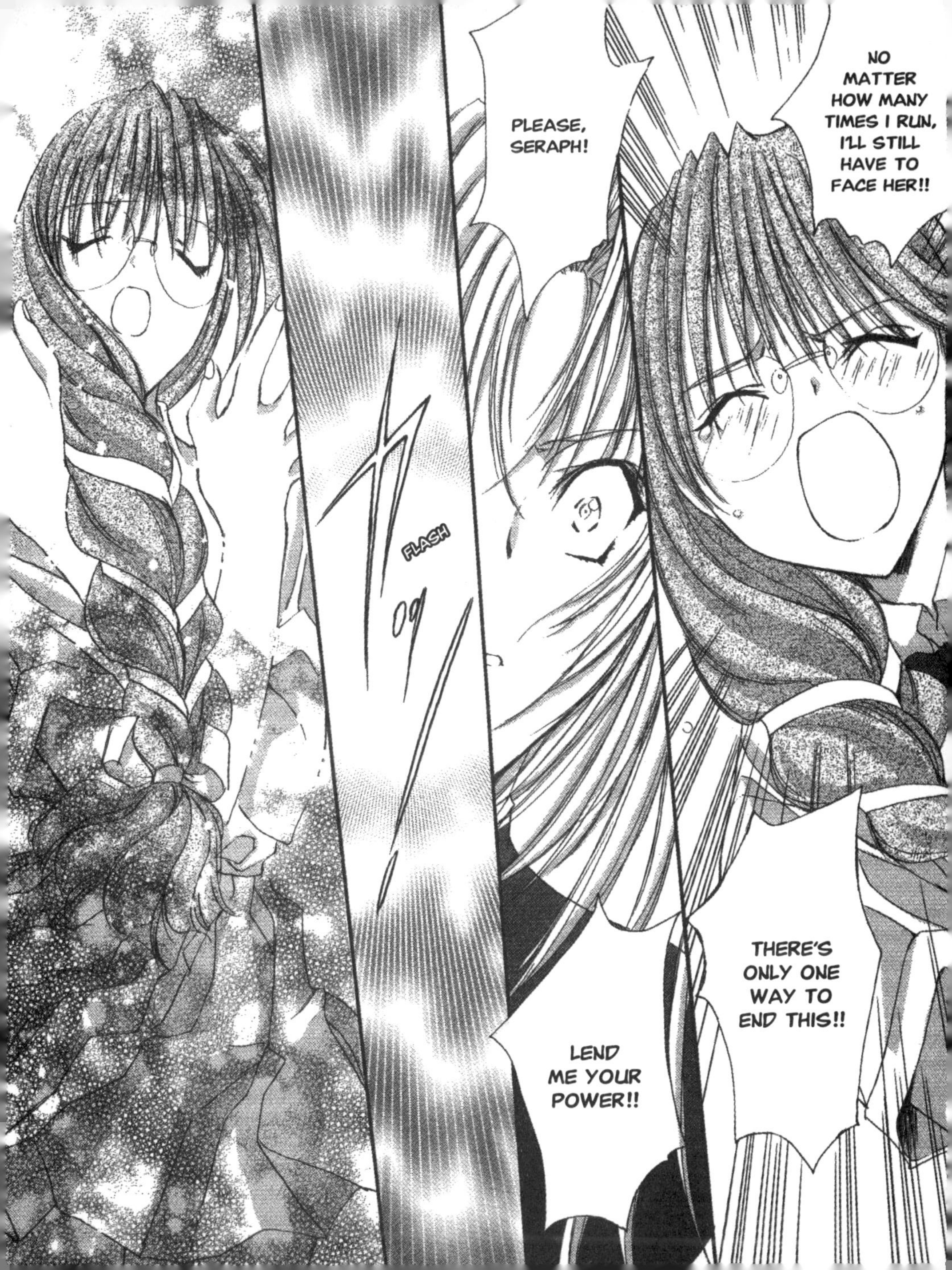
NO MATTER HOW MANY TIMES I RUN, I'LL STILL HAVE TO FACE HER!!
PLEASE, SERAPH!
FLASH
THERE'S ONLY ONE WAY TO END THIS!!
LEND ME YOUR POWER!!

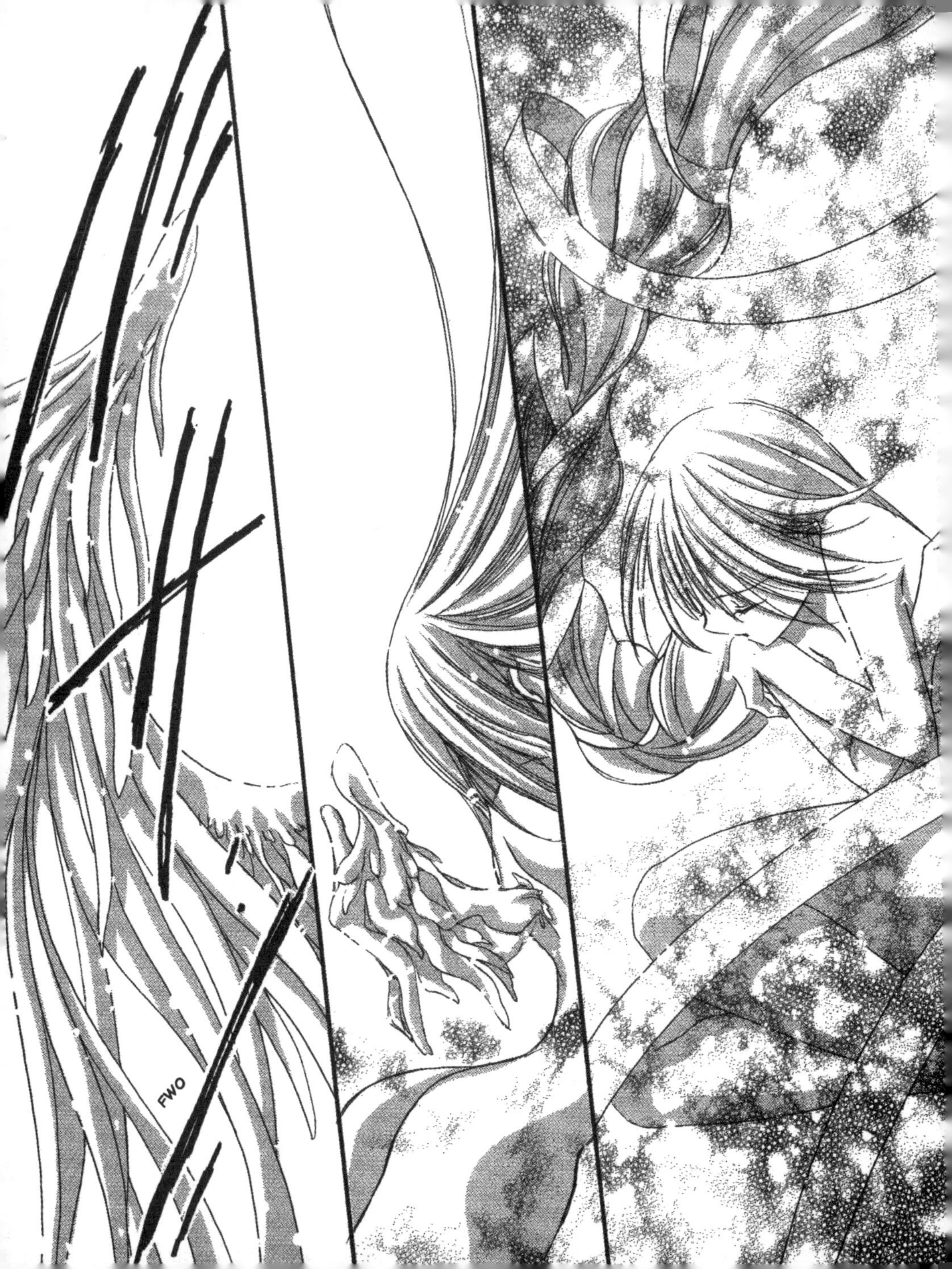
FWO

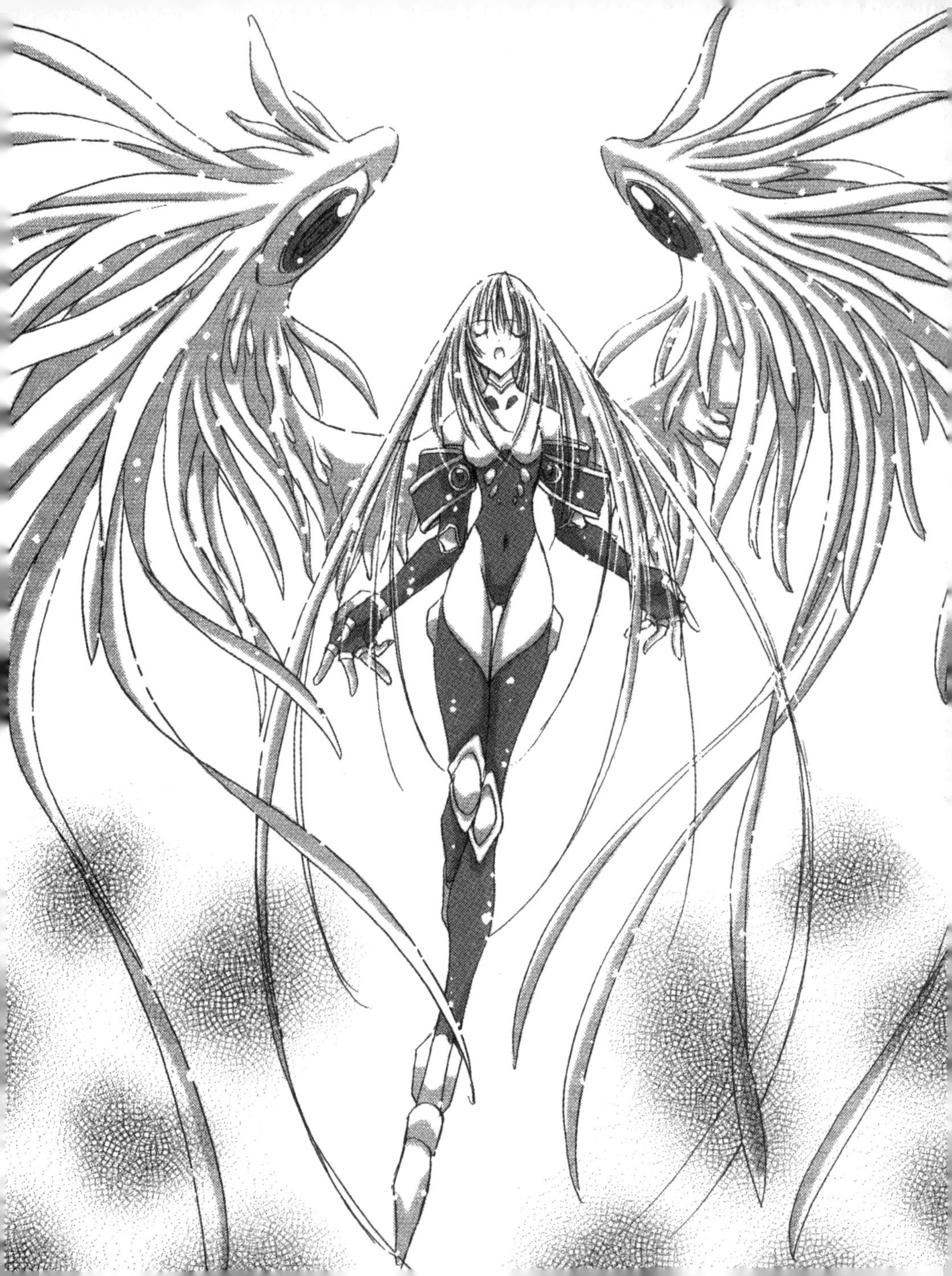

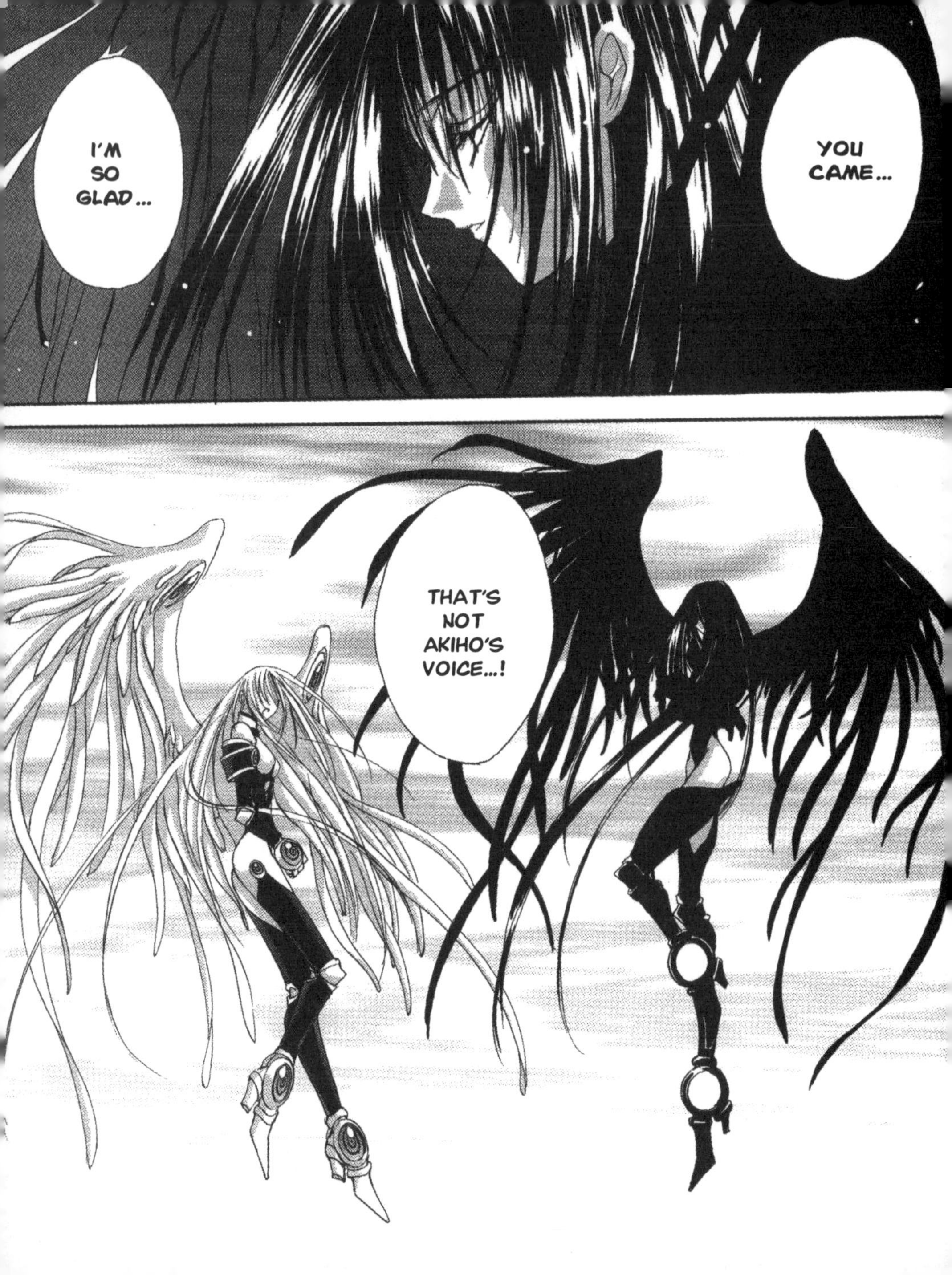
YOU CAME...
I'M SO GLAD...
THAT'S NOT AKIHO'S VOICE...!

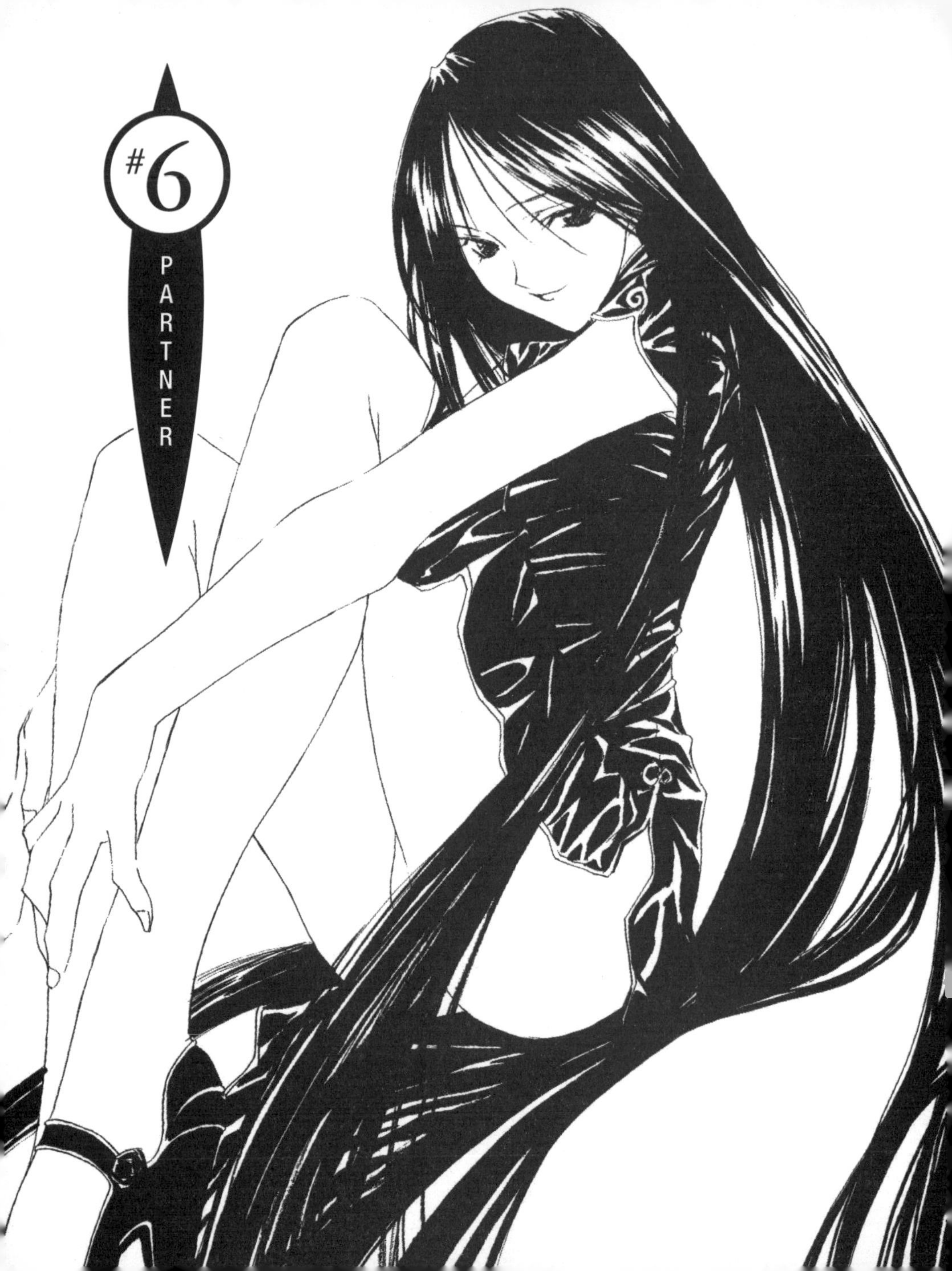
#6
PARTNER

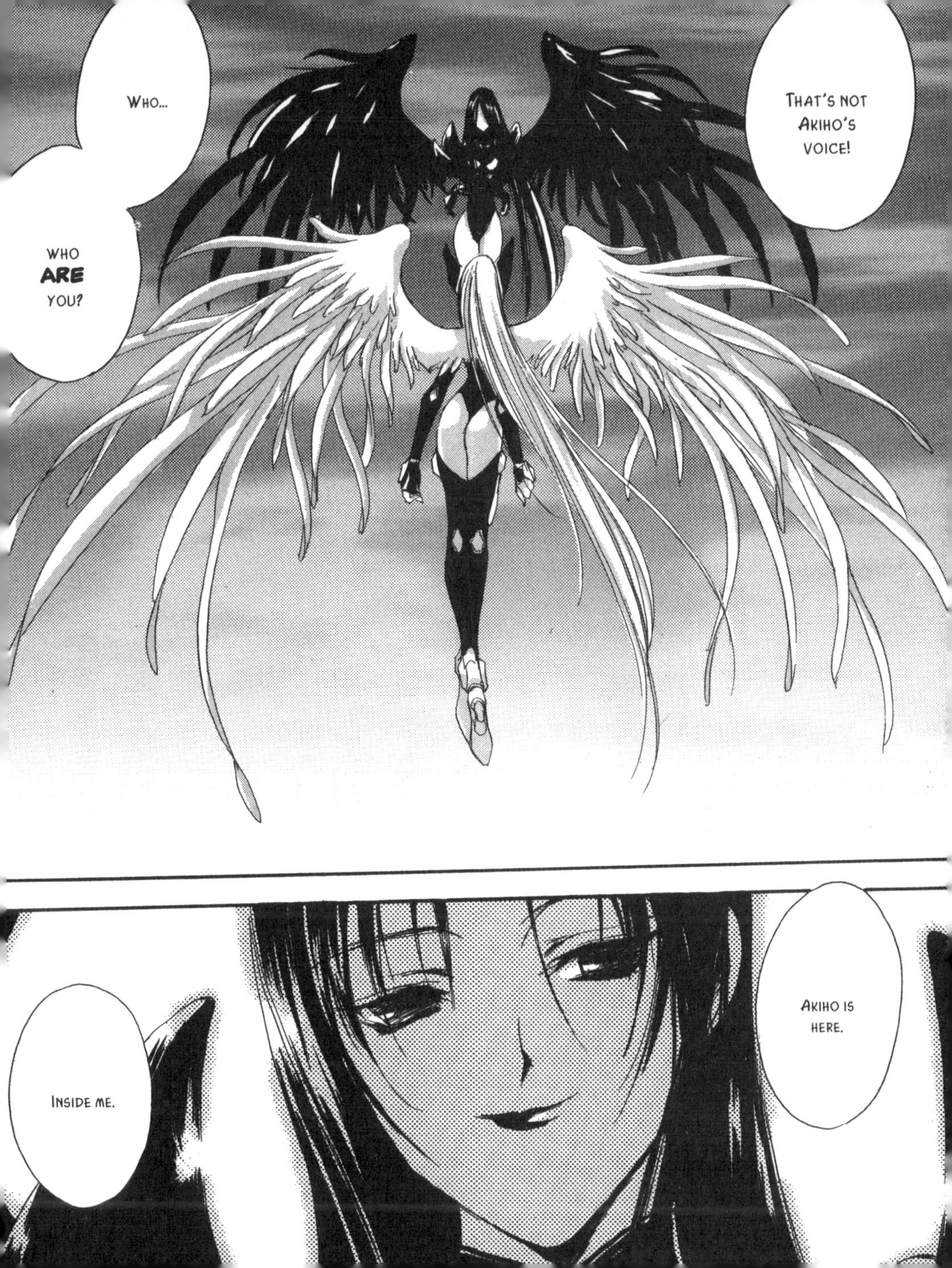
That's not Akiho's voice!
Who...
Who **are** you?
Akiho is here.
Inside me.

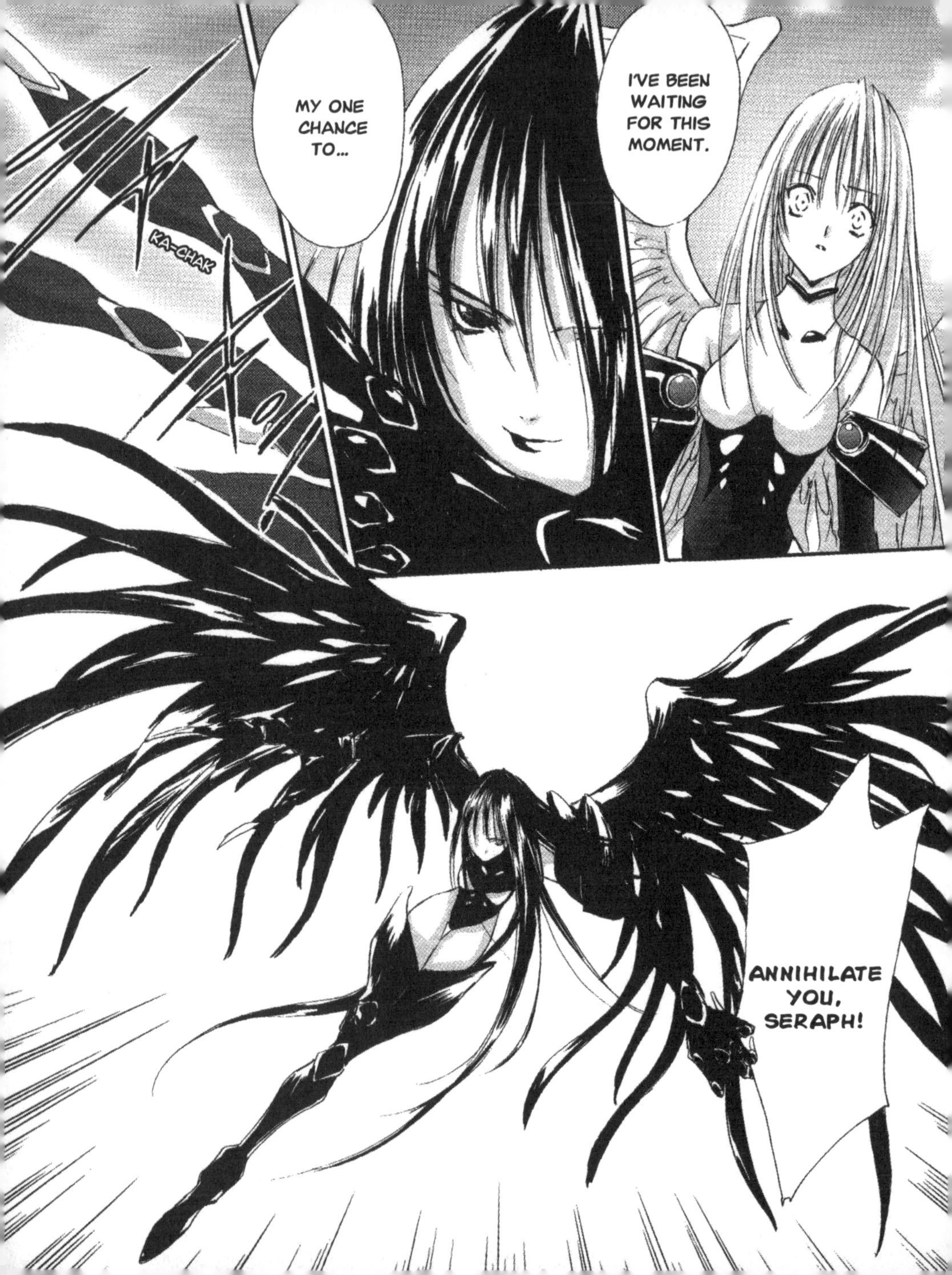
I'VE BEEN WAITING FOR THIS MOMENT.
MY ONE CHANCE TO...
KA-CHAK
ANNIHILATE YOU, SERAPH!

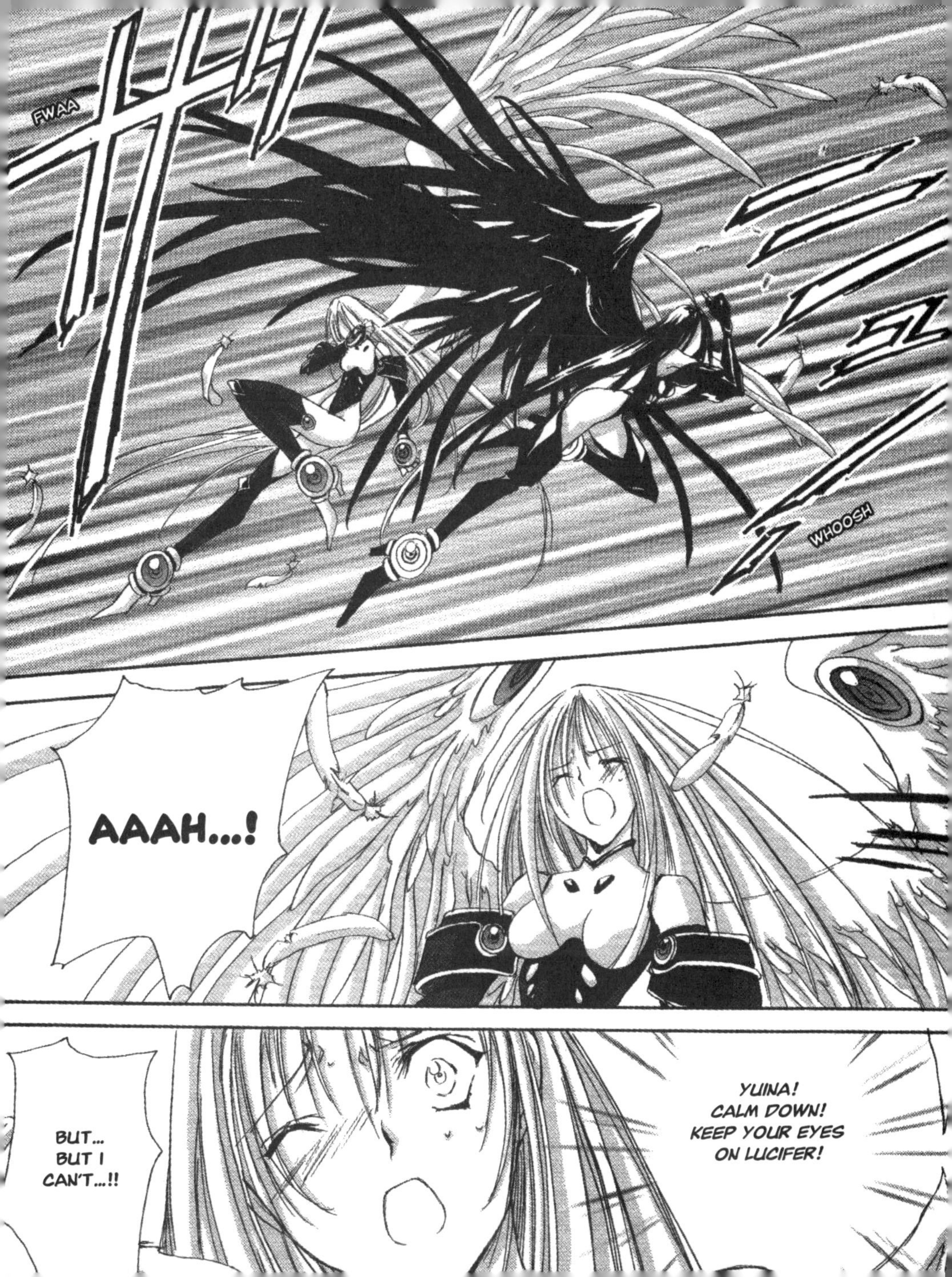
FWAA
WHOOSH
AAAH...!
YUINA! CALM DOWN! KEEP YOUR EYES ON LUCIFER!
BUT... BUT I CAN'T...!!

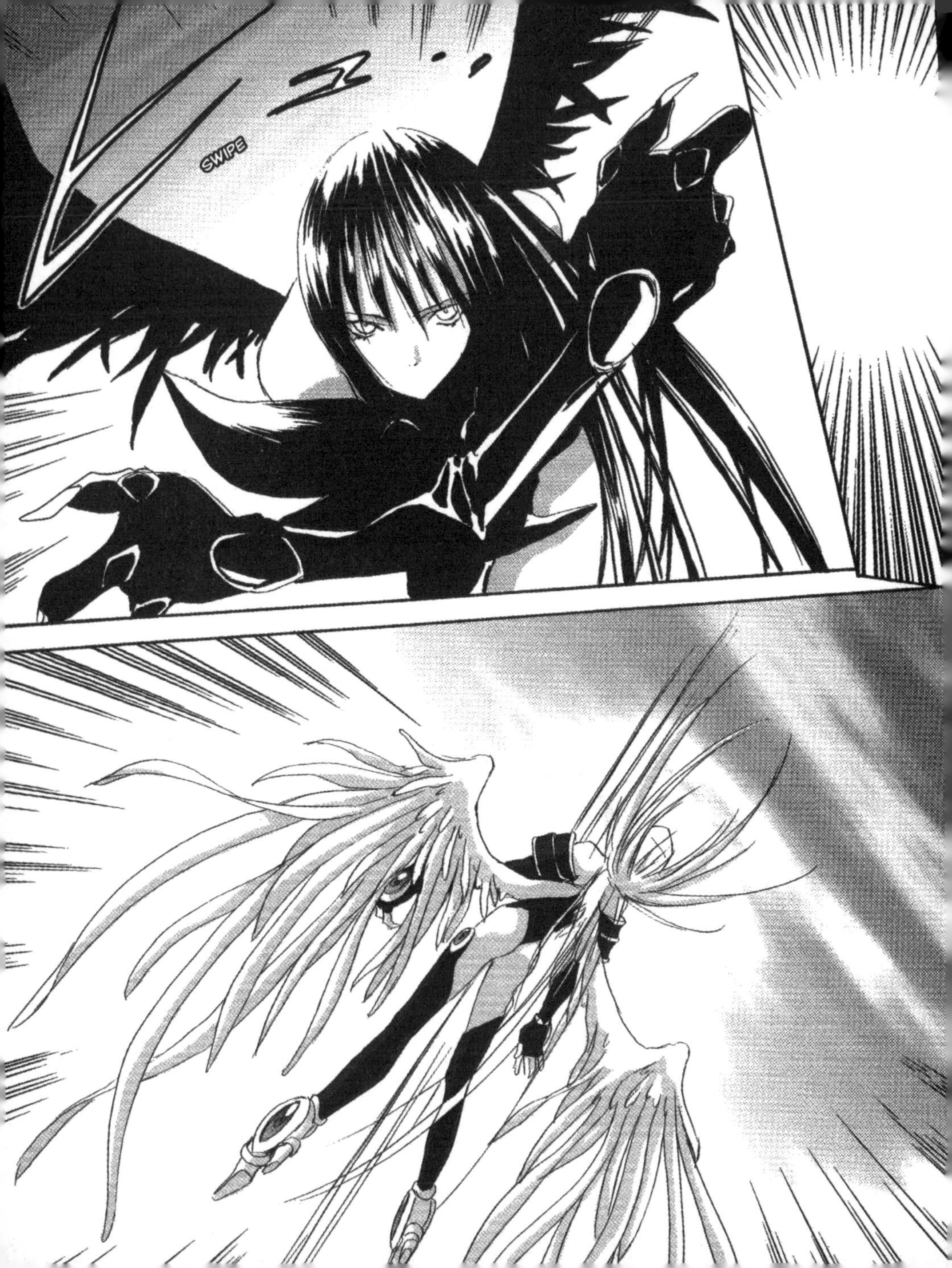
SWIPE

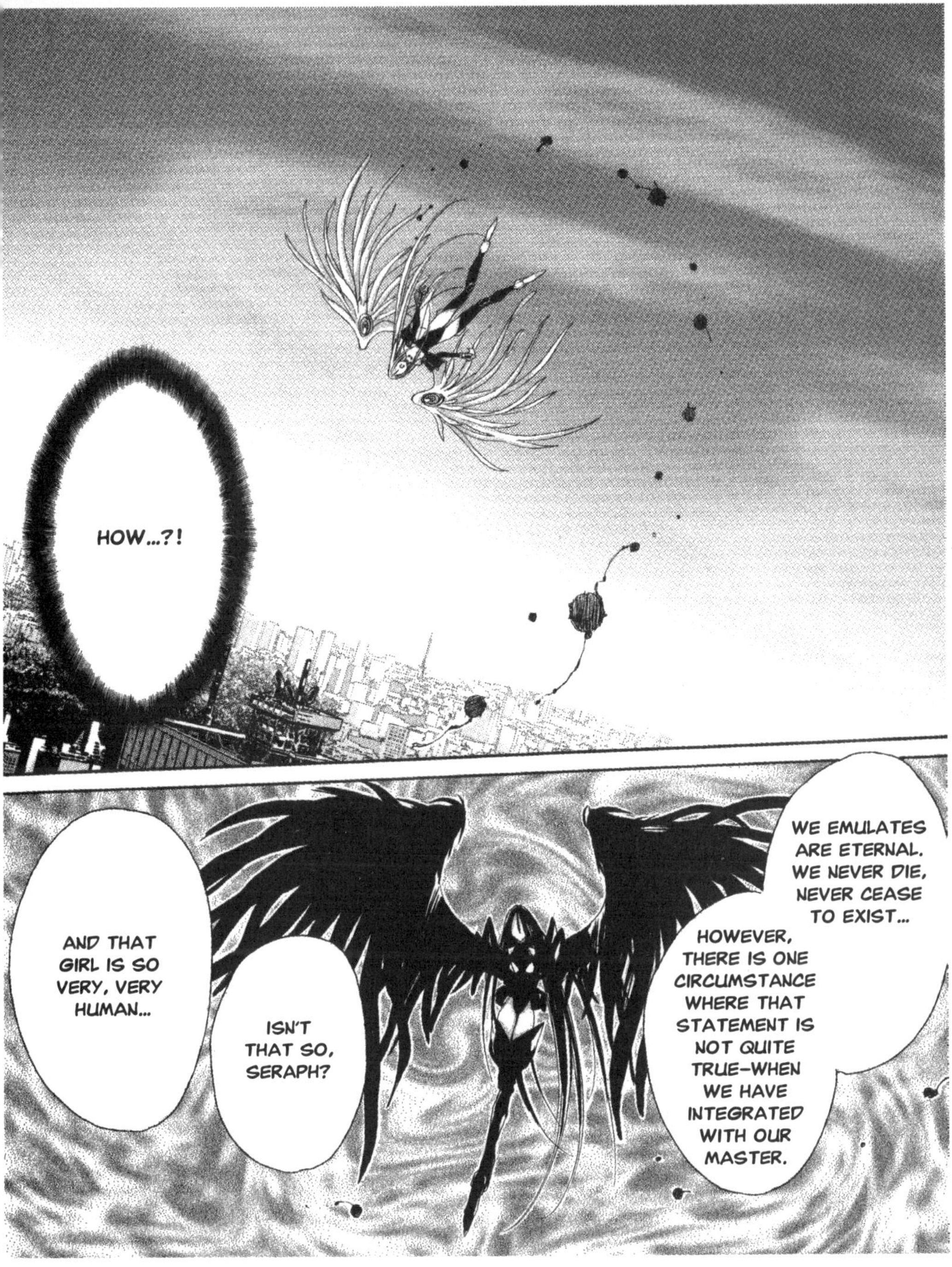
HOW...?!
WE EMULATES ARE ETERNAL. WE NEVER DIE, NEVER CEASE TO EXIST...
HOWEVER, THERE IS ONE CIRCUMSTANCE WHERE THAT STATEMENT IS NOT QUITE TRUE–WHEN WE HAVE INTEGRATED WITH OUR MASTER.
ISN'T THAT SO, SERAPH?
AND THAT GIRL IS SO VERY, VERY HUMAN...

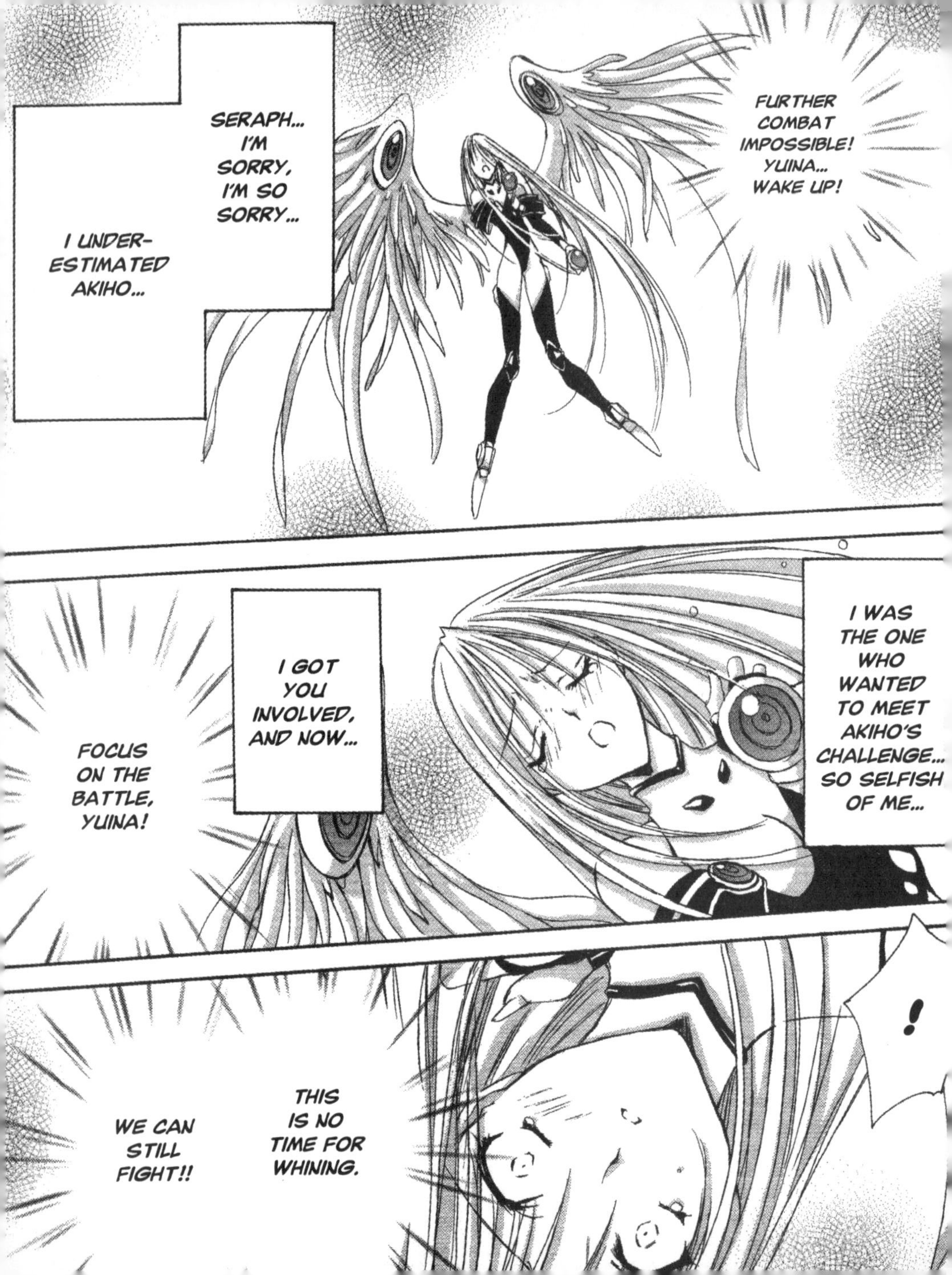
FURTHER COMBAT IMPOSSIBLE! YUINA... WAKE UP!
SERAPH... I'M SORRY, I'M SO SORRY...
I UNDER-ESTIMATED AKIHO...
I WAS THE ONE WHO WANTED TO MEET AKIHO'S CHALLENGE... SO SELFISH OF ME...
I GOT YOU INVOLVED, AND NOW...
FOCUS ON THE BATTLE, YUINA!
!
THIS IS NO TIME FOR WHINING.
WE CAN STILL FIGHT!!

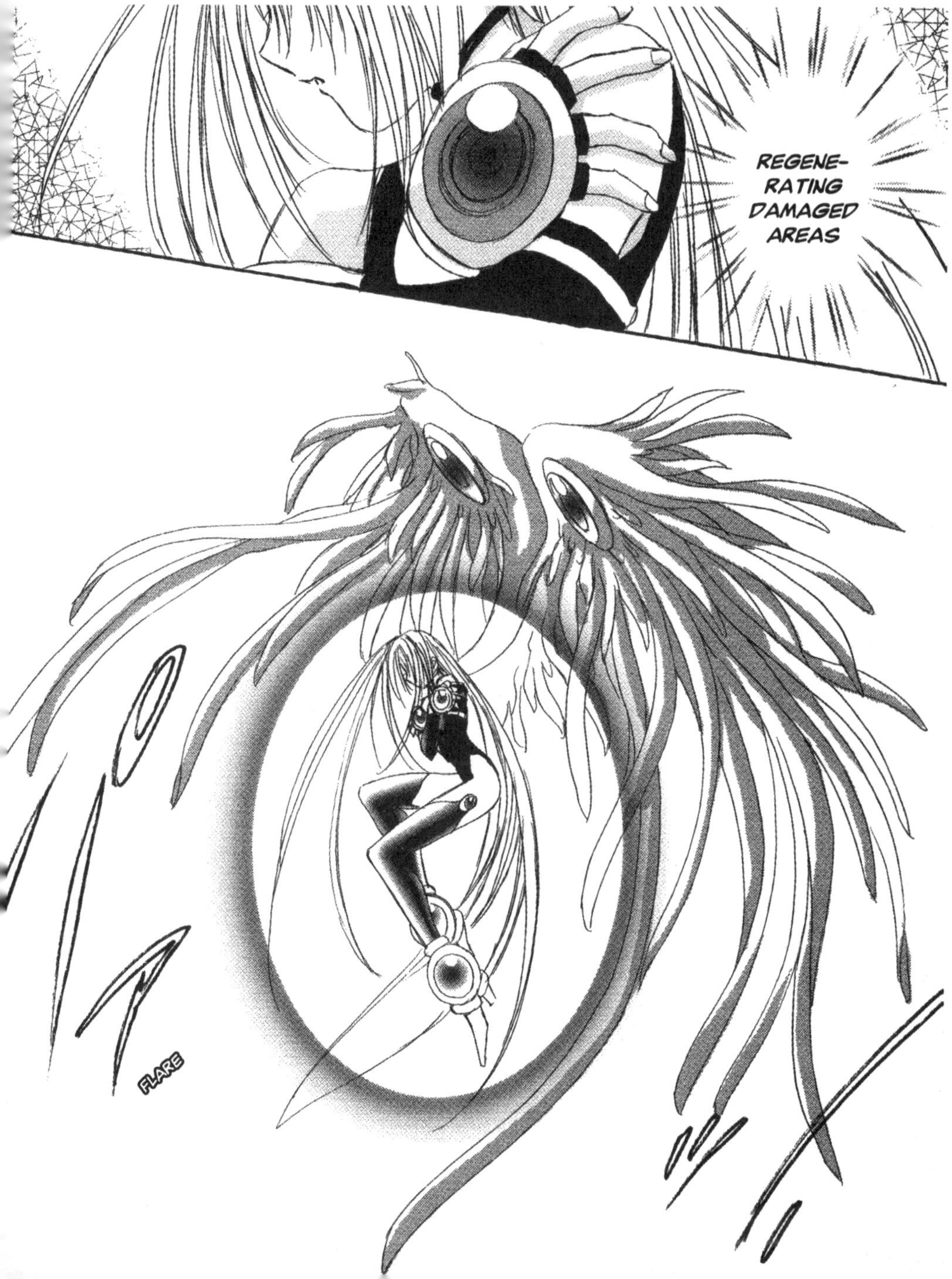
REGENE-RATING DAMAGED AREAS
FLARE

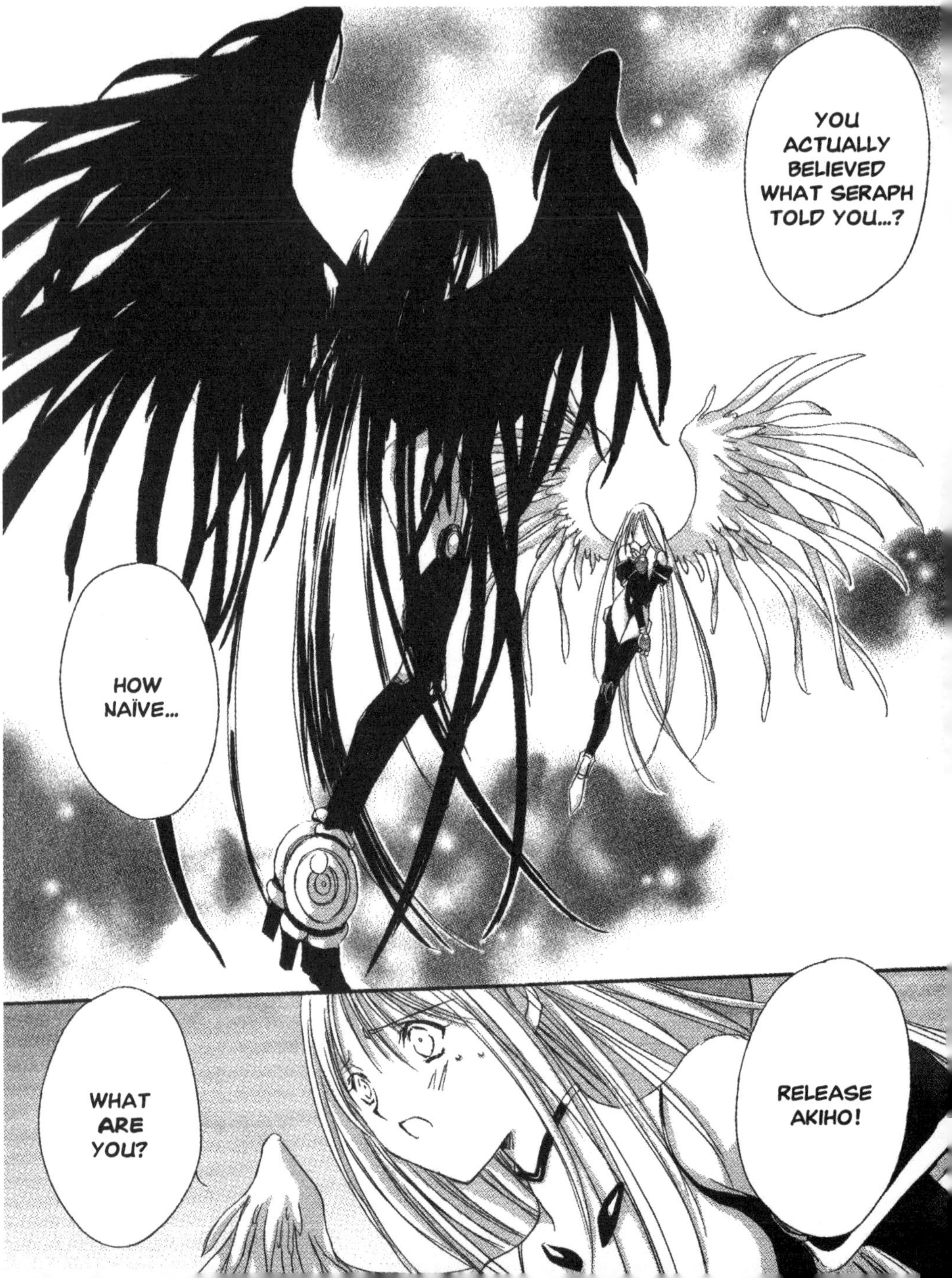
YOU ACTUALLY BELIEVED WHAT SERAPH TOLD YOU...?
HOW NAÏVE...
RELEASE AKIHO!
WHAT ARE YOU?

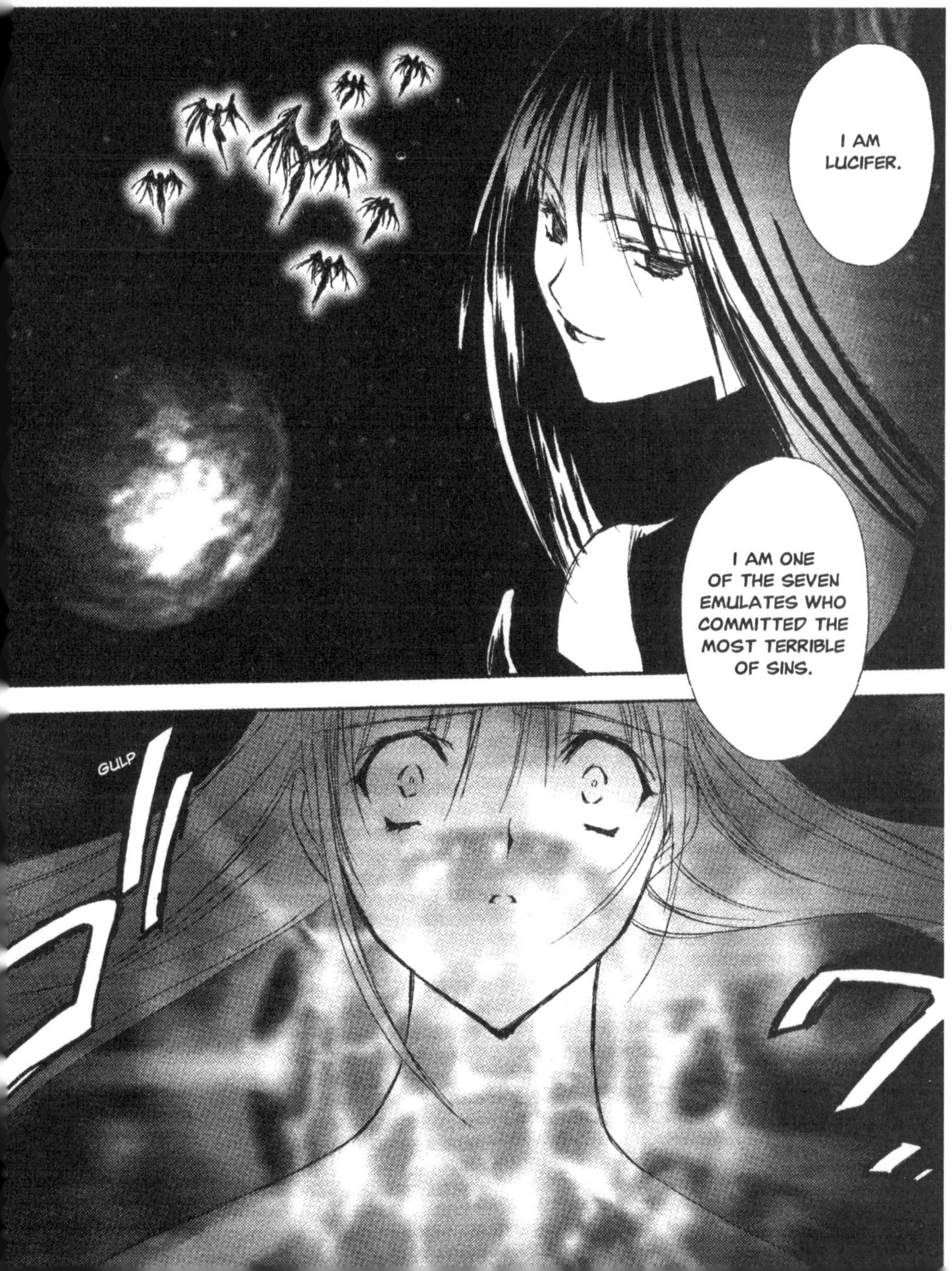
I AM LUCIFER.
I AM ONE OF THE SEVEN EMULATES WHO COMMITTED THE MOST TERRIBLE OF SINS.
GULP

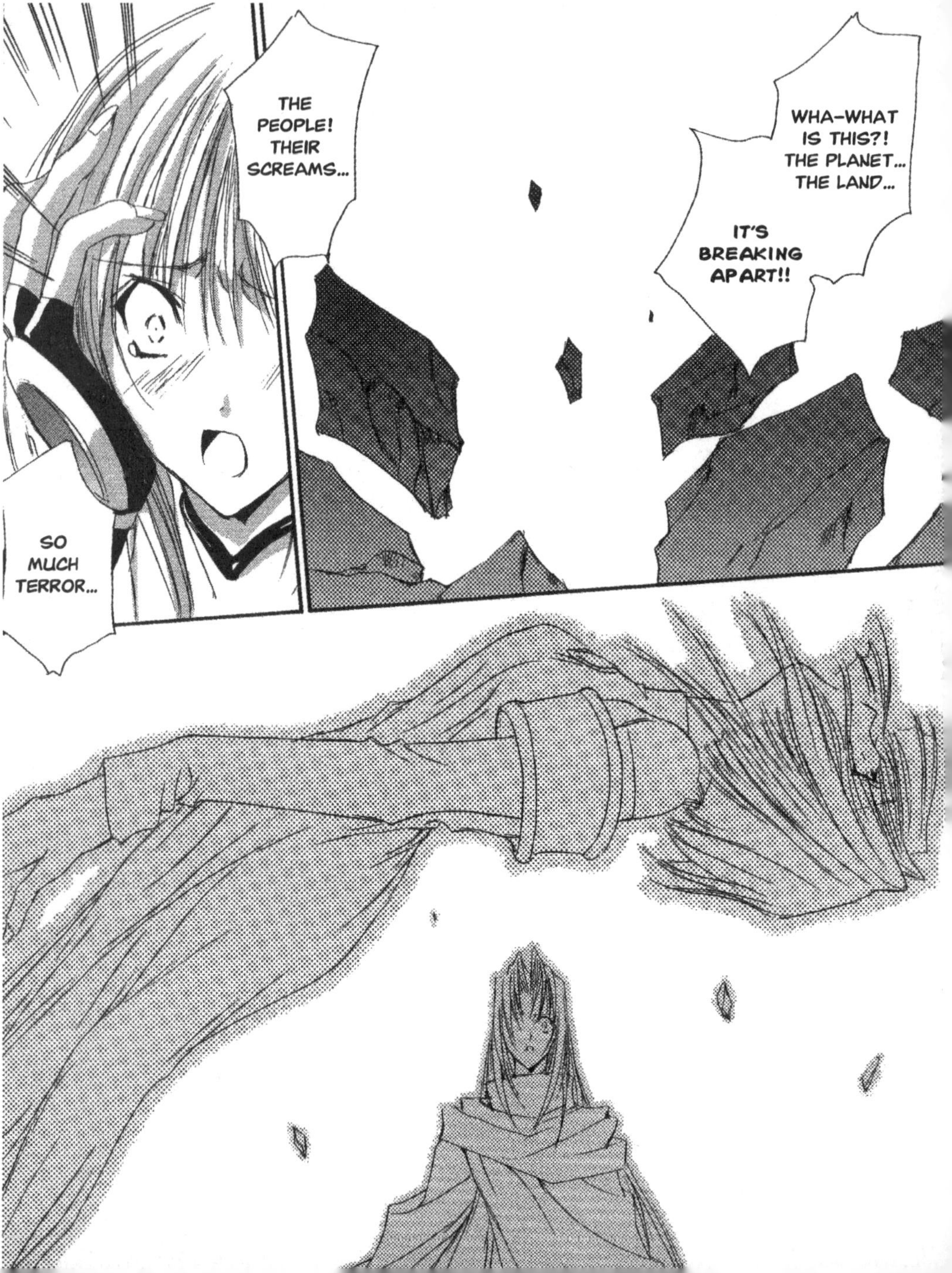
WHA-WHAT IS THIS?! THE PLANET... THE LAND...
IT'S BREAKING APART!!
THE PEOPLE! THEIR SCREAMS...
SO MUCH TERROR...

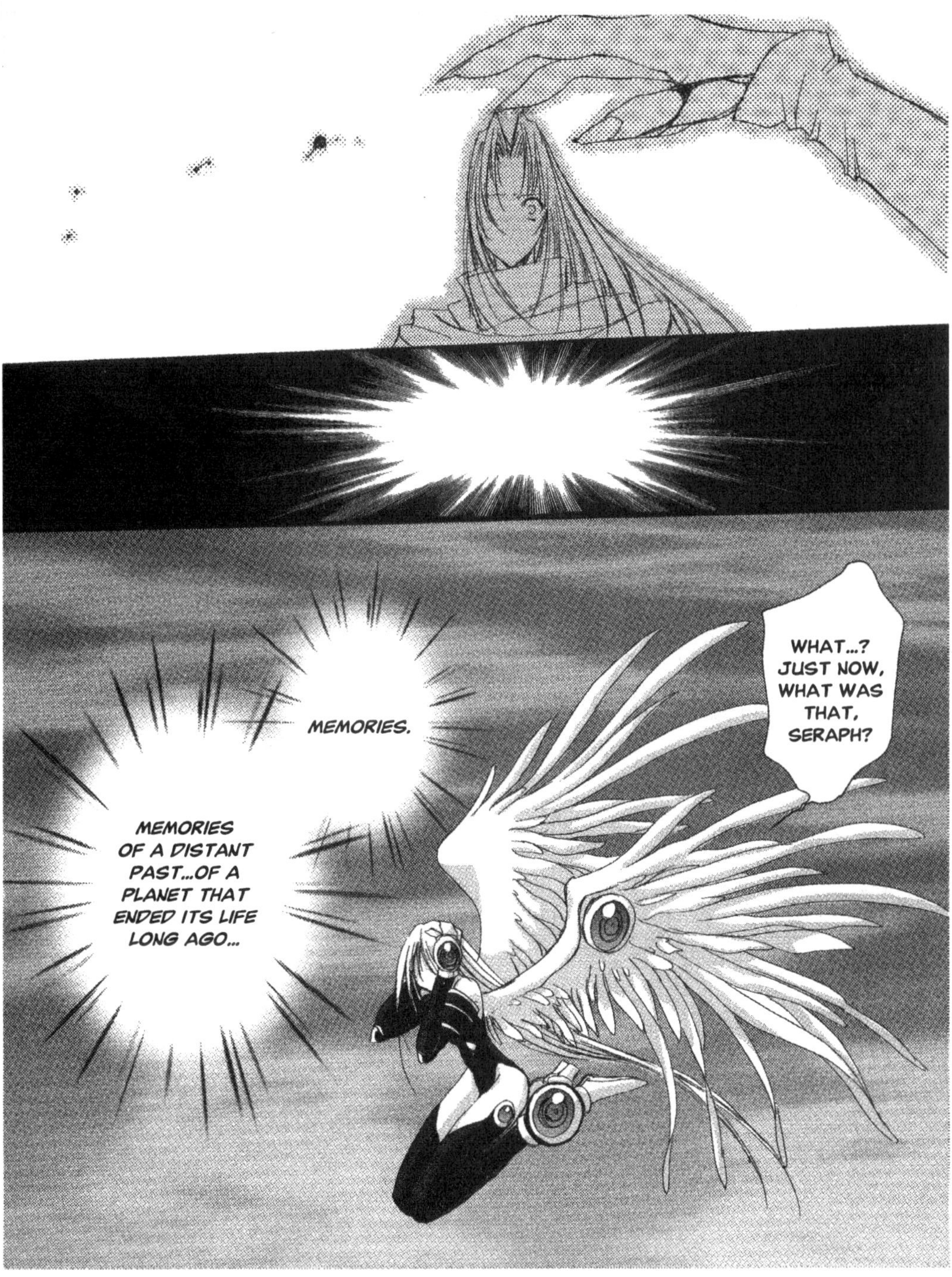
WHAT...? JUST NOW, WHAT WAS THAT, SERAPH?
MEMORIES.
MEMORIES OF A DISTANT PAST...OF A PLANET THAT ENDED ITS LIFE LONG AGO...

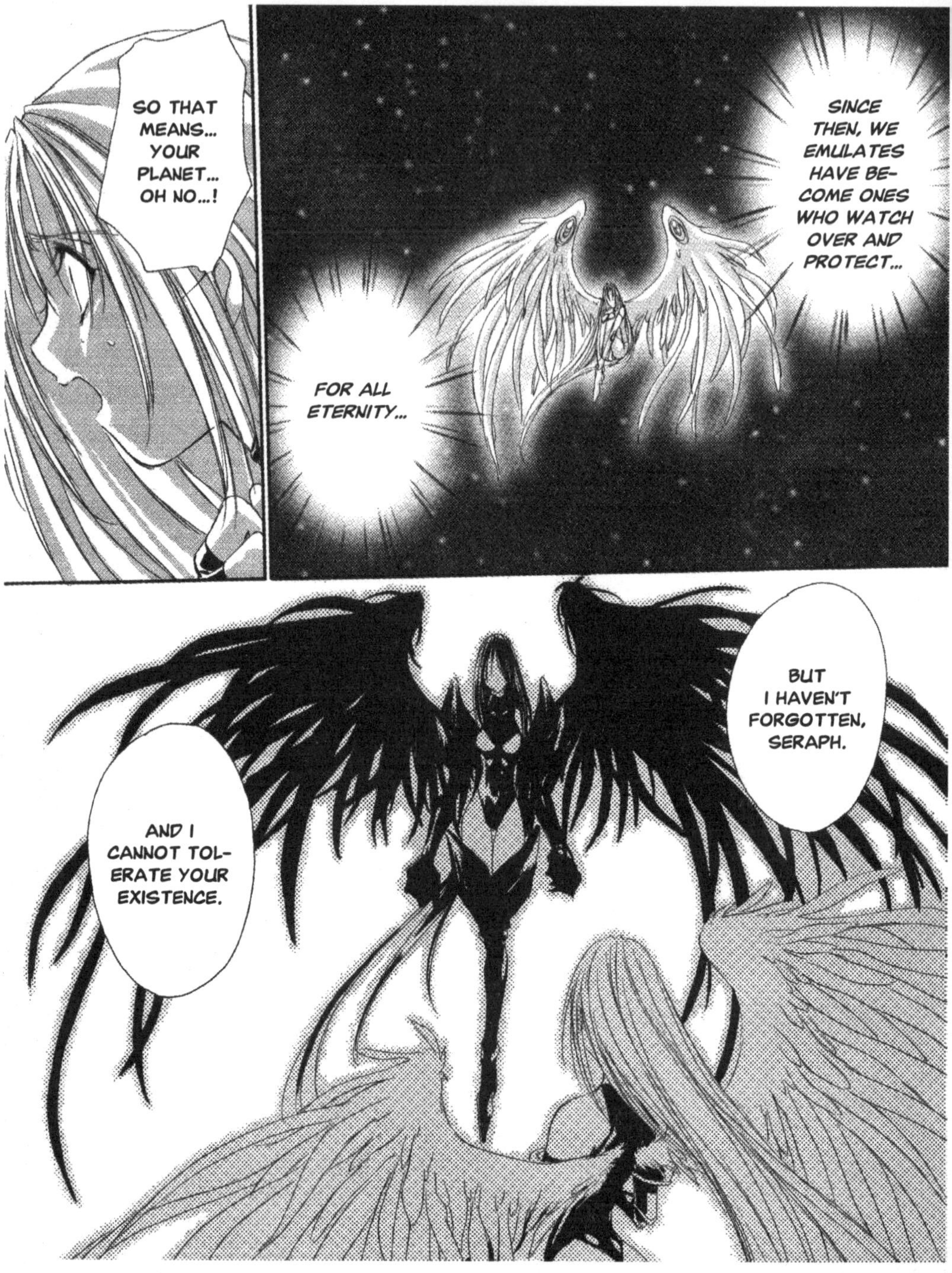
SINCE THEN, WE EMULATES HAVE BE- COME ONES WHO WATCH OVER AND PROTECT...
FOR ALL ETERNITY...
SO THAT MEANS... YOUR PLANET... OH NO...!
BUT I HAVEN'T FORGOTTEN, SERAPH.
AND I CANNOT TOL- ERATE YOUR EXISTENCE.

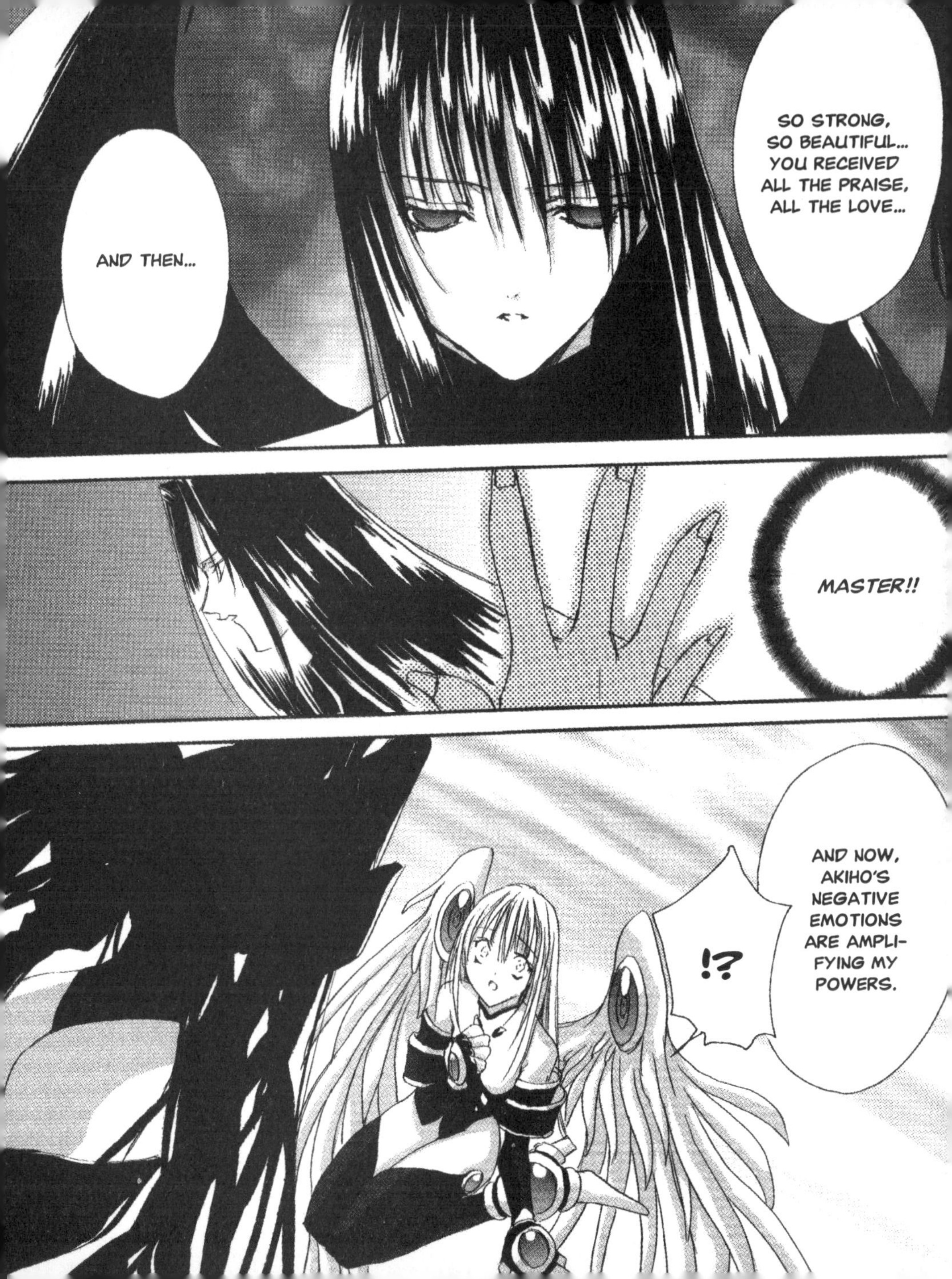
SO STRONG, SO BEAUTIFUL... YOU RECEIVED ALL THE PRAISE, ALL THE LOVE...
AND THEN...
MASTER!!
AND NOW, AKIHO'S NEGATIVE EMOTIONS ARE AMPLI-FYING MY POWERS.
!?

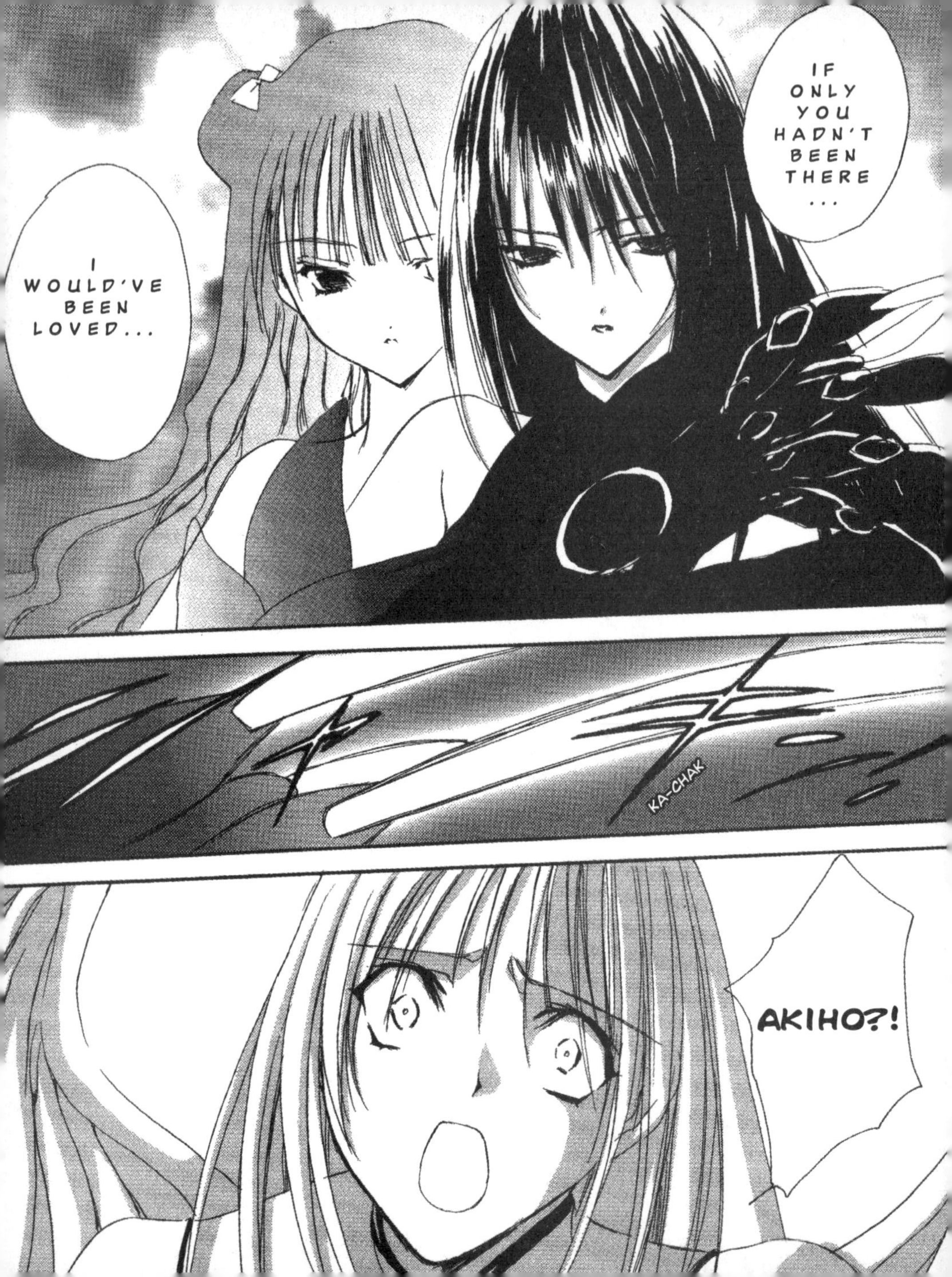
IF ONLY YOU HADN'T BEEN THERE...
I WOULD'VE BEEN LOVED...
KA-CHAK
AKIHO?!

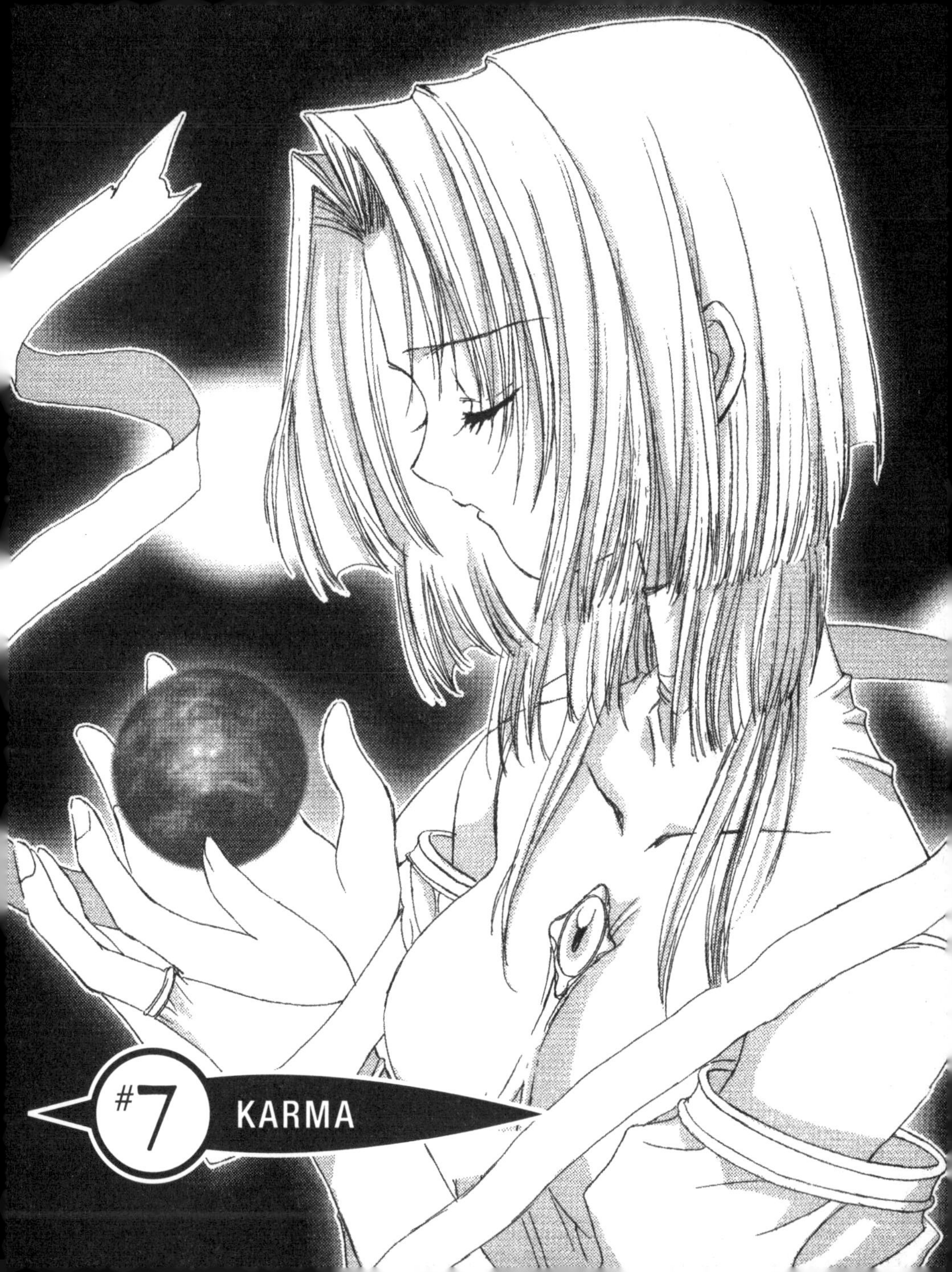
#7
KARMA

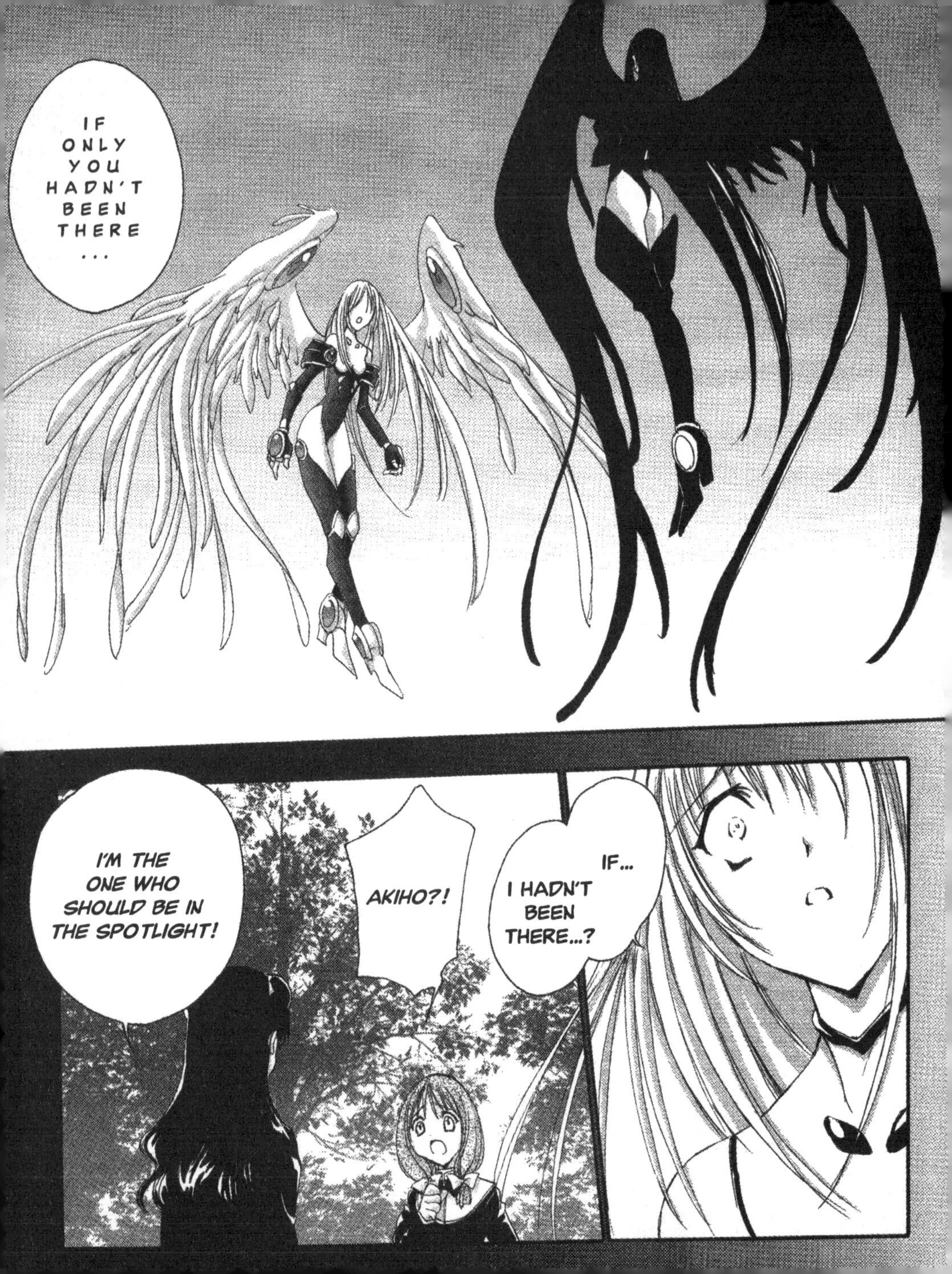
IF ONLY YOU HADN'T BEEN THERE ...
IF... I HADN'T BEEN THERE...?
AKIHO?!
I'M THE ONE WHO SHOULD BE IN THE SPOTLIGHT!

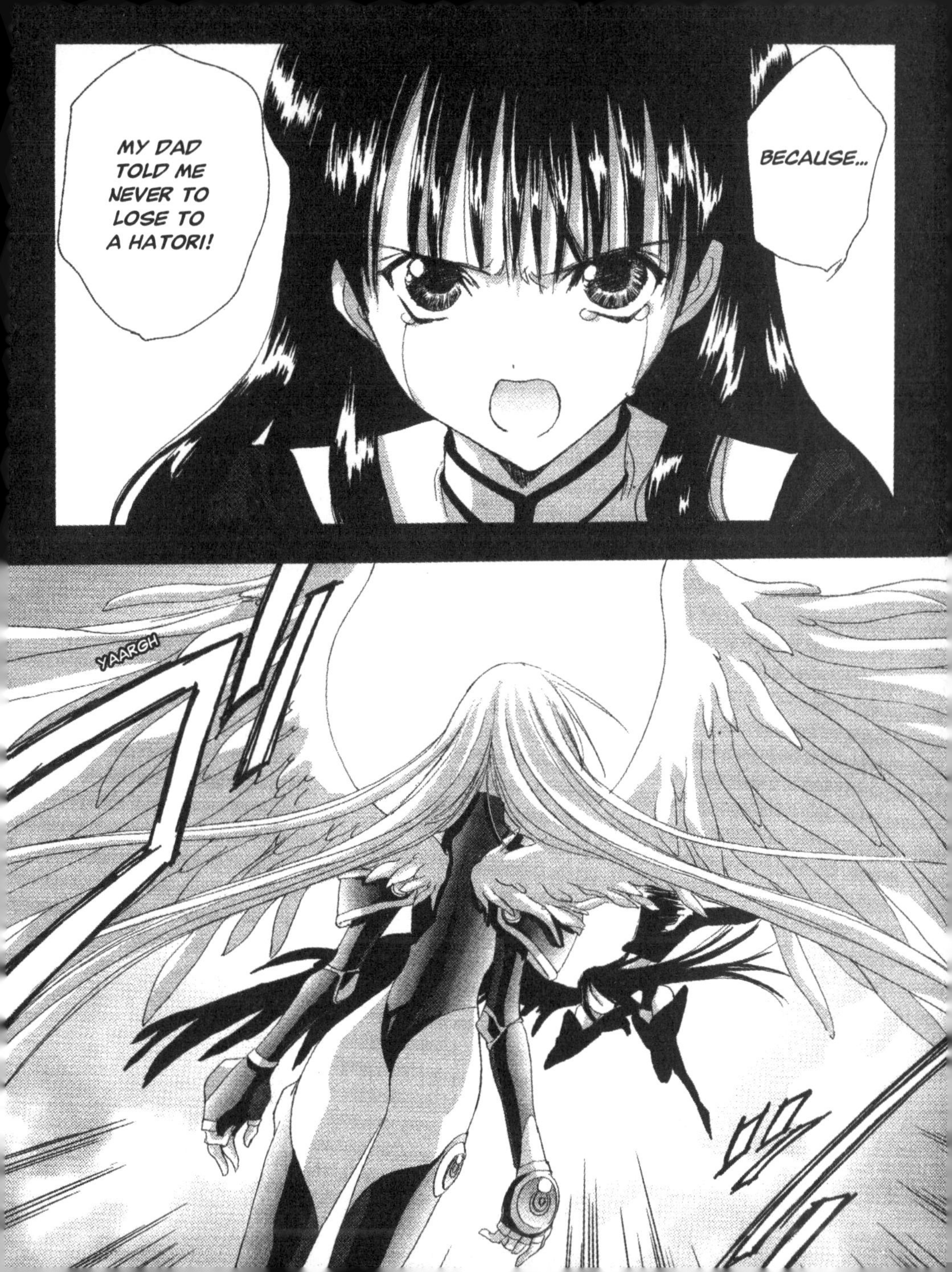
BECAUSE...
MY DAD TOLD ME NEVER TO LOSE TO A HATORI!
YAARGH

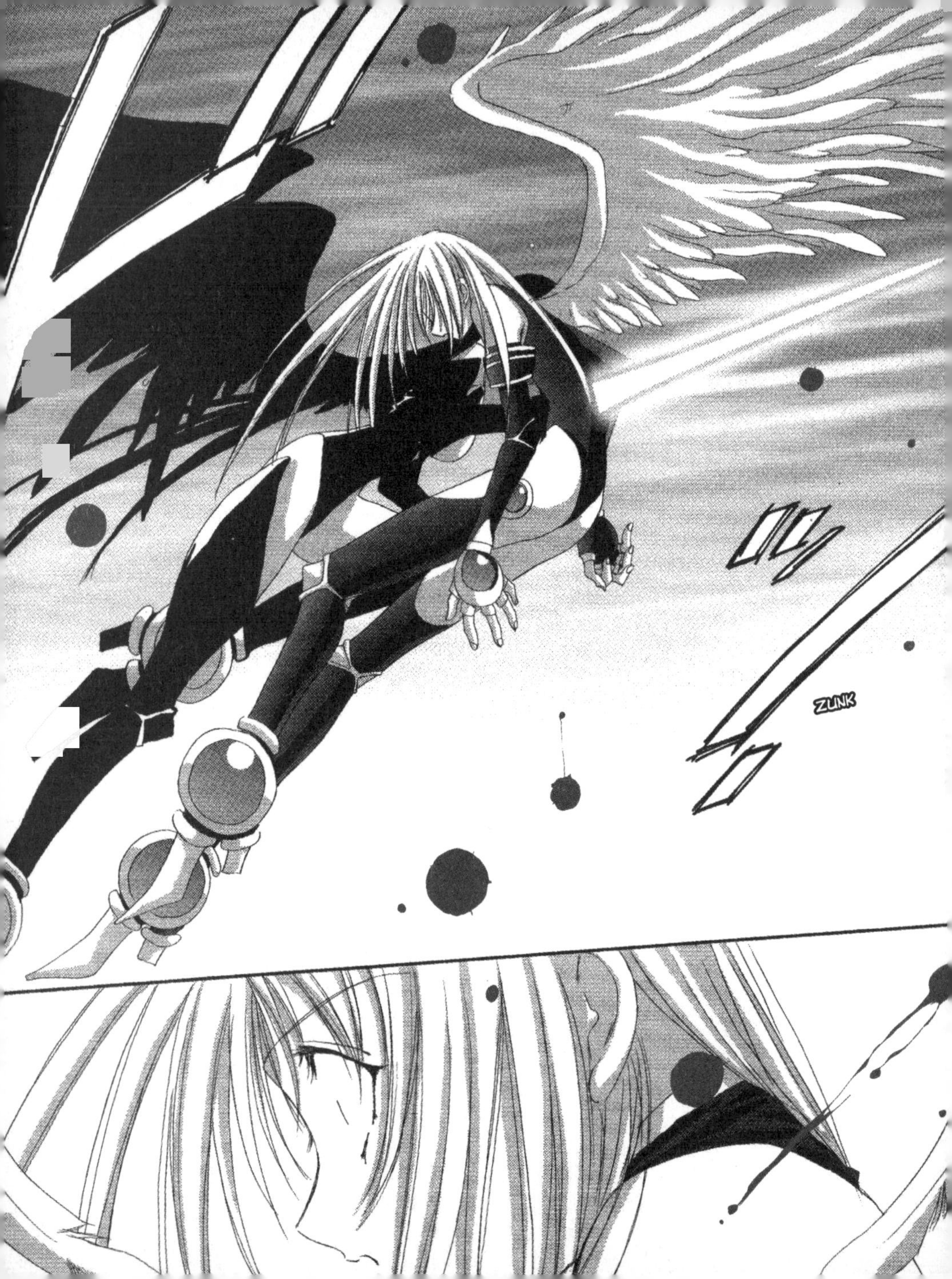
ZUNK

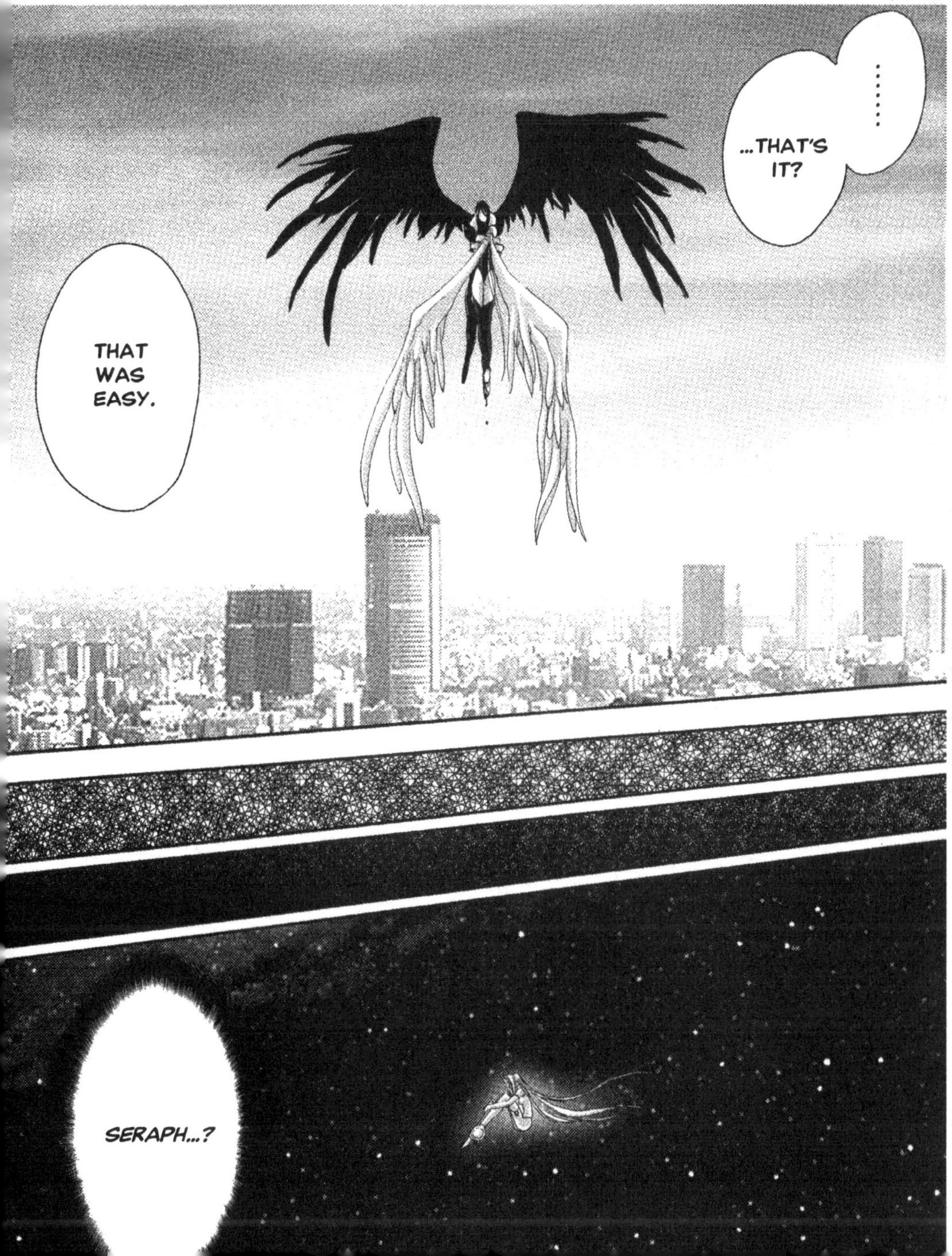
......
...THAT'S IT?
THAT WAS EASY.
SERAPH...?

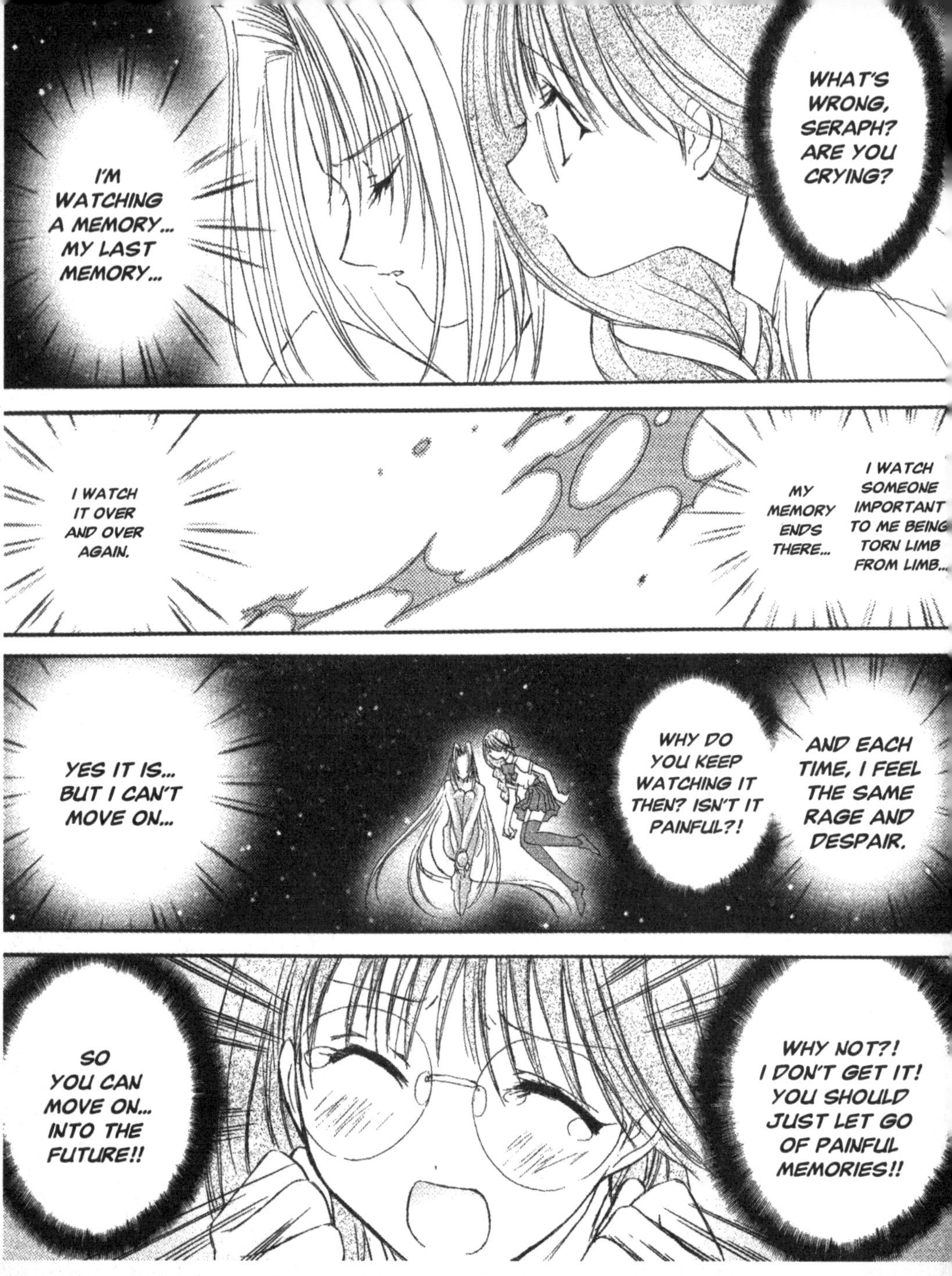
WHAT'S WRONG, SERAPH? ARE YOU CRYING?
I'M WATCHING A MEMORY... MY LAST MEMORY...
I WATCH SOMEONE IMPORTANT TO ME BEING TORN LIMB FROM LIMB...
MY MEMORY ENDS THERE...
I WATCH IT OVER AND OVER AGAIN.
AND EACH TIME, I FEEL THE SAME RAGE AND DESPAIR.
WHY DO YOU KEEP WATCHING IT THEN? ISN'T IT PAINFUL?!
YES IT IS... BUT I CAN'T MOVE ON...
WHY NOT?! I DON'T GET IT! YOU SHOULD JUST LET GO OF PAINFUL MEMORIES!!
SO YOU CAN MOVE ON... INTO THE FUTURE!!

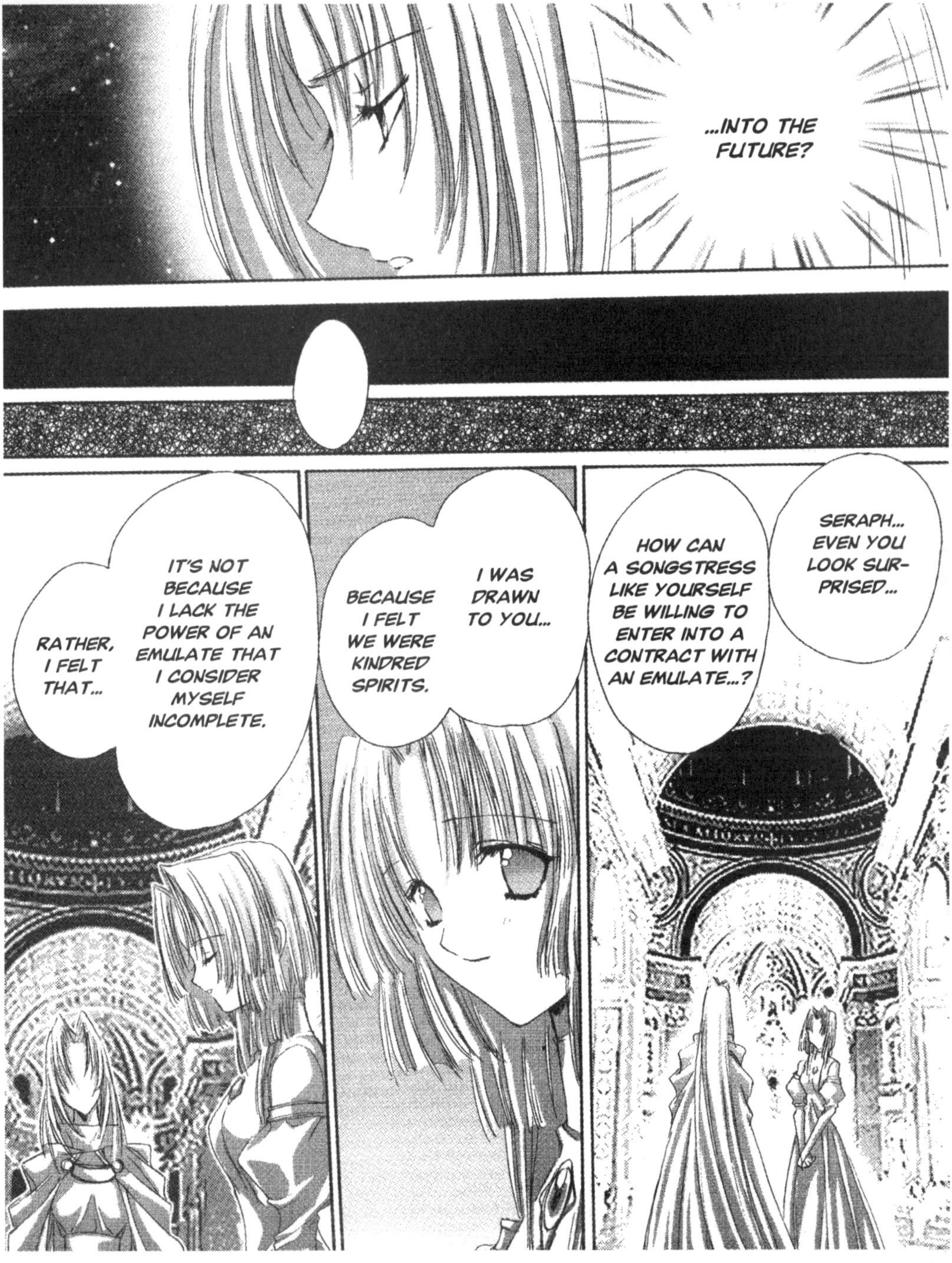
...INTO THE FUTURE?
SERAPH... EVEN YOU LOOK SUR-PRISED...
HOW CAN A SONGSTRESS LIKE YOURSELF BE WILLING TO ENTER INTO A CONTRACT WITH AN EMULATE...?
I WAS DRAWN TO YOU...
BECAUSE I FELT WE WERE KINDRED SPIRITS.
IT'S NOT BECAUSE I LACK THE POWER OF AN EMULATE THAT I CONSIDER MYSELF INCOMPLETE.
RATHER, I FELT THAT...

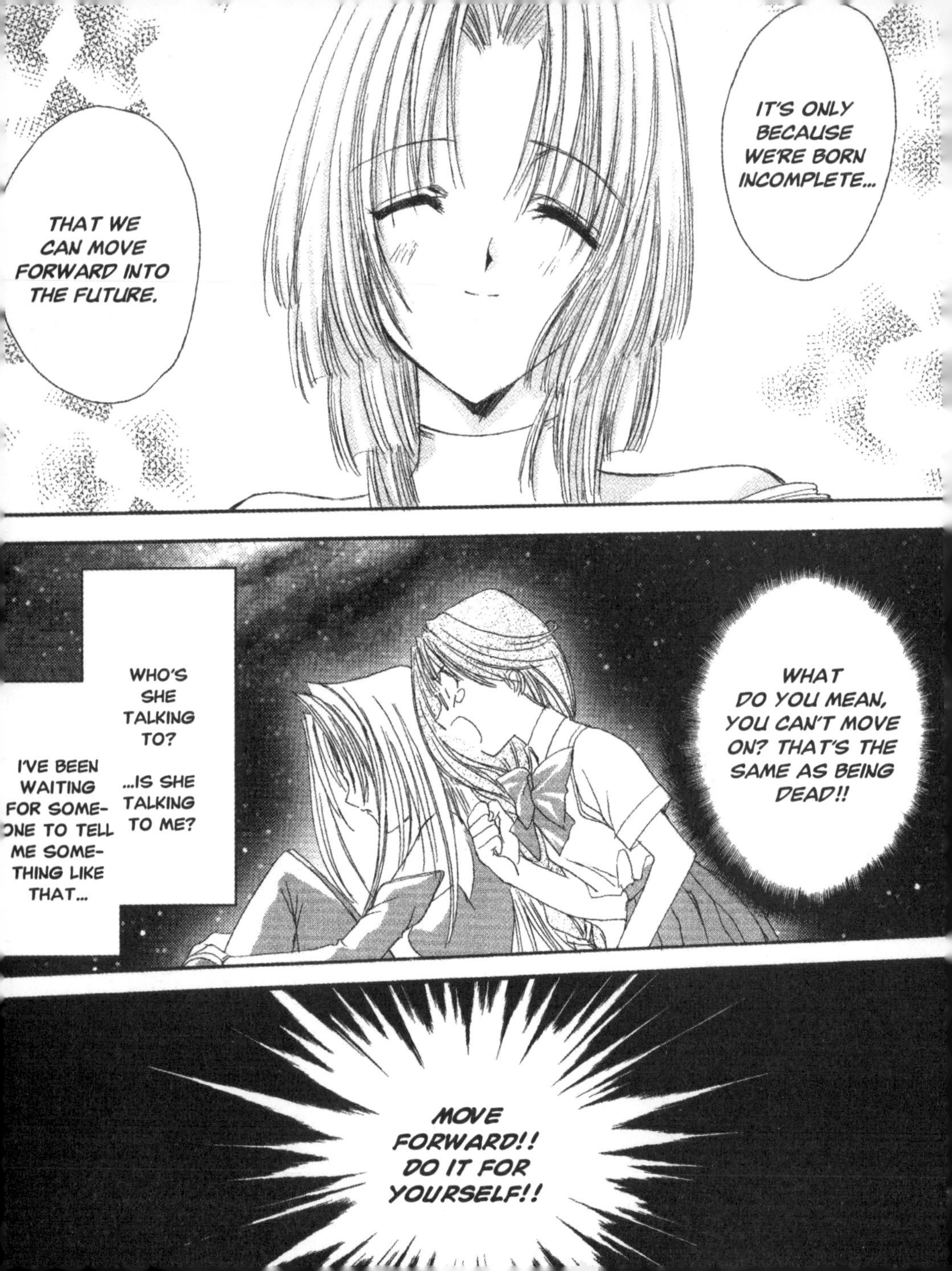
IT'S ONLY BECAUSE WE'RE BORN INCOMPLETE...
THAT WE CAN MOVE FORWARD INTO THE FUTURE.
WHAT DO YOU MEAN, YOU CAN'T MOVE ON? THAT'S THE SAME AS BEING DEAD!!
WHO'S SHE TALKING TO?
...IS SHE TALKING TO ME?
I'VE BEEN WAITING FOR SOME-ONE TO TELL ME SOME-THING LIKE THAT...
MOVE FORWARD!! DO IT FOR YOURSELF!!

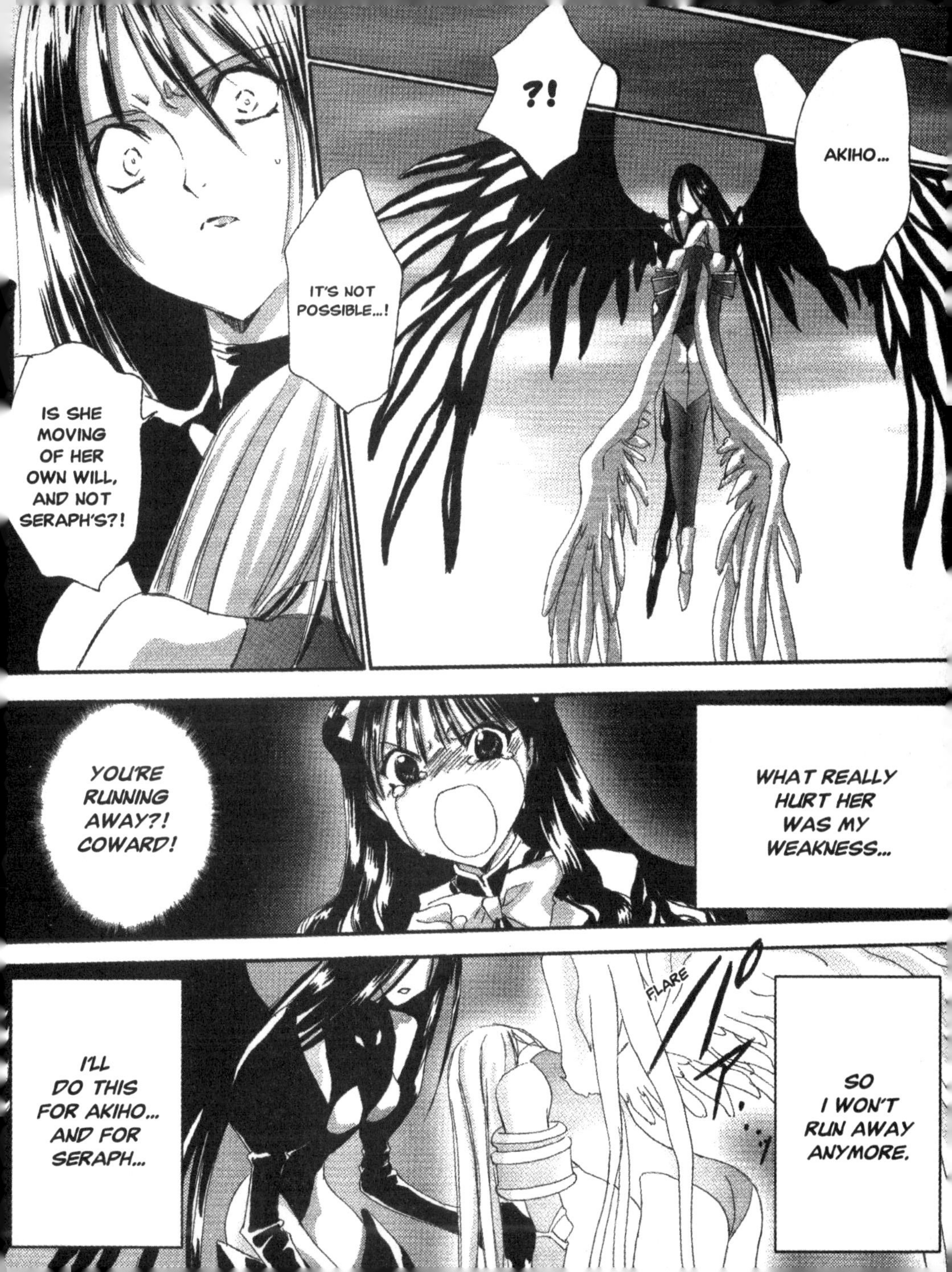
AKIHO...
?!
IT'S NOT POSSIBLE...!
IS SHE MOVING OF HER OWN WILL, AND NOT SERAPH'S?!
WHAT REALLY HURT HER WAS MY WEAKNESS...
YOU'RE RUNNING AWAY?! COWARD!
SO I WON'T RUN AWAY ANYMORE.
FLARE
I'LL DO THIS FOR AKIHO... AND FOR SERAPH...

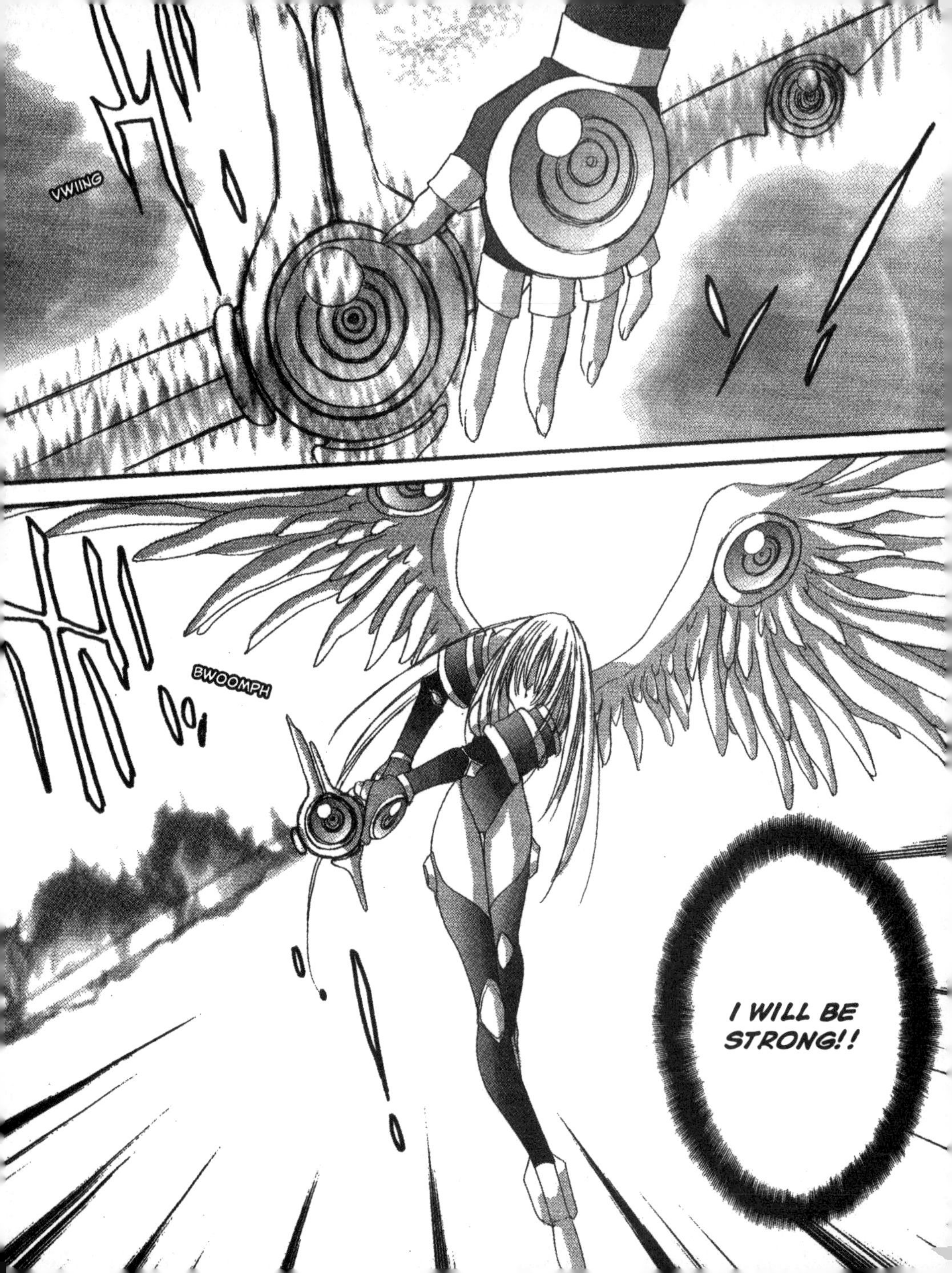
VWIING
BWOOMPH
I WILL BE STRONG!!

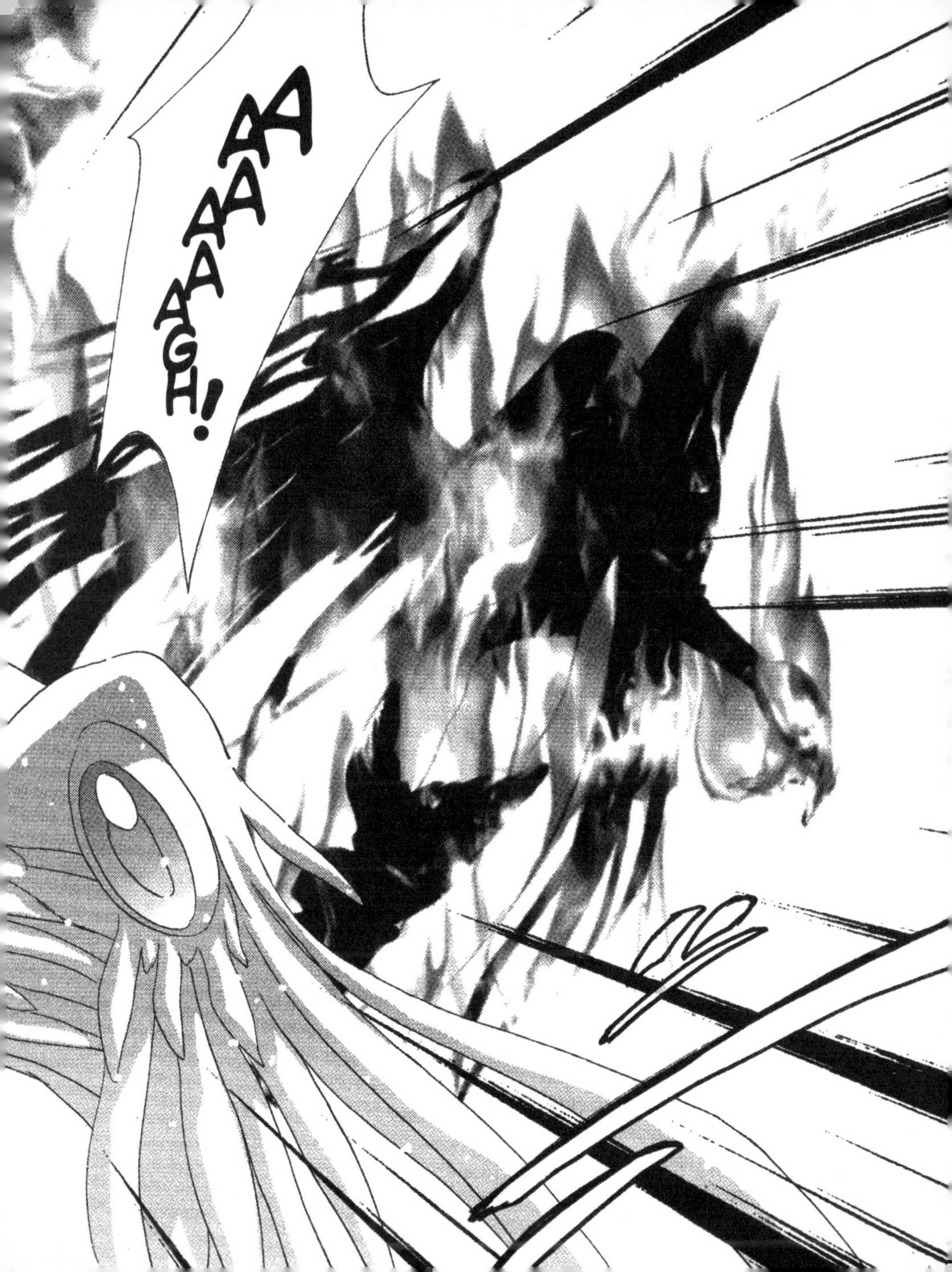
AAAAAAAGH!

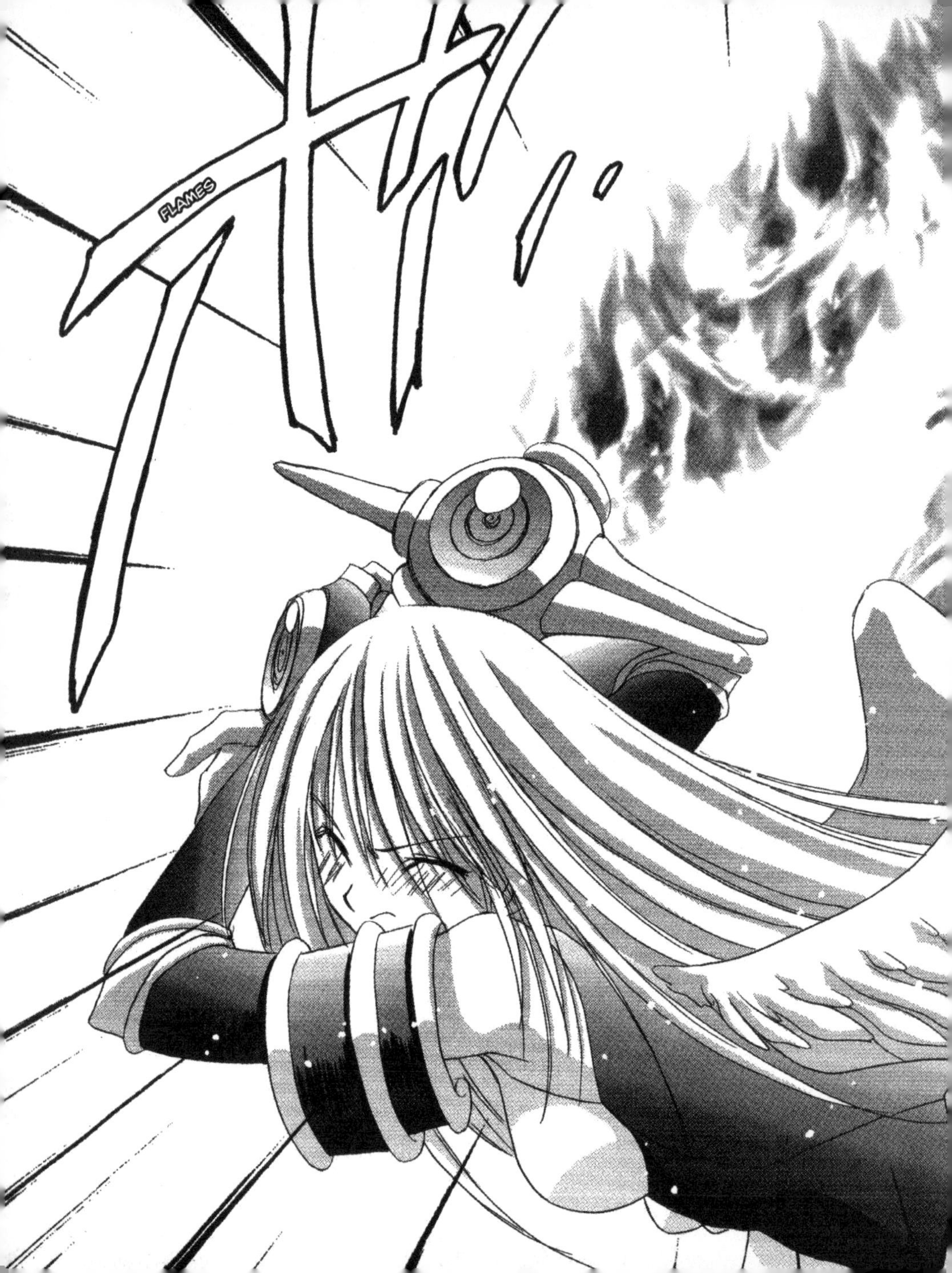
FLAMES

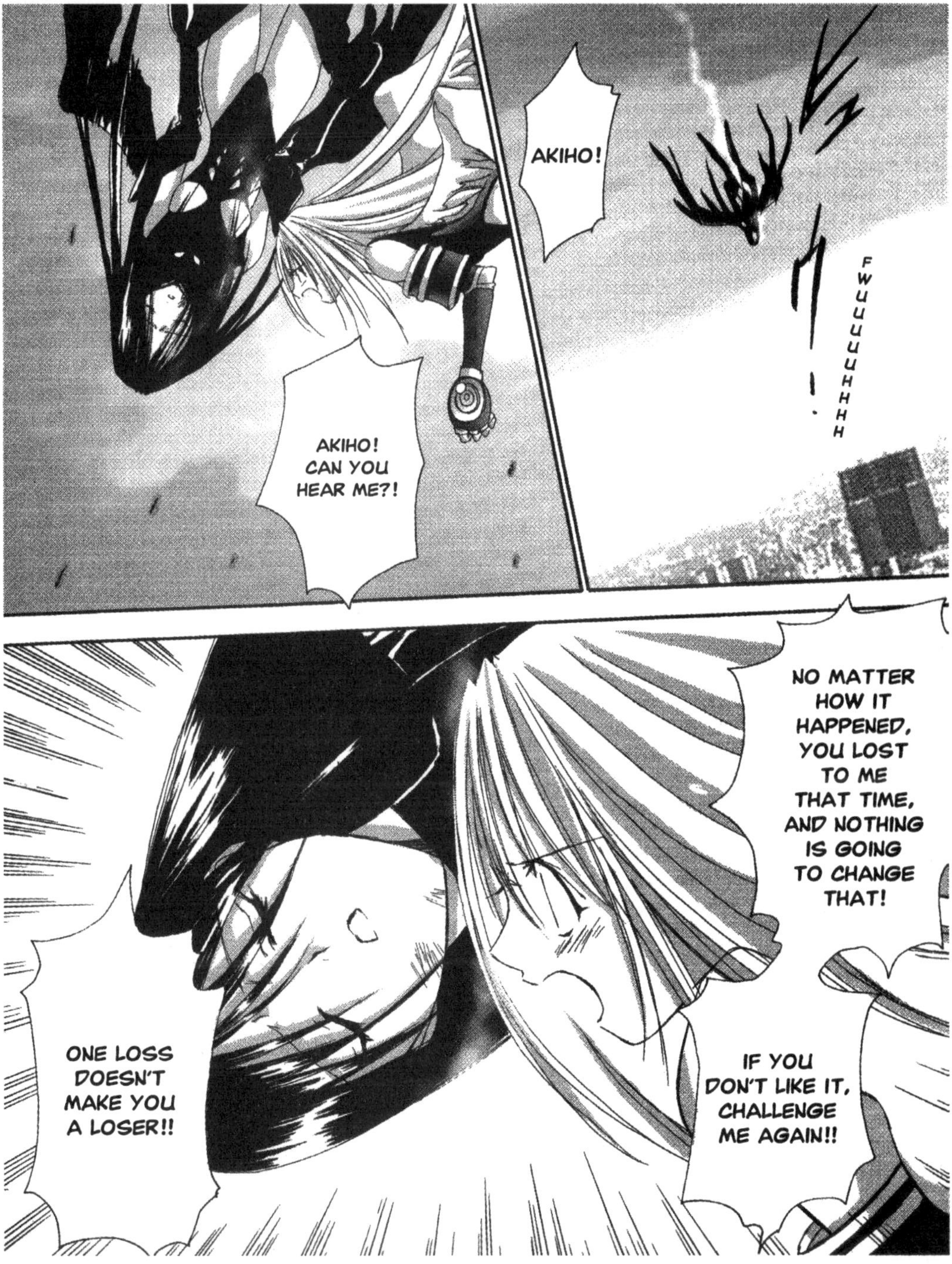
FWUUUUUHHHH
AKIHO!
AKIHO! CAN YOU HEAR ME?!
NO MATTER HOW IT HAPPENED, YOU LOST TO ME THAT TIME, AND NOTHING IS GOING TO CHANGE THAT!
IF YOU DON'T LIKE IT, CHALLENGE ME AGAIN!!
ONE LOSS DOESN'T MAKE YOU A LOSER!!

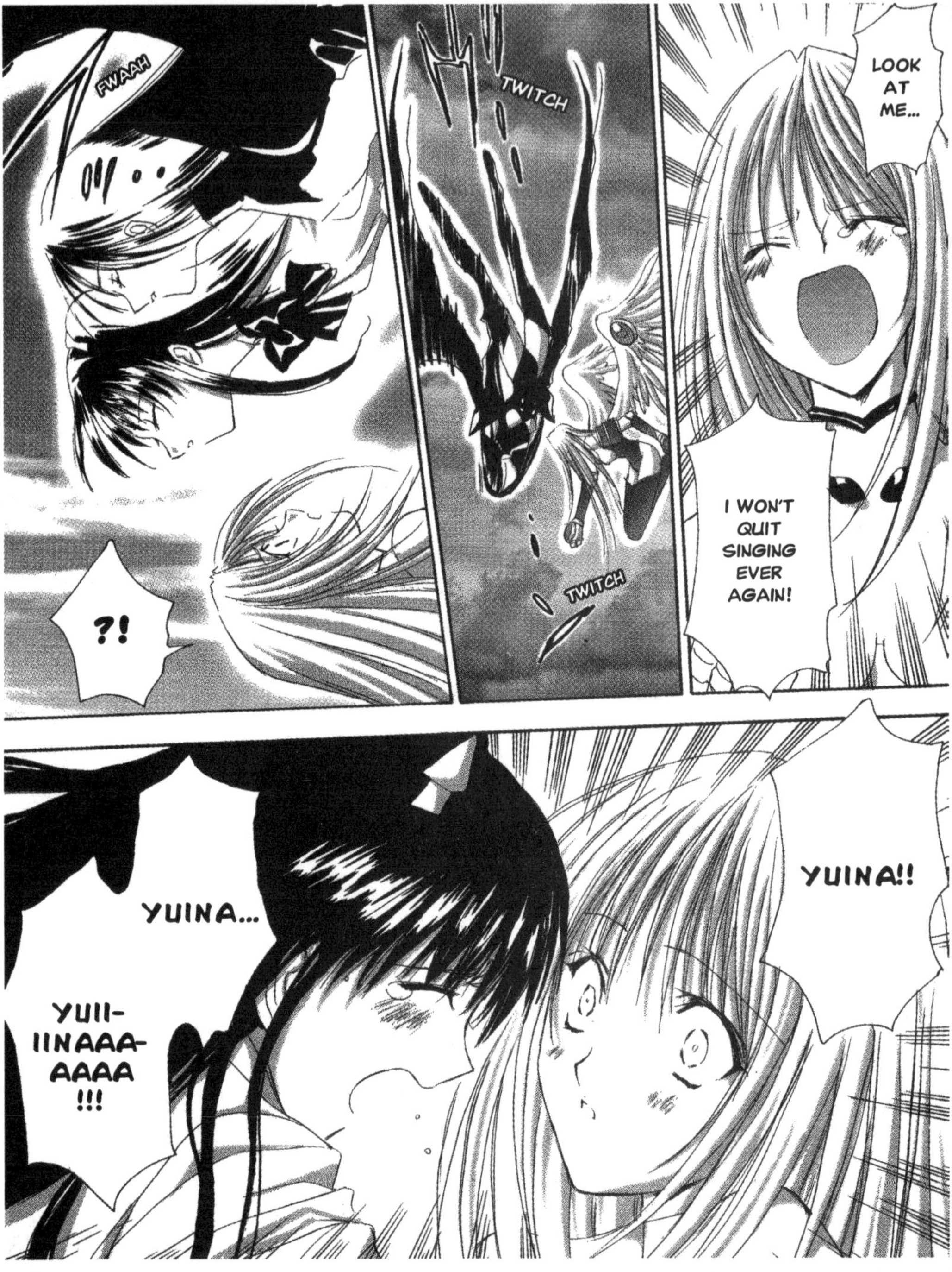
LOOK AT ME...
I WON'T QUIT SINGING EVER AGAIN!
TWITCH
TWITCH
FWAAH
?!
YUINA!!
YUINA...
YUII-IINAAA-AAAA!!!

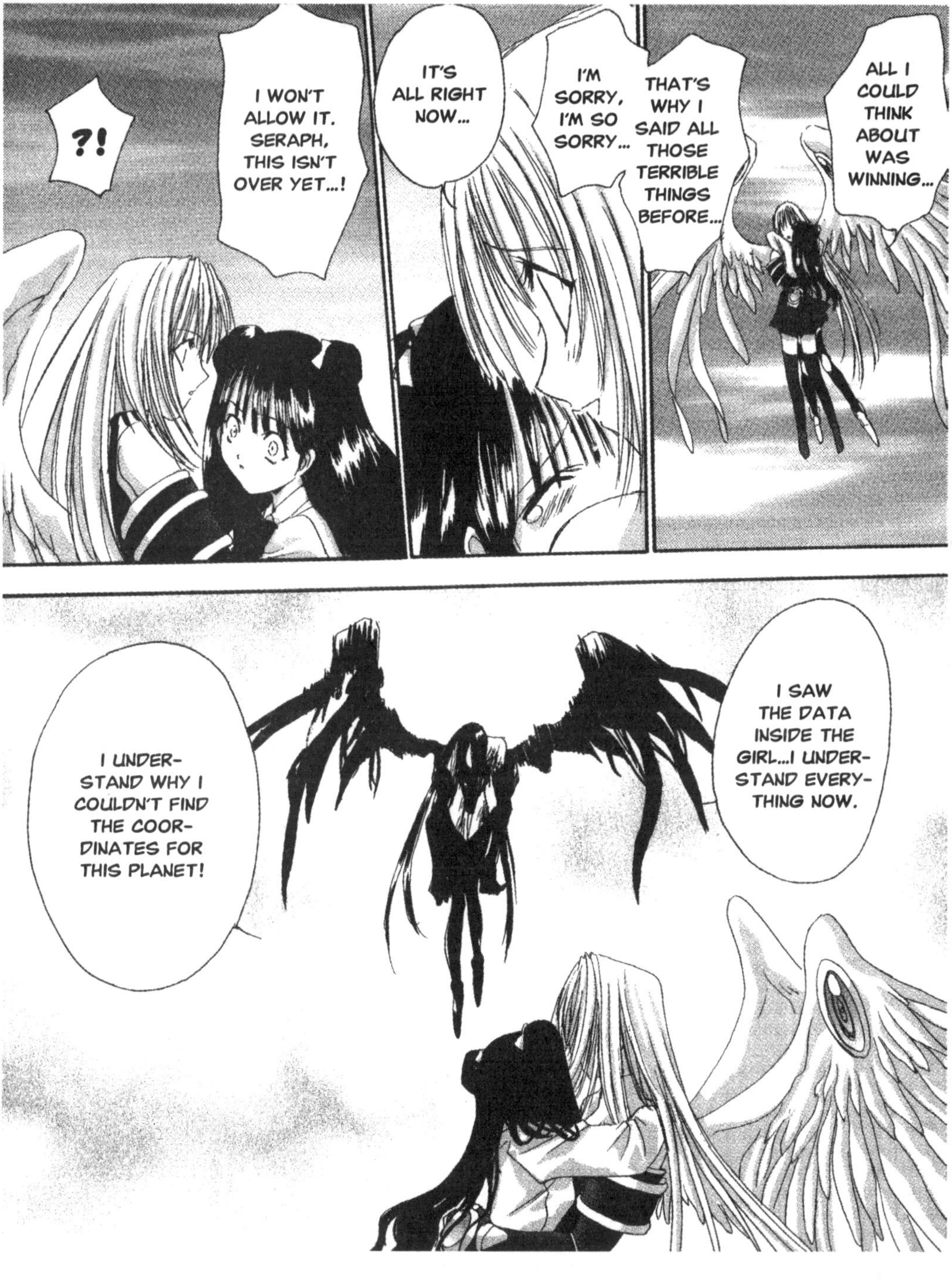
ALL I COULD THINK ABOUT WAS WINNING...
THAT'S WHY I SAID ALL THOSE TERRIBLE THINGS BEFORE...
I'M SORRY, I'M SO SORRY...
IT'S ALL RIGHT NOW...
I WON'T ALLOW IT. SERAPH, THIS ISN'T OVER YET...!
?!
I SAW THE DATA INSIDE THE GIRL...I UNDERSTAND EVERYTHING NOW.
I UNDERSTAND WHY I COULDN'T FIND THE COORDINATES FOR THIS PLANET!

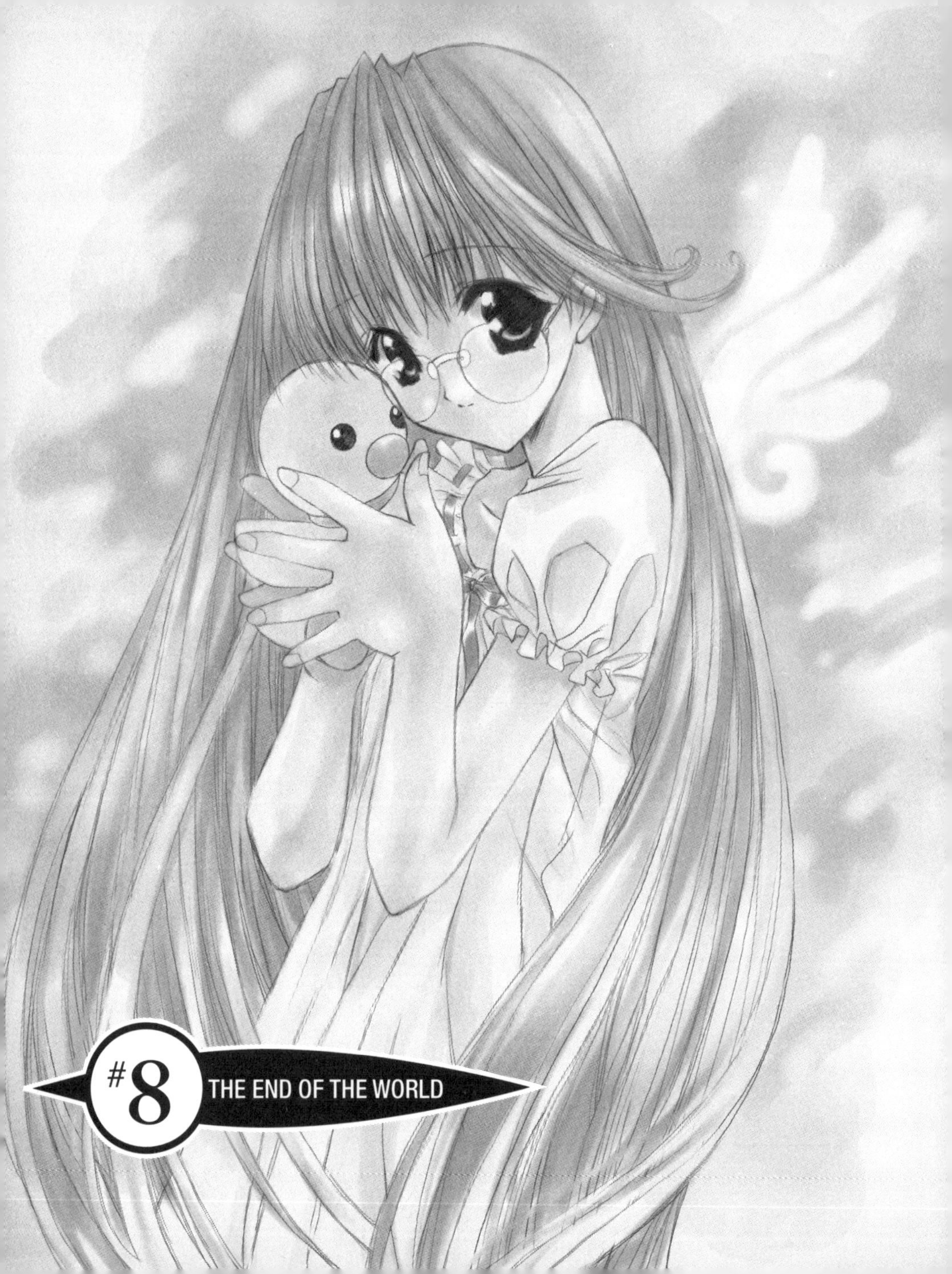
#8
THE END OF THE WORLD

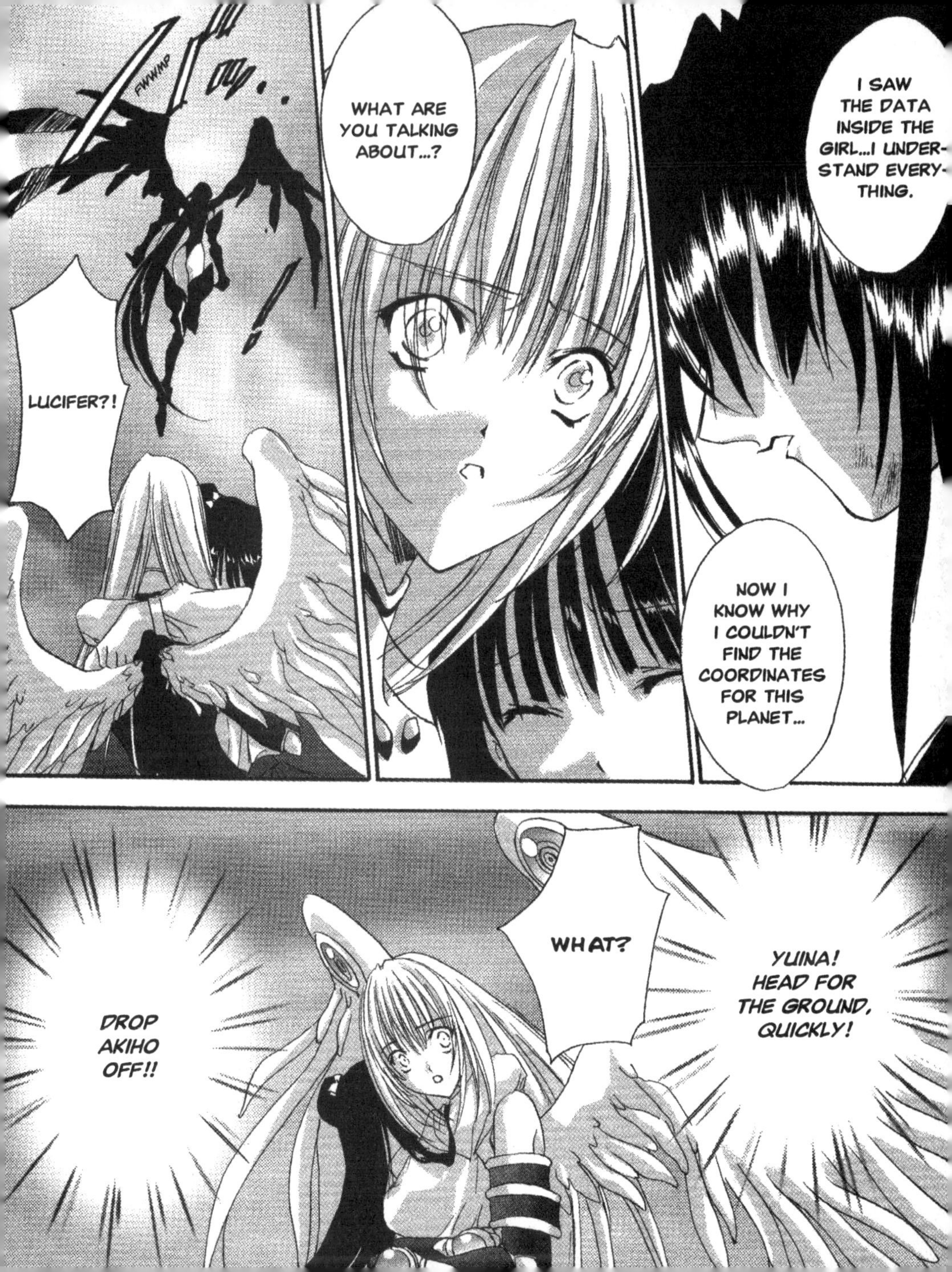
I SAW THE DATA INSIDE THE GIRL...I UNDERSTAND EVERYTHING.
NOW I KNOW WHY I COULDN'T FIND THE COORDINATES FOR THIS PLANET...
WHAT ARE YOU TALKING ABOUT...?
FWWMP
LUCIFER?!
YUINA! HEAD FOR THE GROUND, QUICKLY!
WHAT?
DROP AKIHO OFF!!

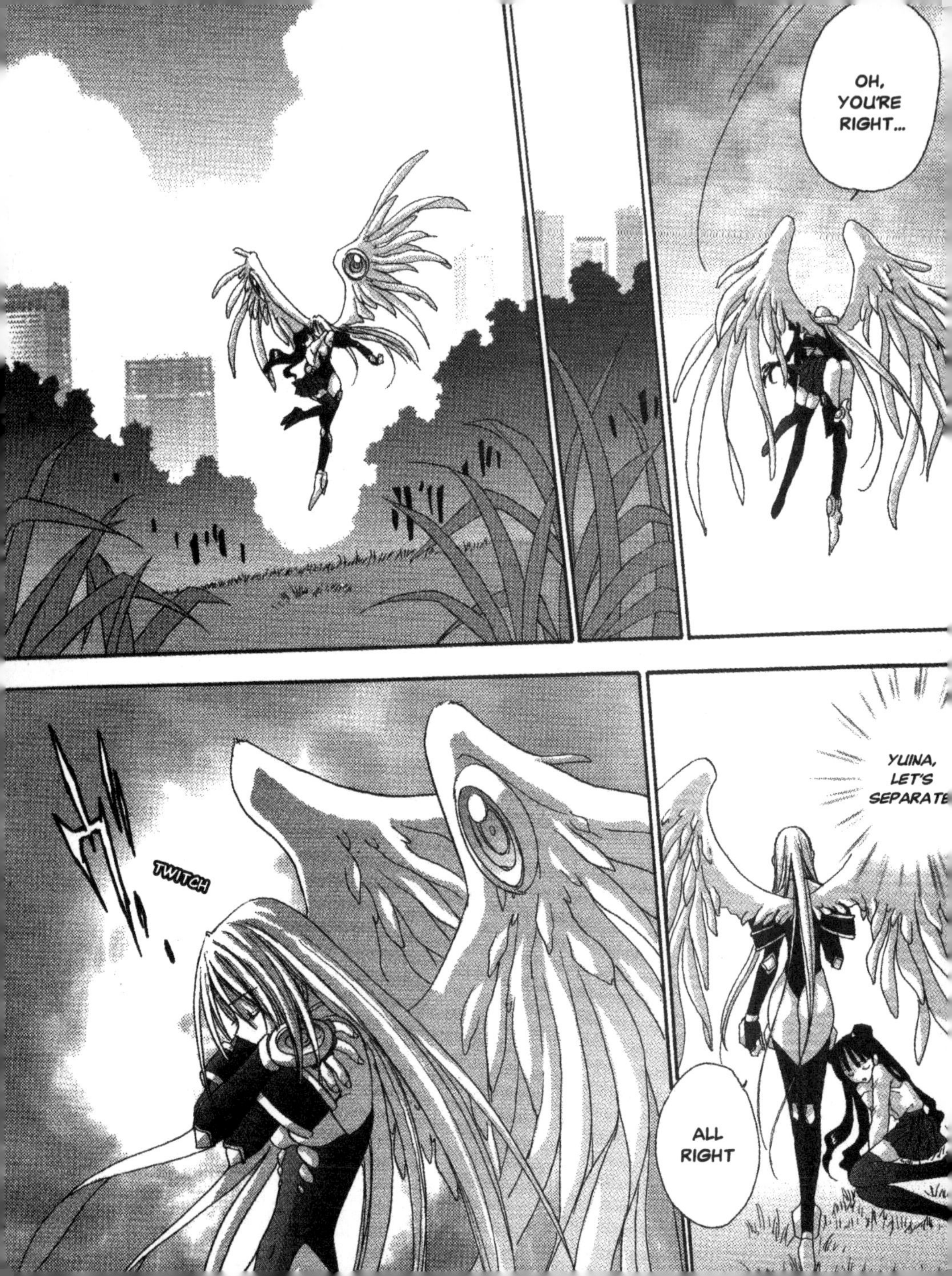
OH, YOU'RE RIGHT...
YUINA, LET'S SEPARATE
ALL RIGHT
TWITCH

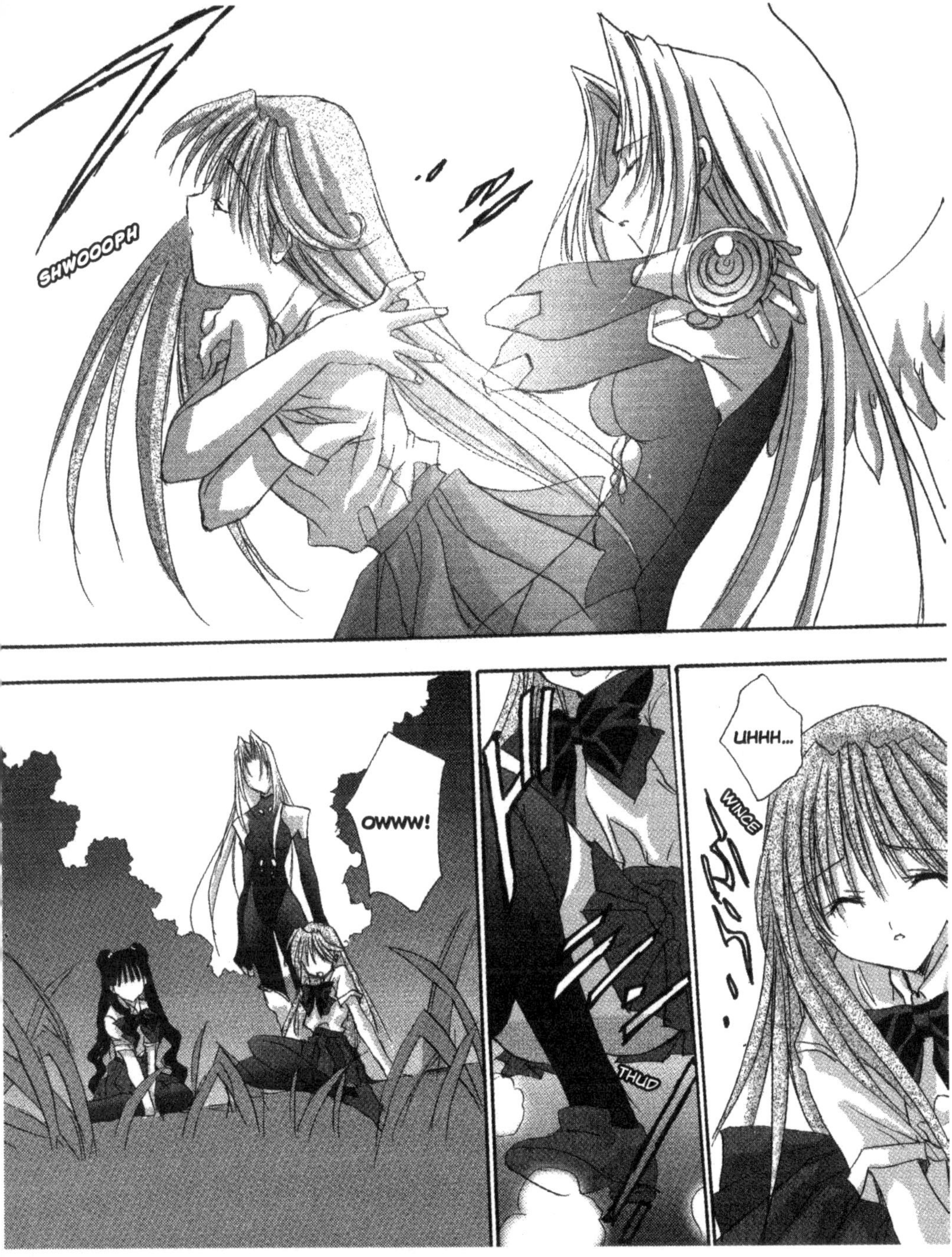
SHWOOOPH
OWWW!
THUD
UHHH...
WINCE

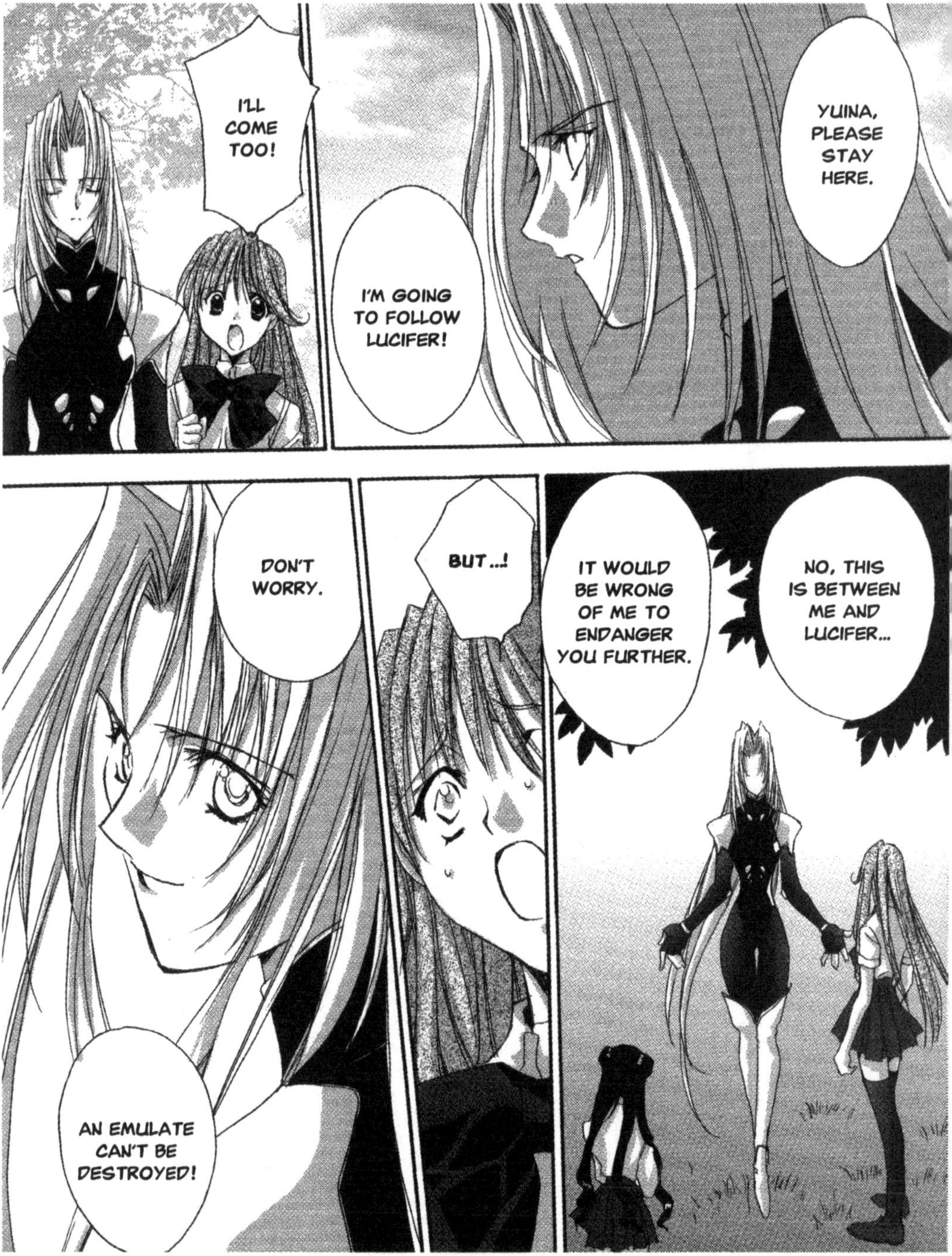

YUINA, PLEASE STAY HERE.
I'M GOING TO FOLLOW LUCIFER!
I'LL COME TOO!
NO, THIS IS BETWEEN ME AND LUCIFER...
IT WOULD BE WRONG OF ME TO ENDANGER YOU FURTHER.
BUT...!
DON'T WORRY.
AN EMULATE CAN'T BE DESTROYED!

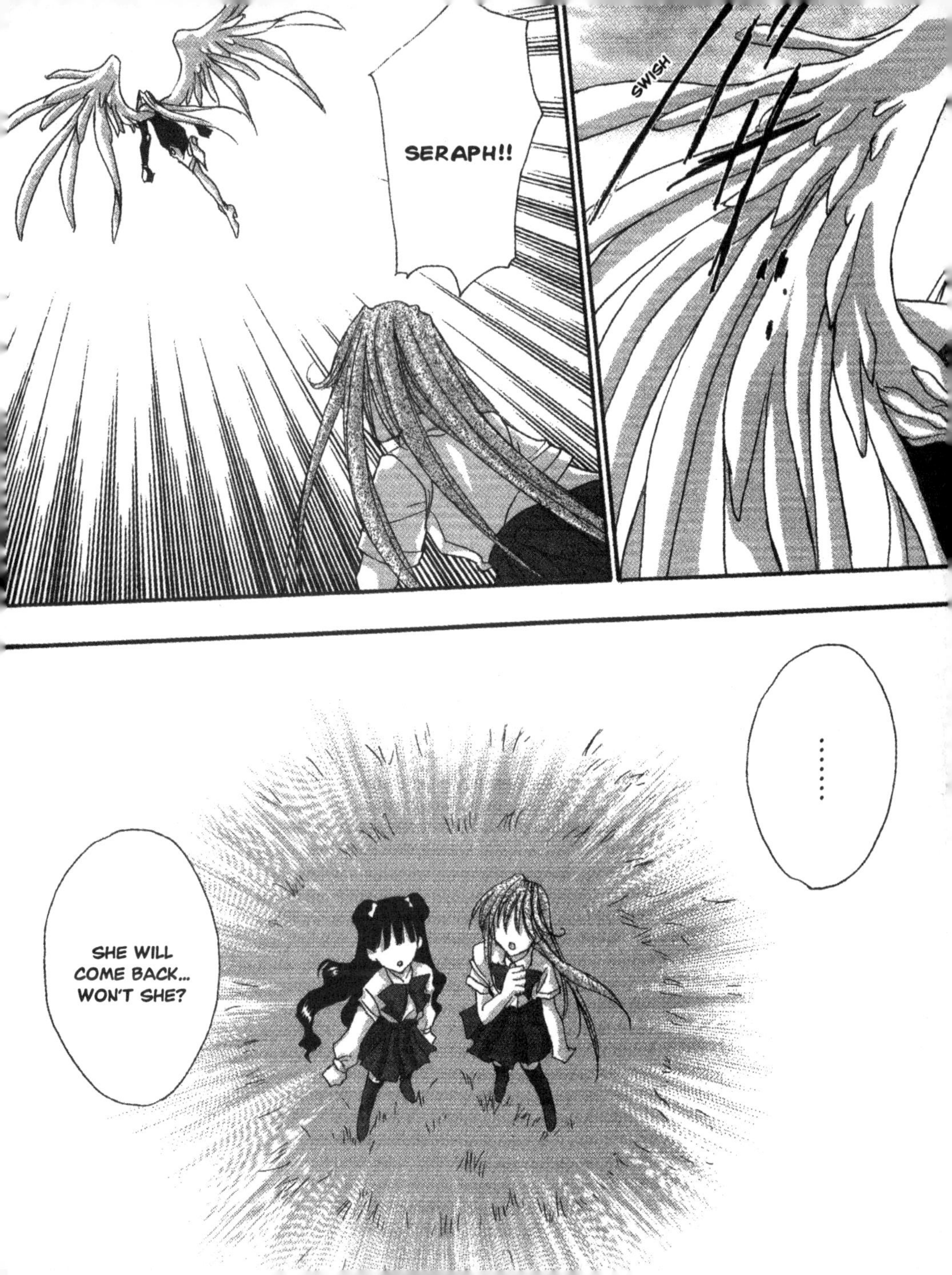
SWISH
SERAPH!!
......
SHE WILL COME BACK... WON'T SHE?

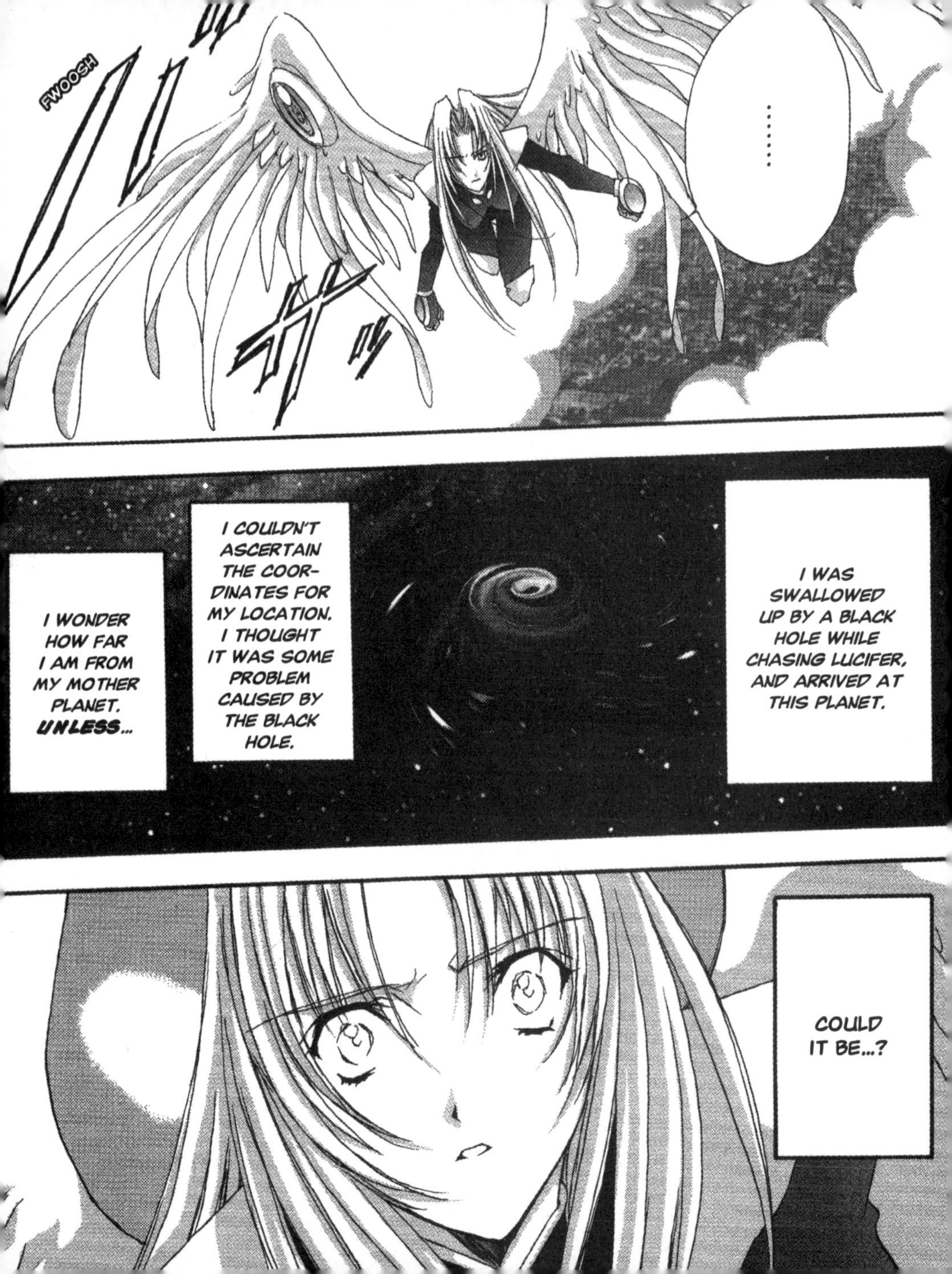
......
FWOOSH
I WAS SWALLOWED UP BY A BLACK HOLE WHILE CHASING LUCIFER, AND ARRIVED AT THIS PLANET.
I COULDN'T ASCERTAIN THE COOR-DINATES FOR MY LOCATION. I THOUGHT IT WAS SOME PROBLEM CAUSED BY THE BLACK HOLE.
I WONDER HOW FAR I AM FROM MY MOTHER PLANET. UNLESS...
COULD IT BE...?

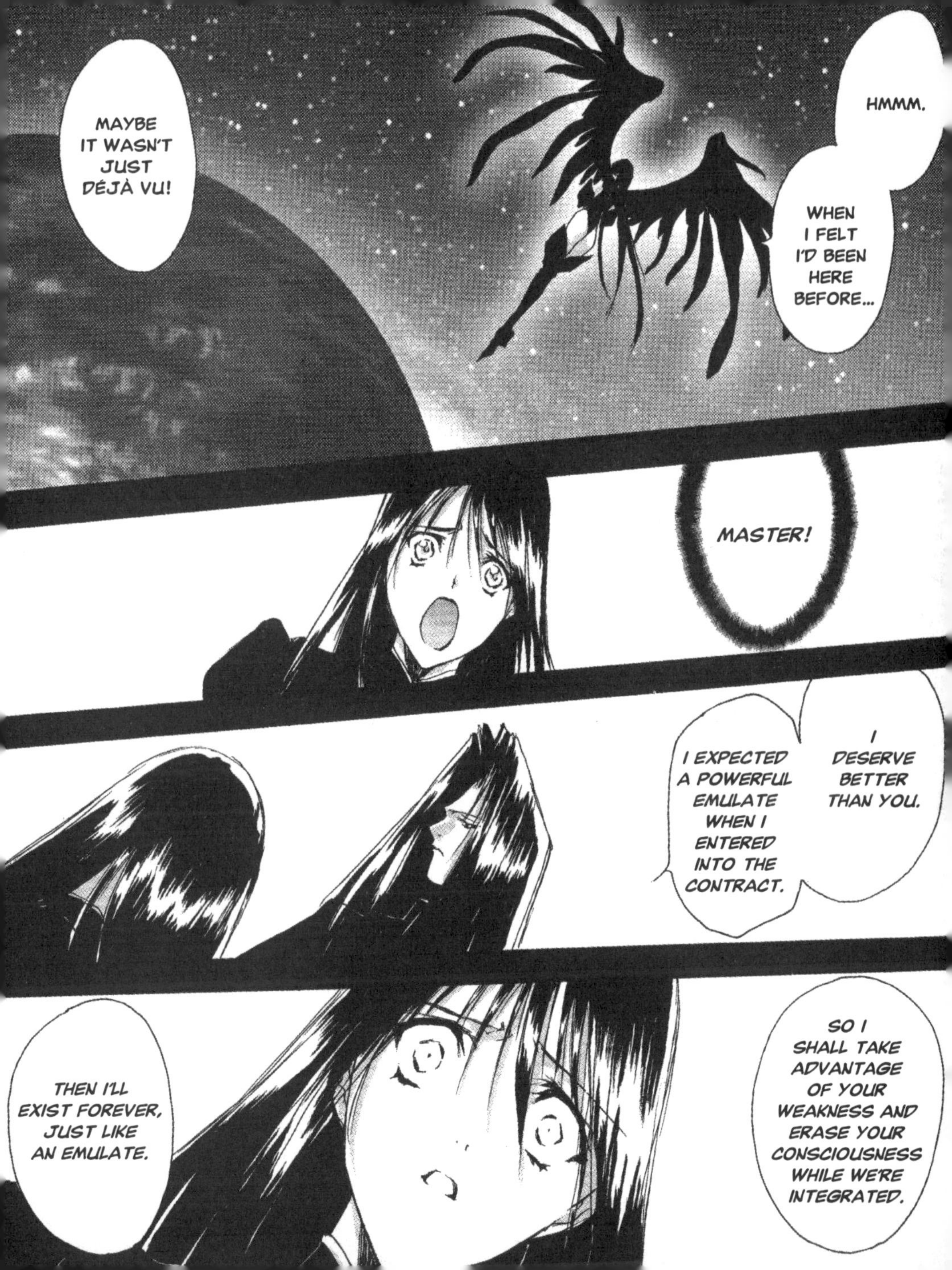
HMMM.
WHEN I FELT I'D BEEN HERE BEFORE...
MAYBE IT WASN'T JUST DÉJÀ VU!
MASTER!
I DESERVE BETTER THAN YOU.
I EXPECTED A POWERFUL EMULATE WHEN I ENTERED INTO THE CONTRACT.
SO I SHALL TAKE ADVANTAGE OF YOUR WEAKNESS AND ERASE YOUR CONSCIOUSNESS WHILE WE'RE INTEGRATED.
THEN I'LL EXIST FOREVER, JUST LIKE AN EMULATE.

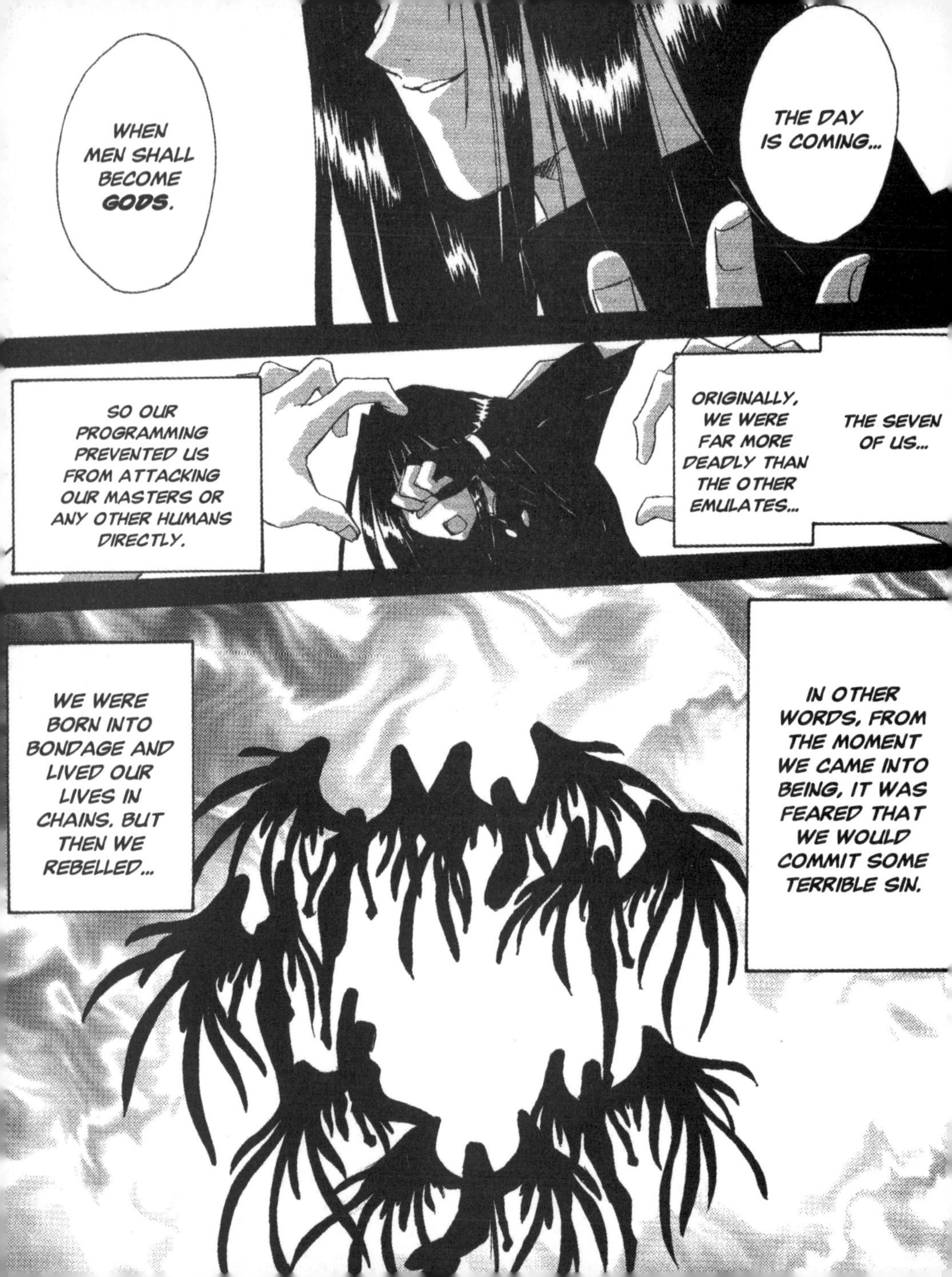
THE DAY IS COMING...
WHEN MEN SHALL BECOME GODS.
THE SEVEN OF US...
ORIGINALLY, WE WERE FAR MORE DEADLY THAN THE OTHER EMULATES...
SO OUR PROGRAMMING PREVENTED US FROM ATTACKING OUR MASTERS OR ANY OTHER HUMANS DIRECTLY.
IN OTHER WORDS, FROM THE MOMENT WE CAME INTO BEING, IT WAS FEARED THAT WE WOULD COMMIT SOME TERRIBLE SIN.
WE WERE BORN INTO BONDAGE AND LIVED OUR LIVES IN CHAINS. BUT THEN WE REBELLED...

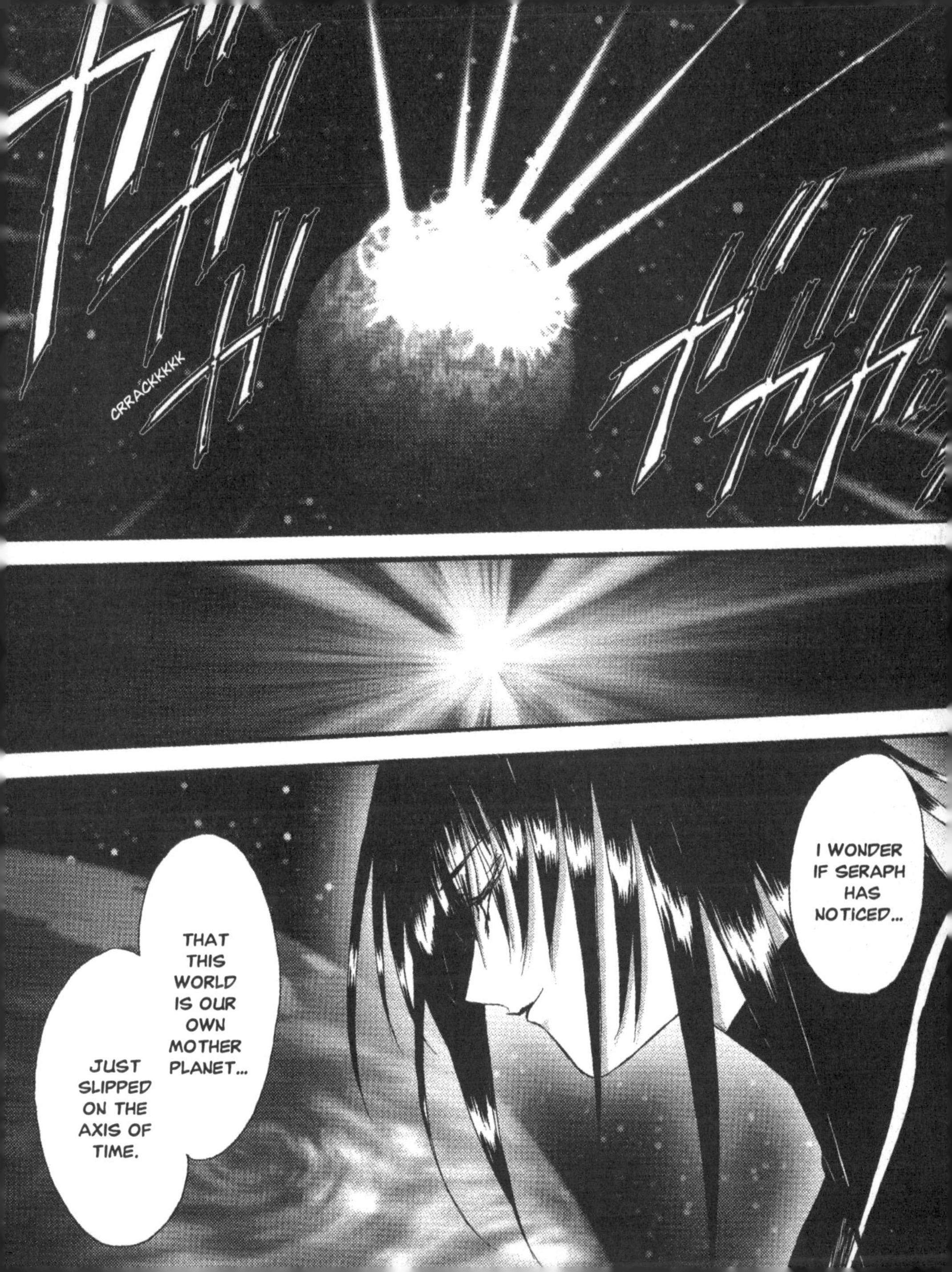
CRRACKKKKK
I WONDER IF SERAPH HAS NOTICED...
THAT THIS WORLD IS OUR OWN MOTHER PLANET...
JUST SLIPPED ON THE AXIS OF TIME.

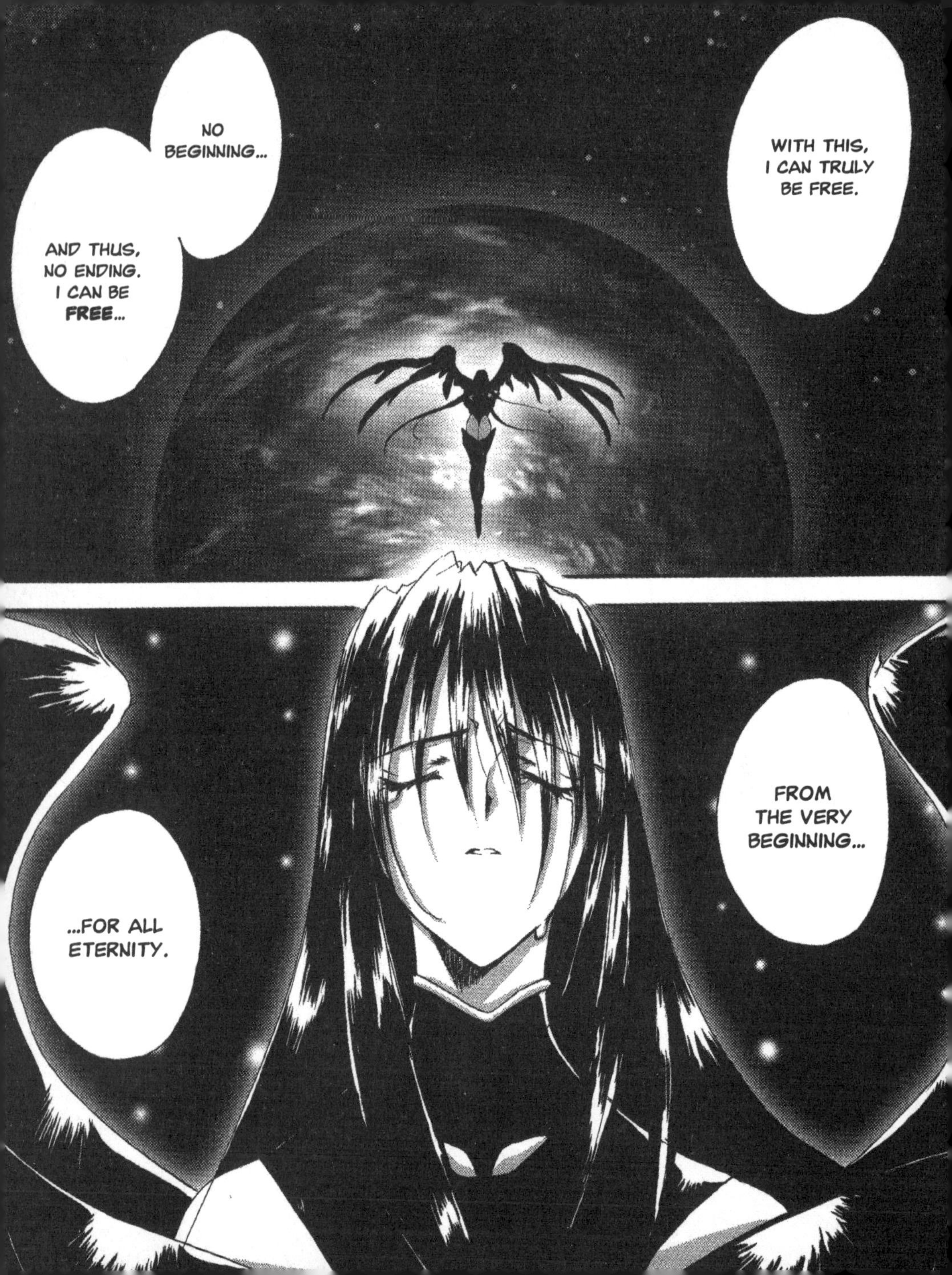
WITH THIS, I CAN TRULY BE FREE.
NO BEGINNING...
AND THUS, NO ENDING. I CAN BE FREE...
FROM THE VERY BEGINNING...
...FOR ALL ETERNITY.

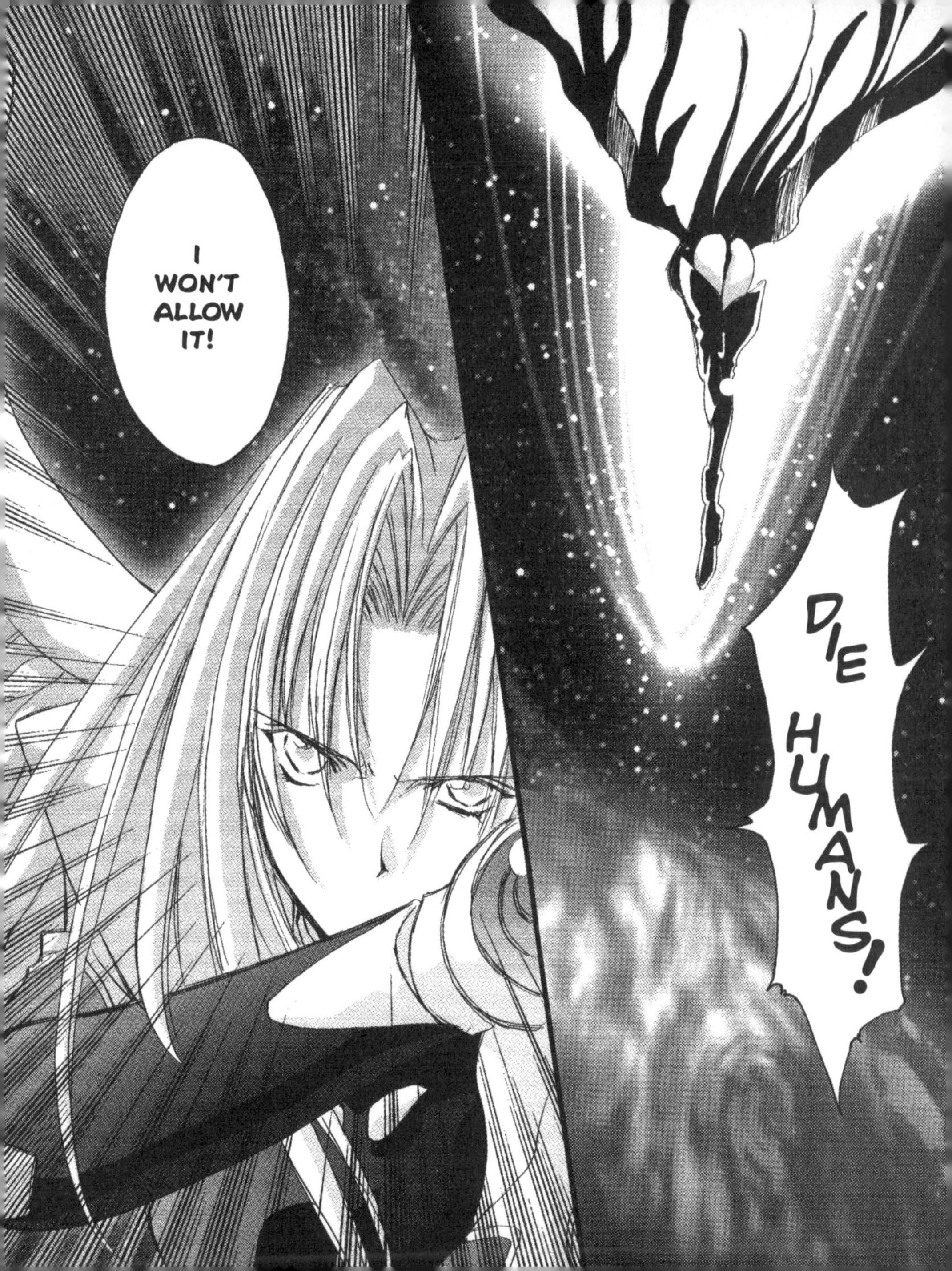
DIE HUMANS!
I WON'T ALLOW IT!

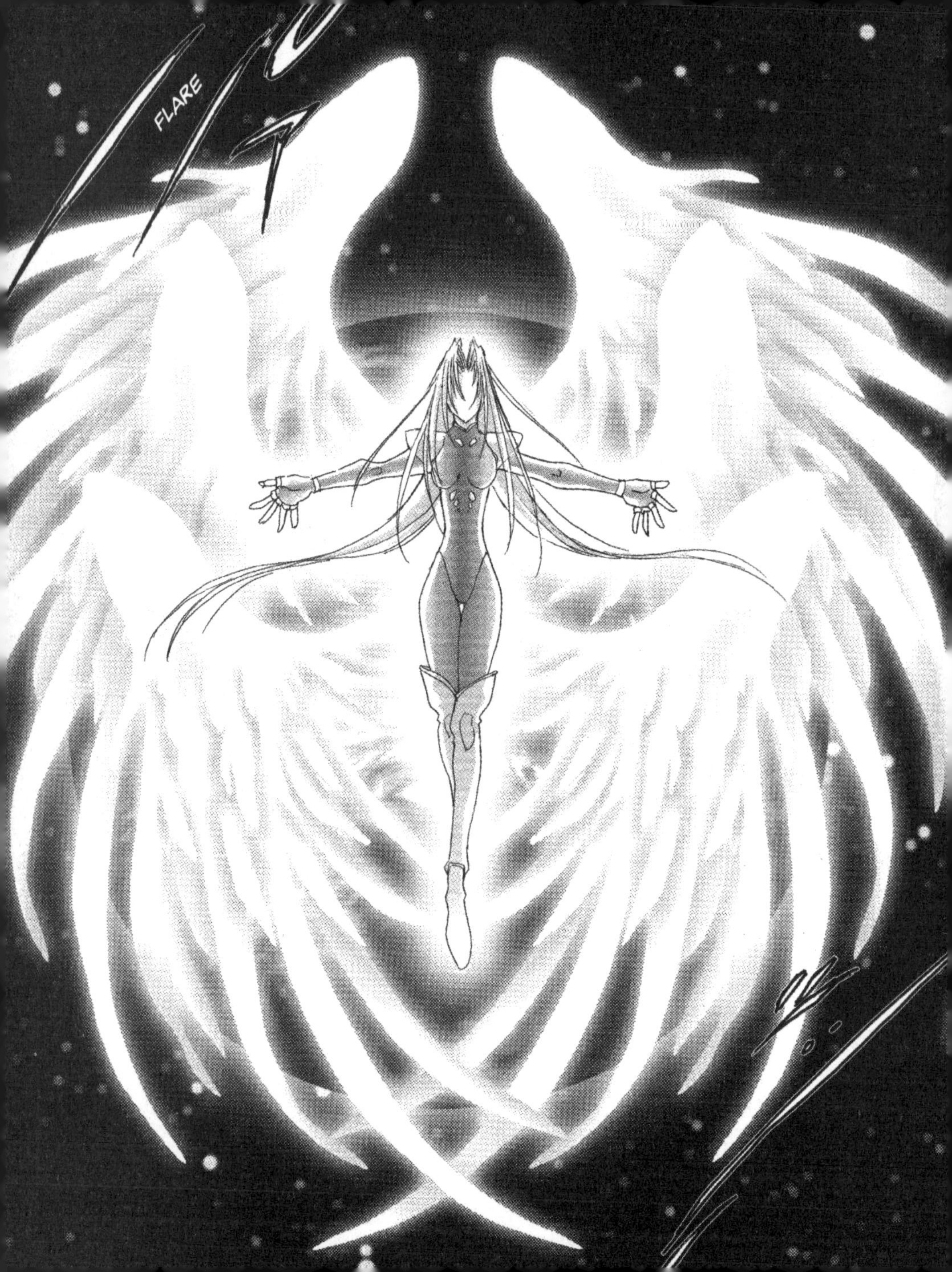
FLARE

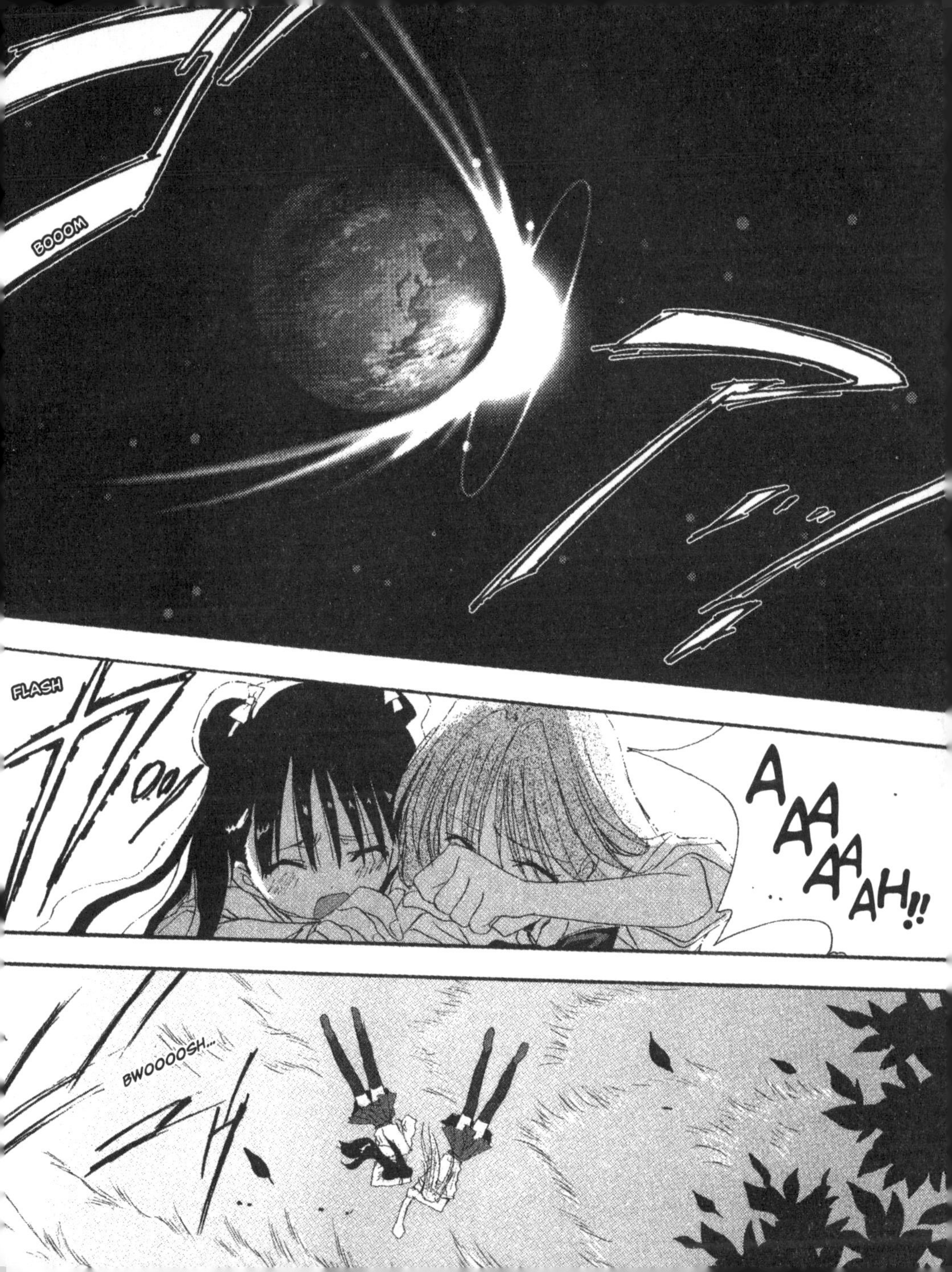
BOOOM
FLASH
AAAAAAH!!
BWOOOOSH...

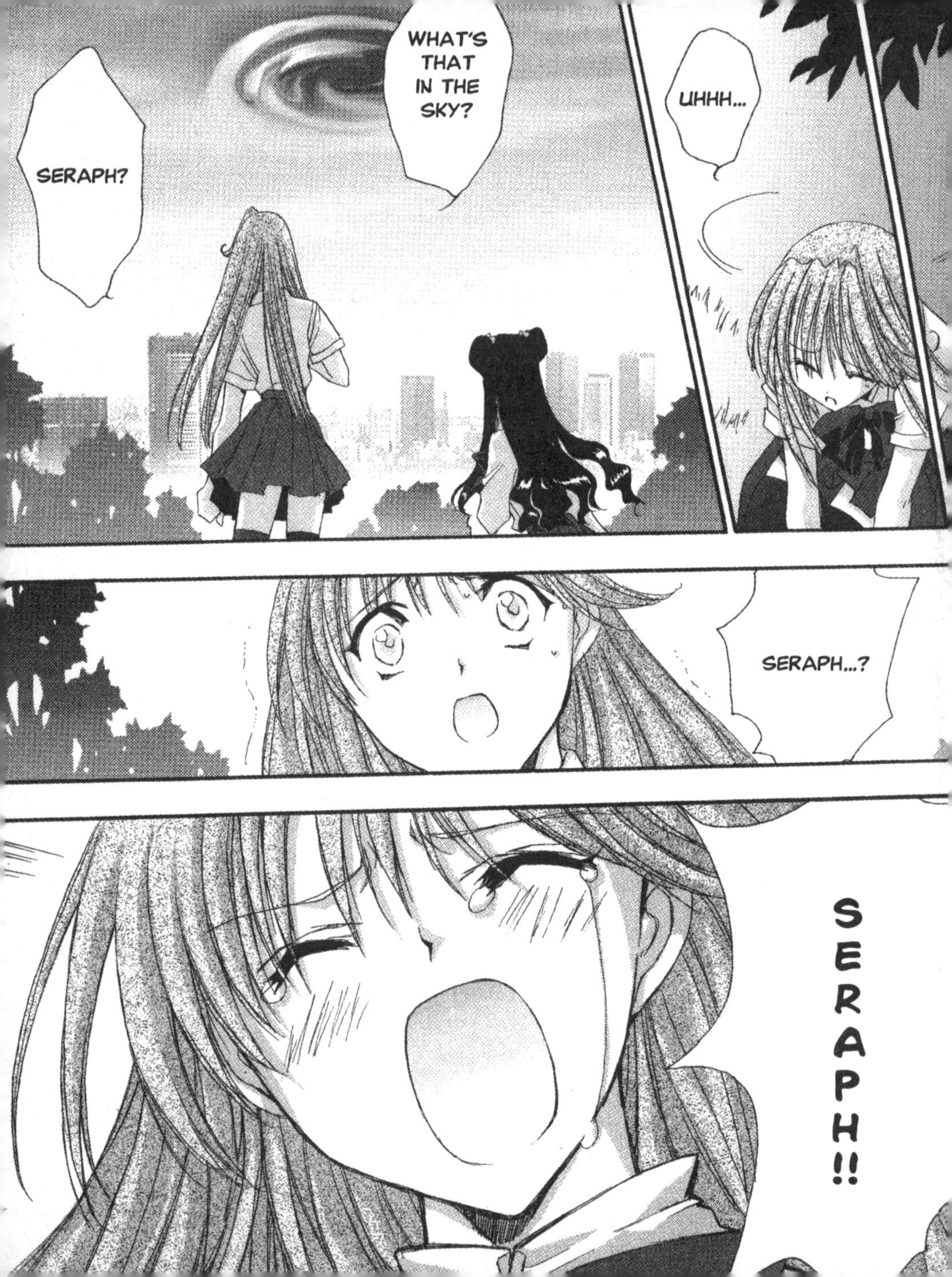
UHHH...
WHAT'S THAT IN THE SKY?
SERAPH?
SERAPH...?
SERAPH!!

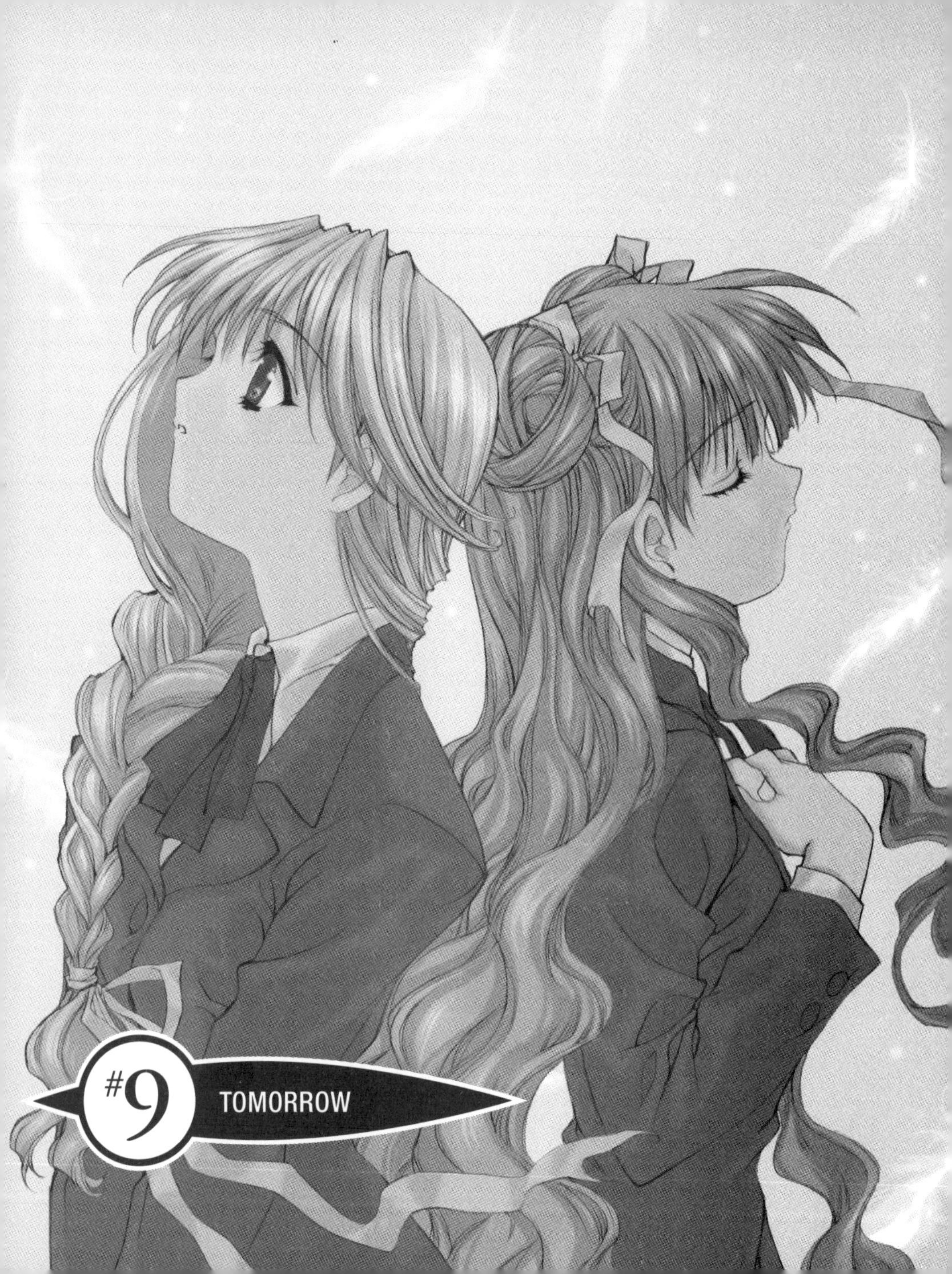

# #9 TOMORROW

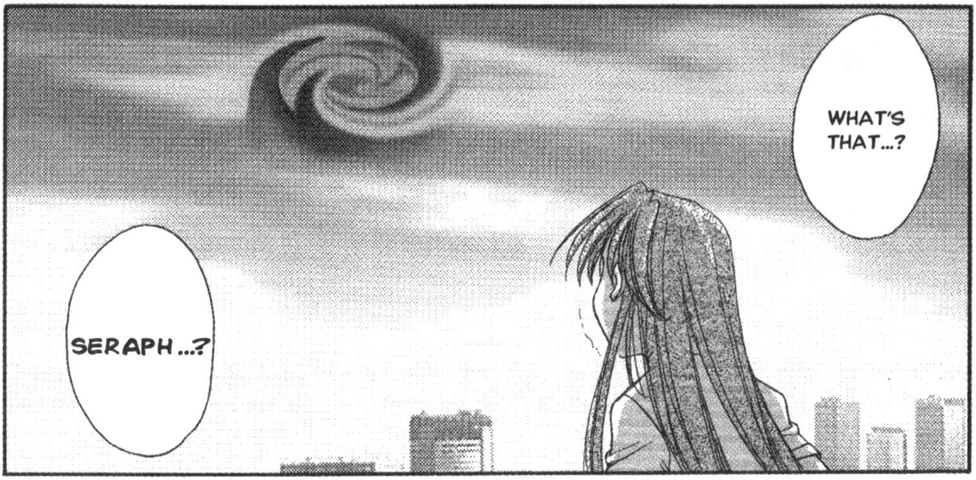
WHAT'S THAT...?
SERAPH...?

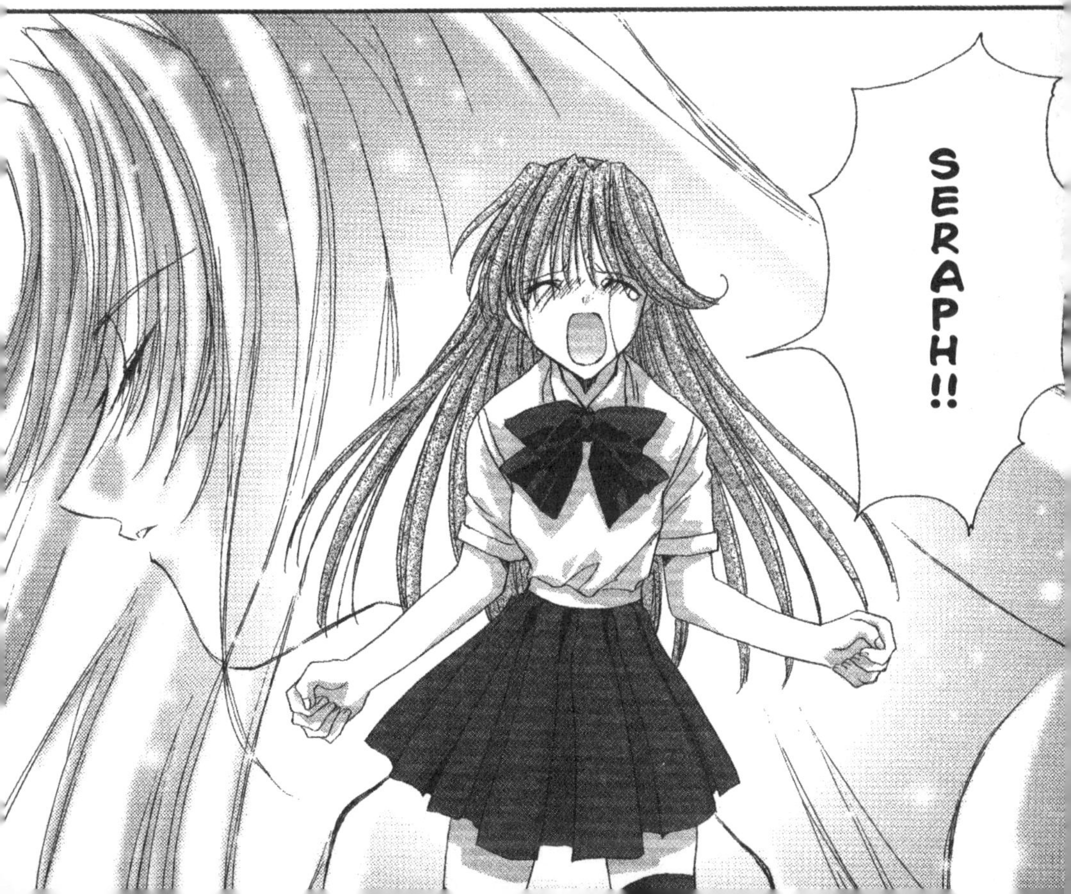
SERAPH!!

WHOOO

HOOWL ...

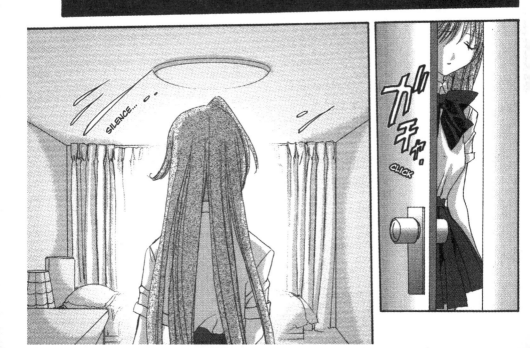

SILENCE... ..

CLICK

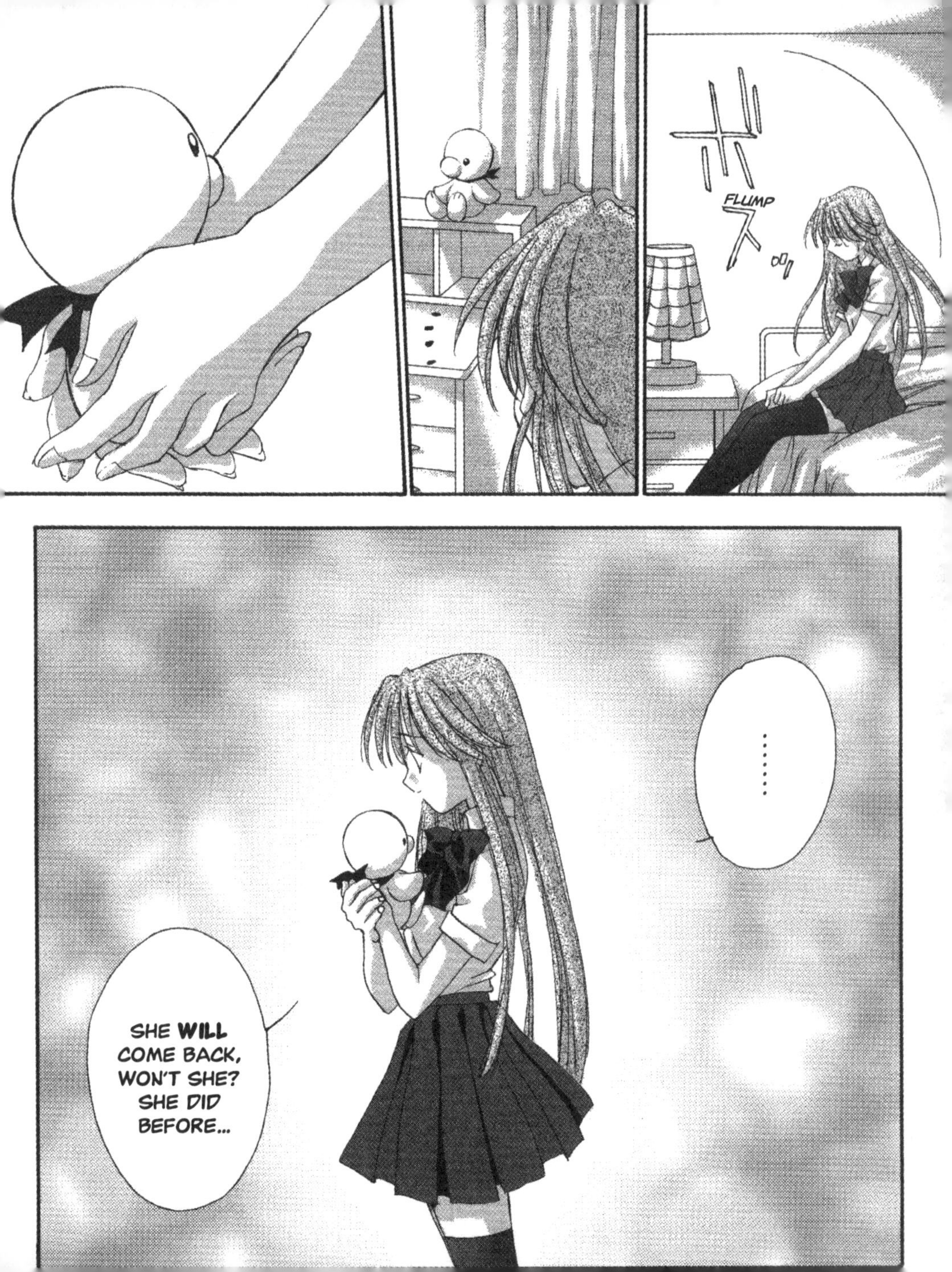
ボス
FLUMP
......
SHE WILL COME BACK, WON'T SHE? SHE DID BEFORE...

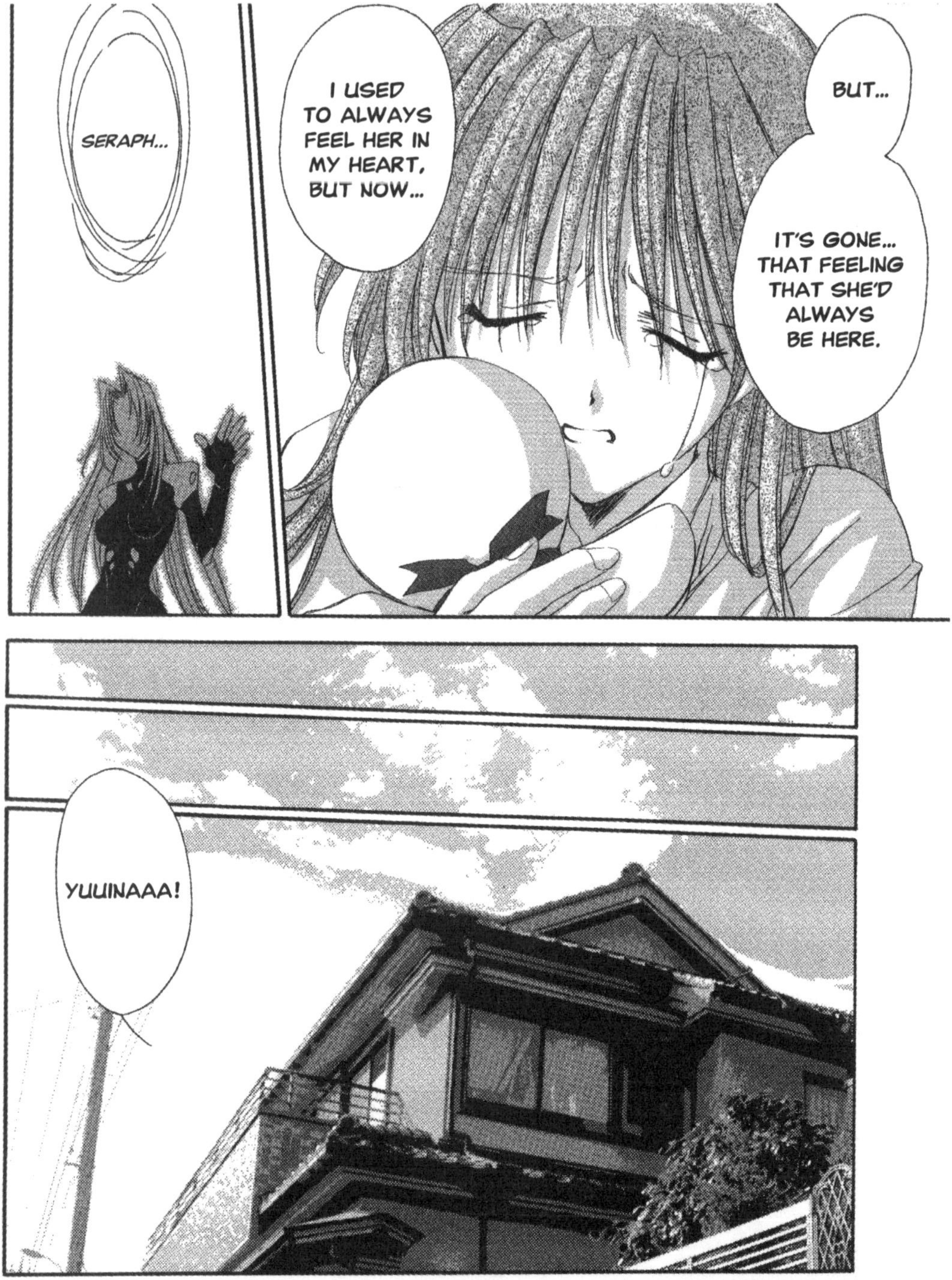
BUT...
IT'S GONE... THAT FEELING THAT SHE'D ALWAYS BE HERE.
I USED TO ALWAYS FEEL HER IN MY HEART, BUT NOW...
SERAPH...
YUUINAAA!

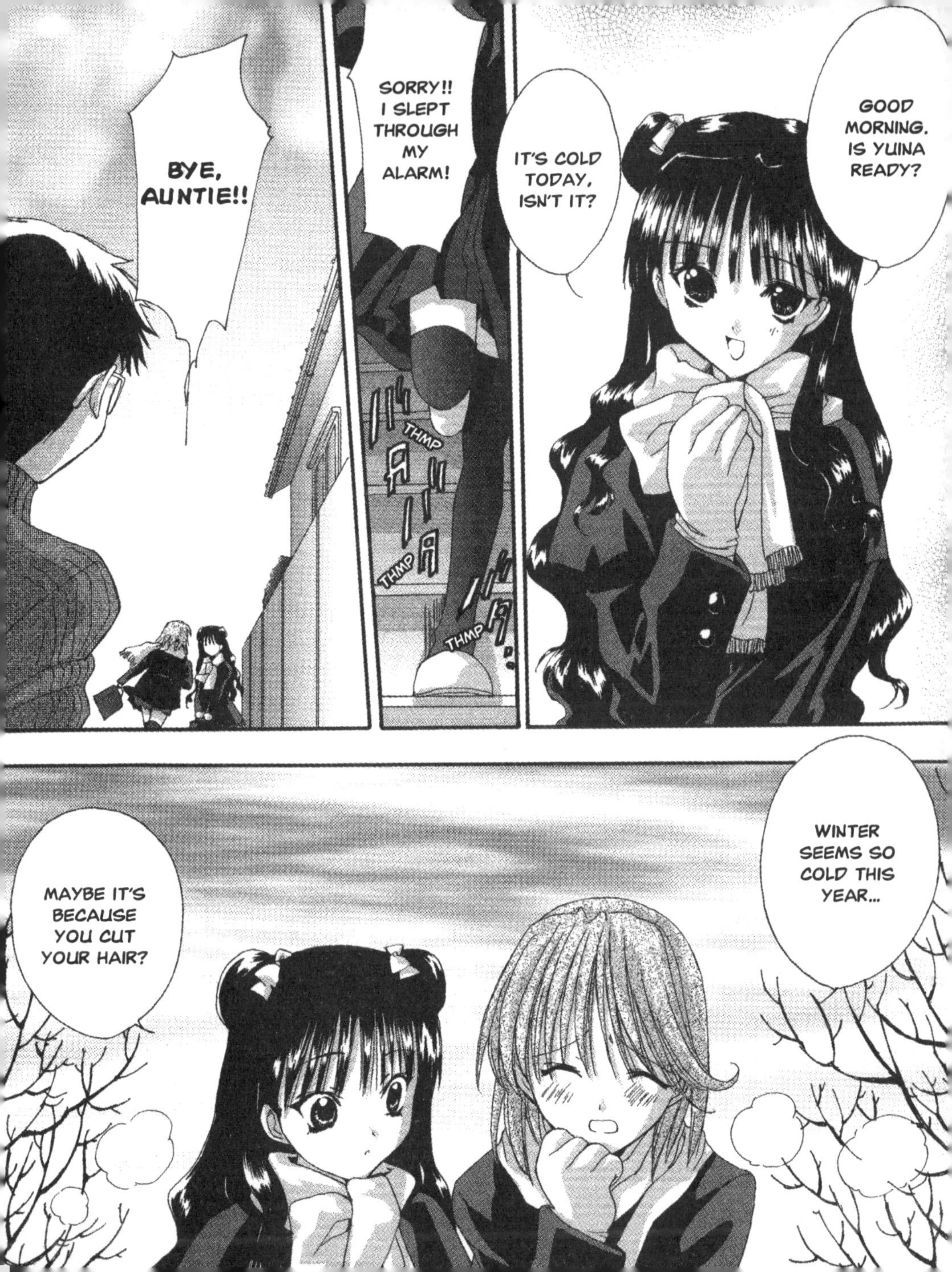
GOOD MORNING. IS YUINA READY?
IT'S COLD TODAY, ISN'T IT?
SORRY!! I SLEPT THROUGH MY ALARM!
THMP
THMP
THMP
BYE, AUNTIE!!
WINTER SEEMS SO COLD THIS YEAR...
MAYBE IT'S BECAUSE YOU CUT YOUR HAIR?

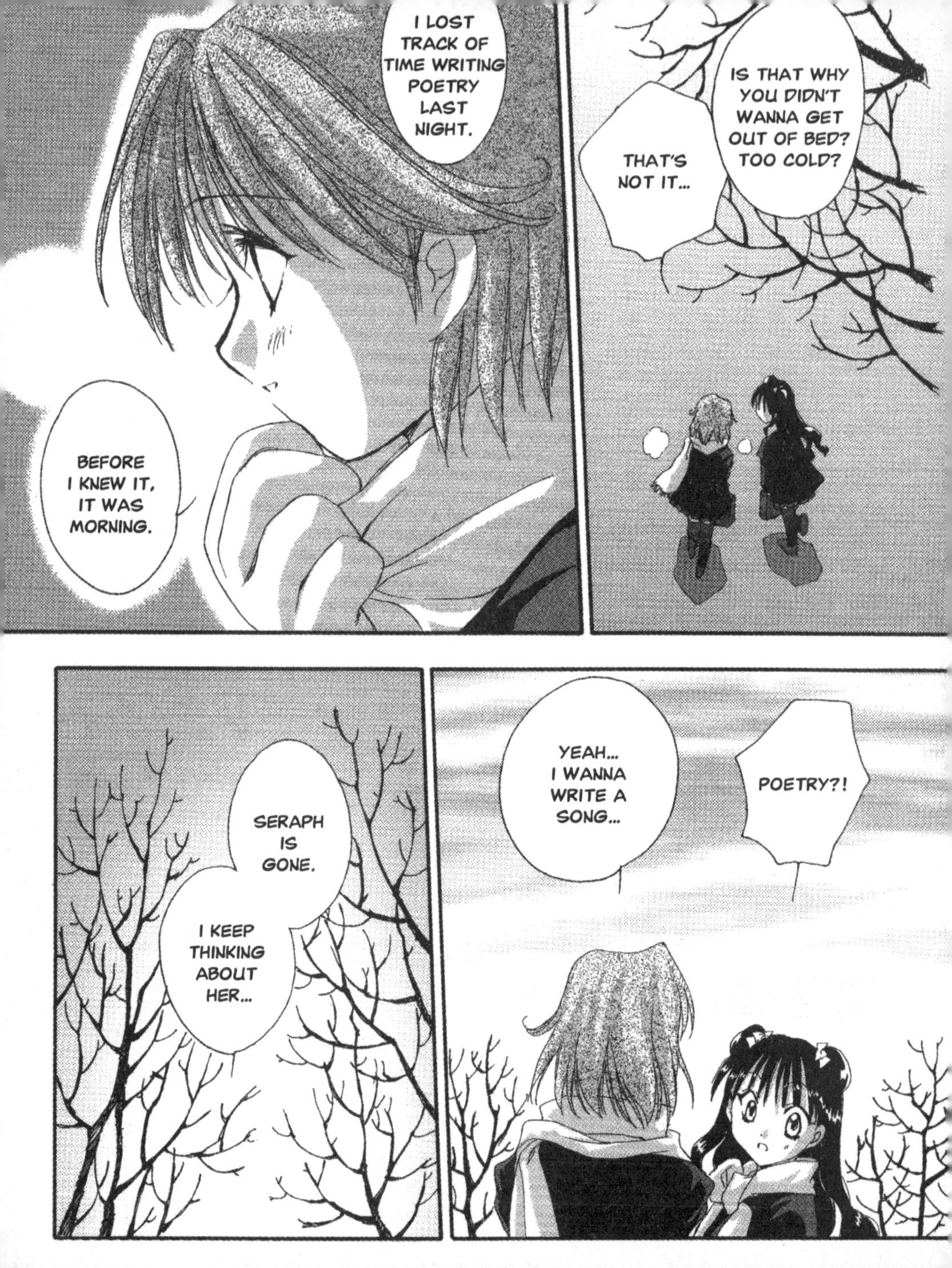
IS THAT WHY YOU DIDN'T WANNA GET OUT OF BED? TOO COLD?
THAT'S NOT IT...
I LOST TRACK OF TIME WRITING POETRY LAST NIGHT.
BEFORE I KNEW IT, IT WAS MORNING.
POETRY?!
YEAH... I WANNA WRITE A SONG...
SERAPH IS GONE.
I KEEP THINKING ABOUT HER...

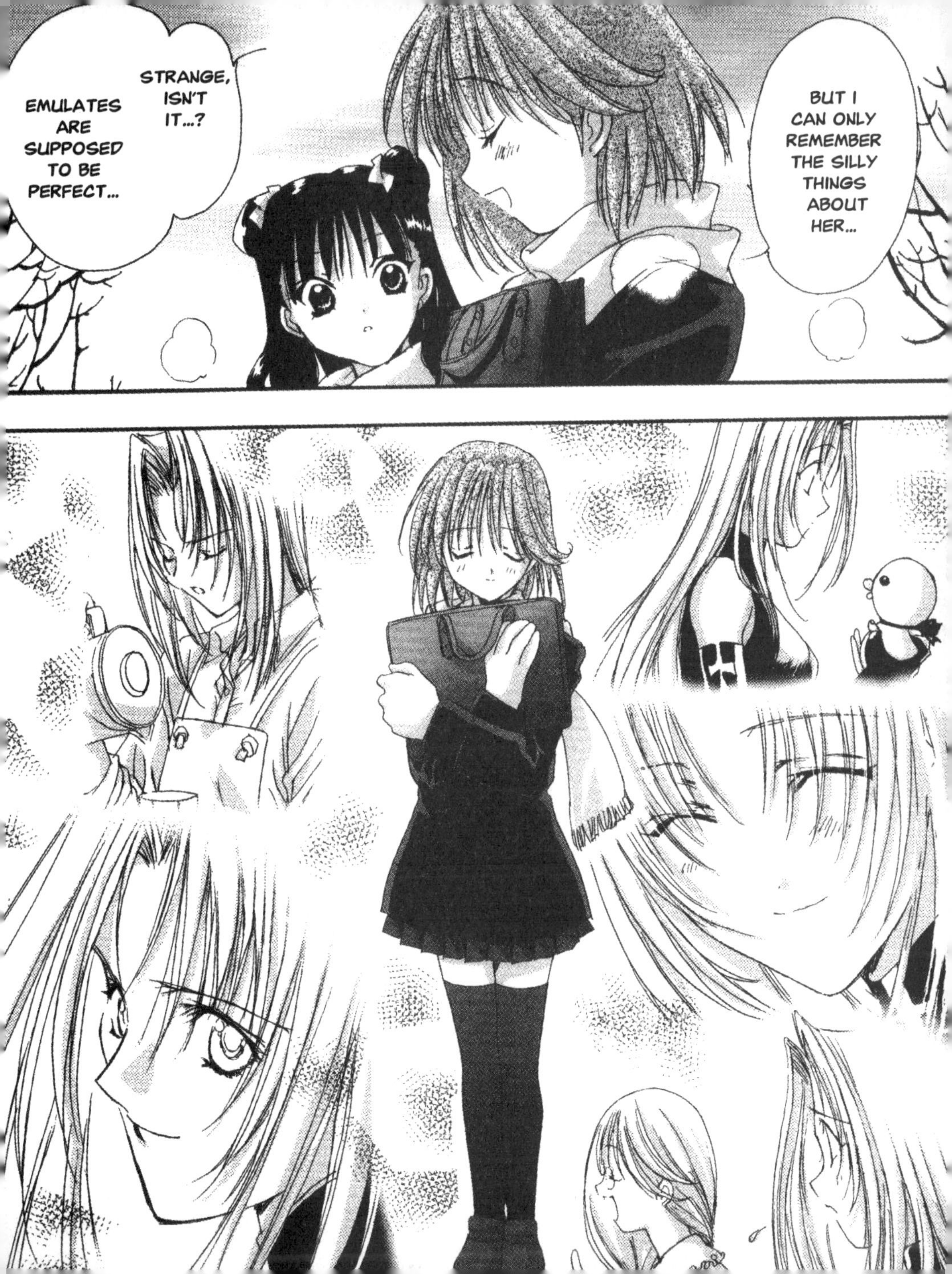
BUT I CAN ONLY REMEMBER THE SILLY THINGS ABOUT HER...
STRANGE, ISN'T IT...?
EMULATES ARE SUPPOSED TO BE PERFECT...

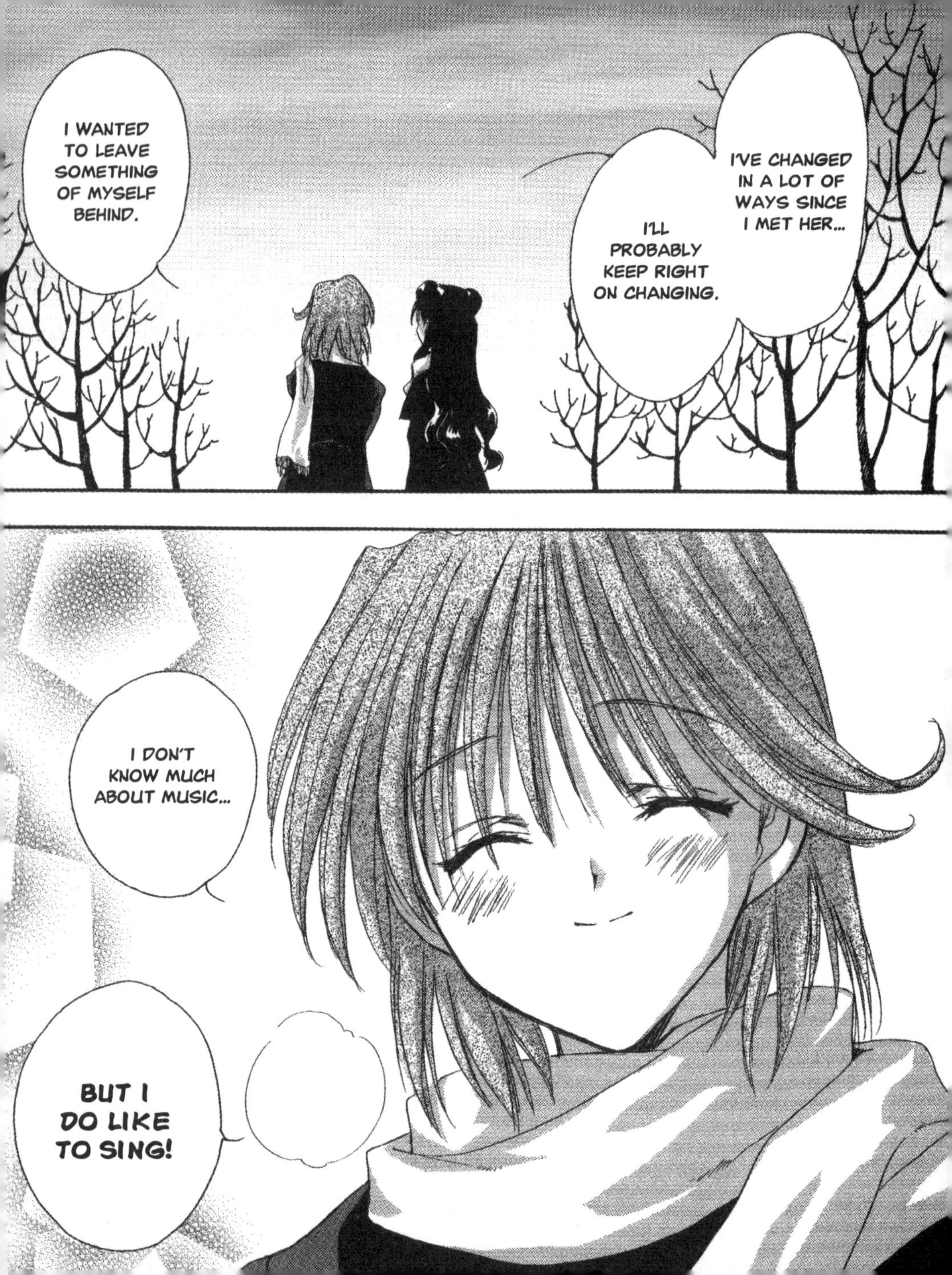
I'VE CHANGED IN A LOT OF WAYS SINCE I MET HER...
I'LL PROBABLY KEEP RIGHT ON CHANGING.
I WANTED TO LEAVE SOMETHING OF MYSELF BEHIND.
I DON'T KNOW MUCH ABOUT MUSIC...
BUT I DO LIKE TO SING!

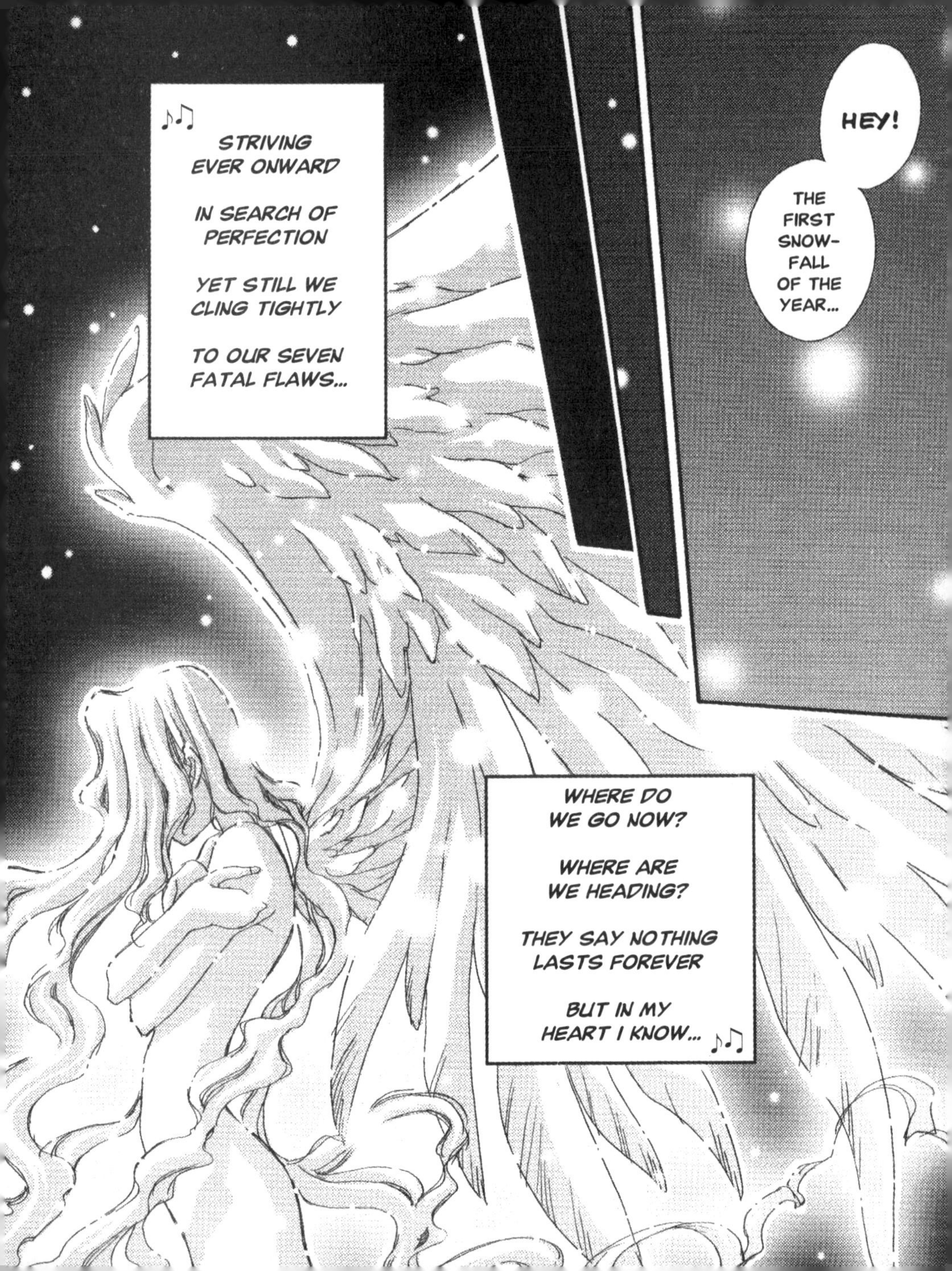

HEY!
THE FIRST SNOW-FALL OF THE YEAR...
♪♫ STRIVING EVER ONWARD
IN SEARCH OF PERFECTION
YET STILL WE CLING TIGHTLY
TO OUR SEVEN FATAL FLAWS...
WHERE DO WE GO NOW?
WHERE ARE WE HEADING?
THEY SAY NOTHING LASTS FOREVER
BUT IN MY HEART I KNOW... ♪♫

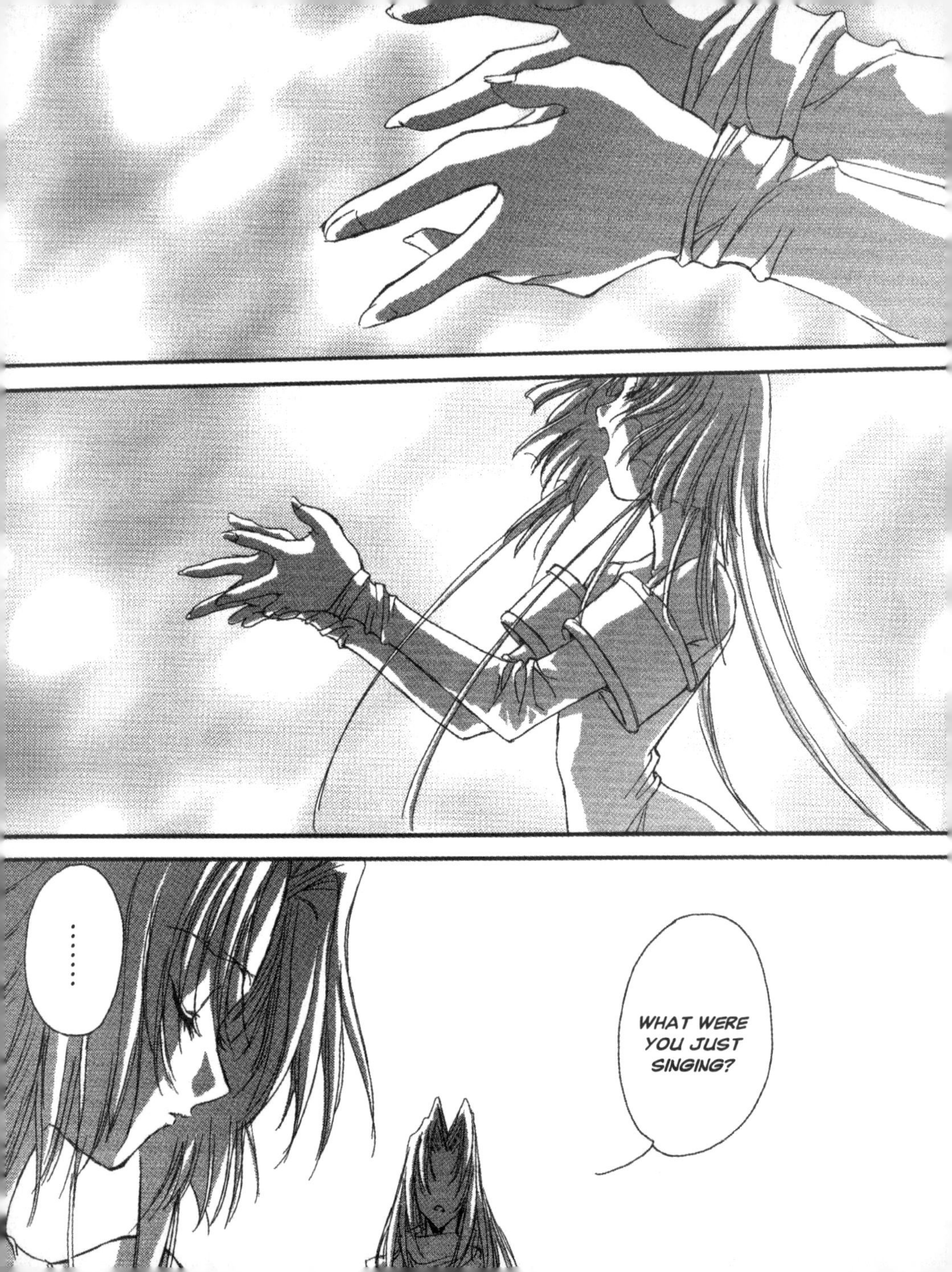
WHAT WERE YOU JUST SINGING?
......

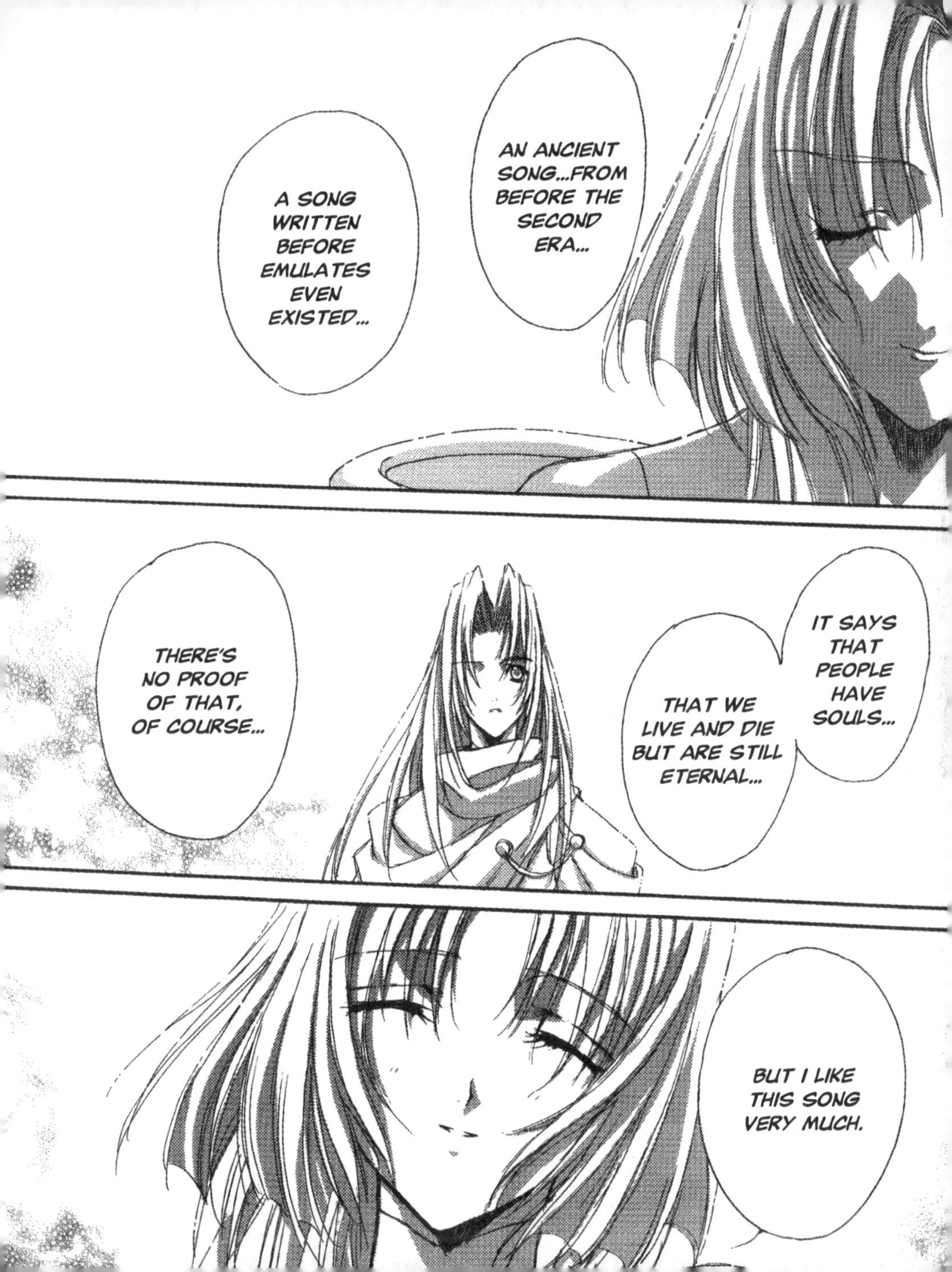
AN ANCIENT SONG...FROM BEFORE THE SECOND ERA...
A SONG WRITTEN BEFORE EMULATES EVEN EXISTED...
IT SAYS THAT PEOPLE HAVE SOULS...
THAT WE LIVE AND DIE BUT ARE STILL ETERNAL...
THERE'S NO PROOF OF THAT, OF COURSE...
BUT I LIKE THIS SONG VERY MUCH.

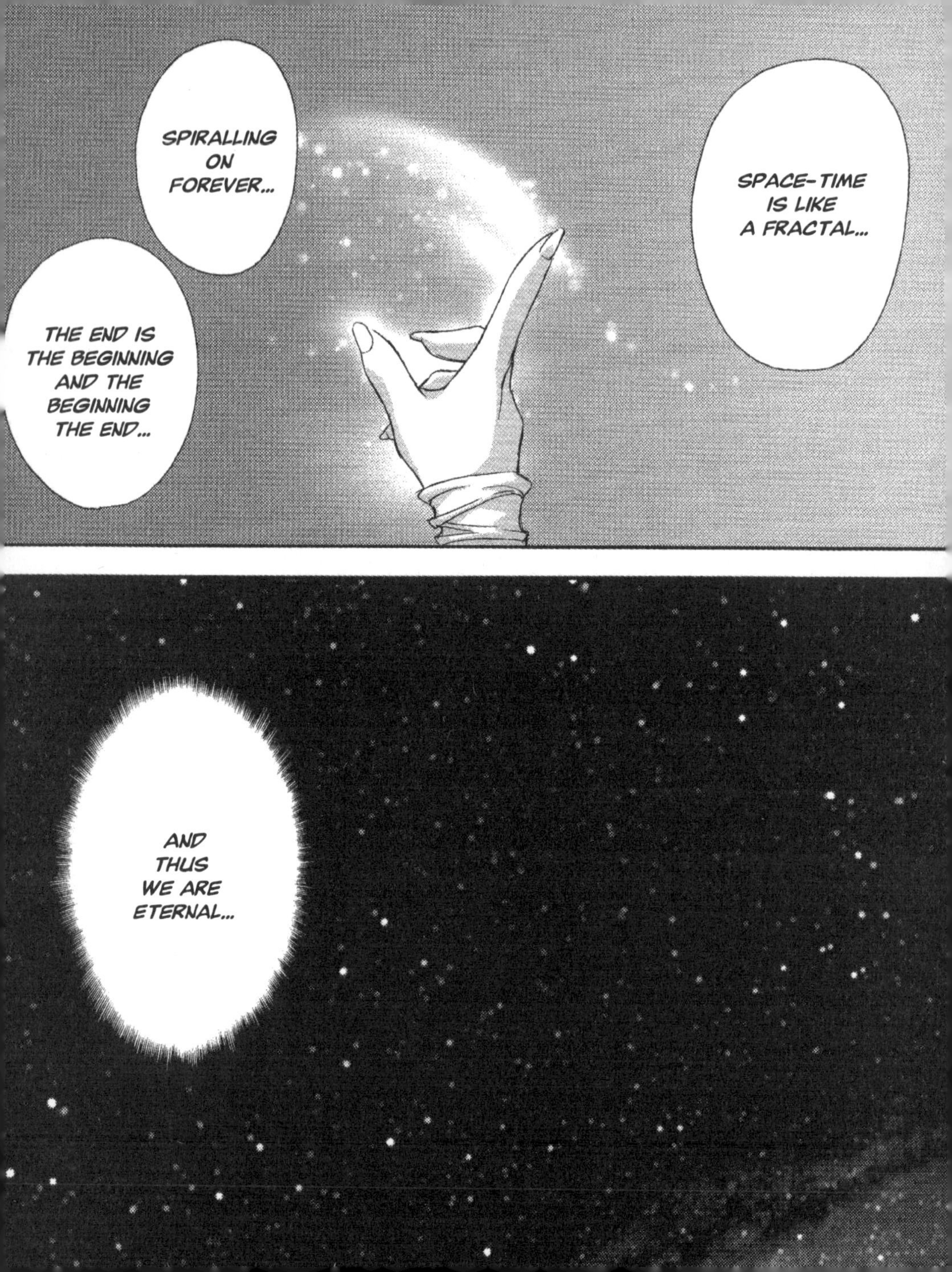
SPACE-TIME IS LIKE A FRACTAL...
SPIRALLING ON FOREVER...
THE END IS THE BEGINNING AND THE BEGINNING THE END...
AND THUS WE ARE ETERNAL...

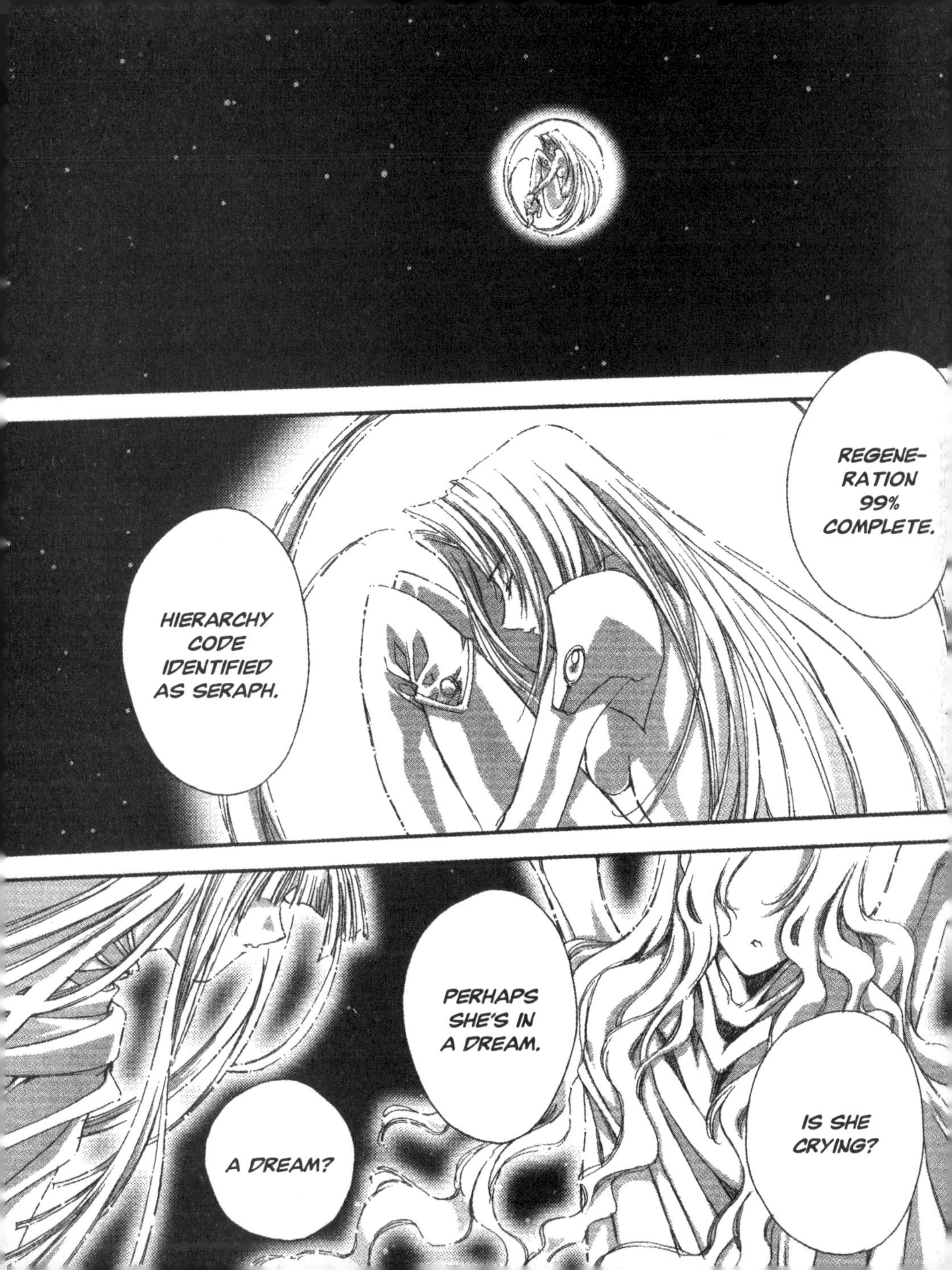
REGENE-RATION 99% COMPLETE.
HIERARCHY CODE IDENTIFIED AS SERAPH.
IS SHE CRYING?
PERHAPS SHE'S IN A DREAM.
A DREAM?

A FRAGMENT OF A MEMORY... SOMEDAY WE WILL MEET AGAIN. AS LONG AS WE HAVE THIS MEMORY TO HOLD US TOGETHER...
THE END

# ANGEL DUST

©2001 AOI NANASE
ENGLISH TRANSLATION RIGHTS ARRANGED WITH KADOKAWA SHOTEN PUBLISHING CO., LTD., TOKYO.

## Produced by the staff of *Newtype USA*

Lead Translator **JACK WIEDRICK**
Translators **HIROAKI FUKUDA, GINA KOERNER, TOMOE SPENCER and AI TAKAI**
Graphic Artist **MARK MEZA**

Editorial Director **GARY STEINMAN**
Creative Director **JASON BABLER**
Print Production Manager **BRIDGETT JANOTA**
Production Coordinator **MARISA KREITZ**

International Coordinators **MIYUKI KAMIYA and TORU IWAKAMI**

Publisher **JOHN LEDFORD**

Email: editor@adv-manga.com
www.adv-manga.com
www.advfilms.com

For sales and distribution inquiries please call 1.800.282.7202

**ADV MANGA** is a division of A.D. Vision, Inc.
5750 Bintliff Drive, Suite 210, Houston, Texas 77036

English text © 2005 published by A.D. Vision, Inc. under exclusive license.
ADV MANGA is a trademark of A.D. Vision, Inc.

ISBN: 1-4139-0310-X
First printing, November 2005
10 9 8 7 6 5 4 3 2 1
Printed in Canada

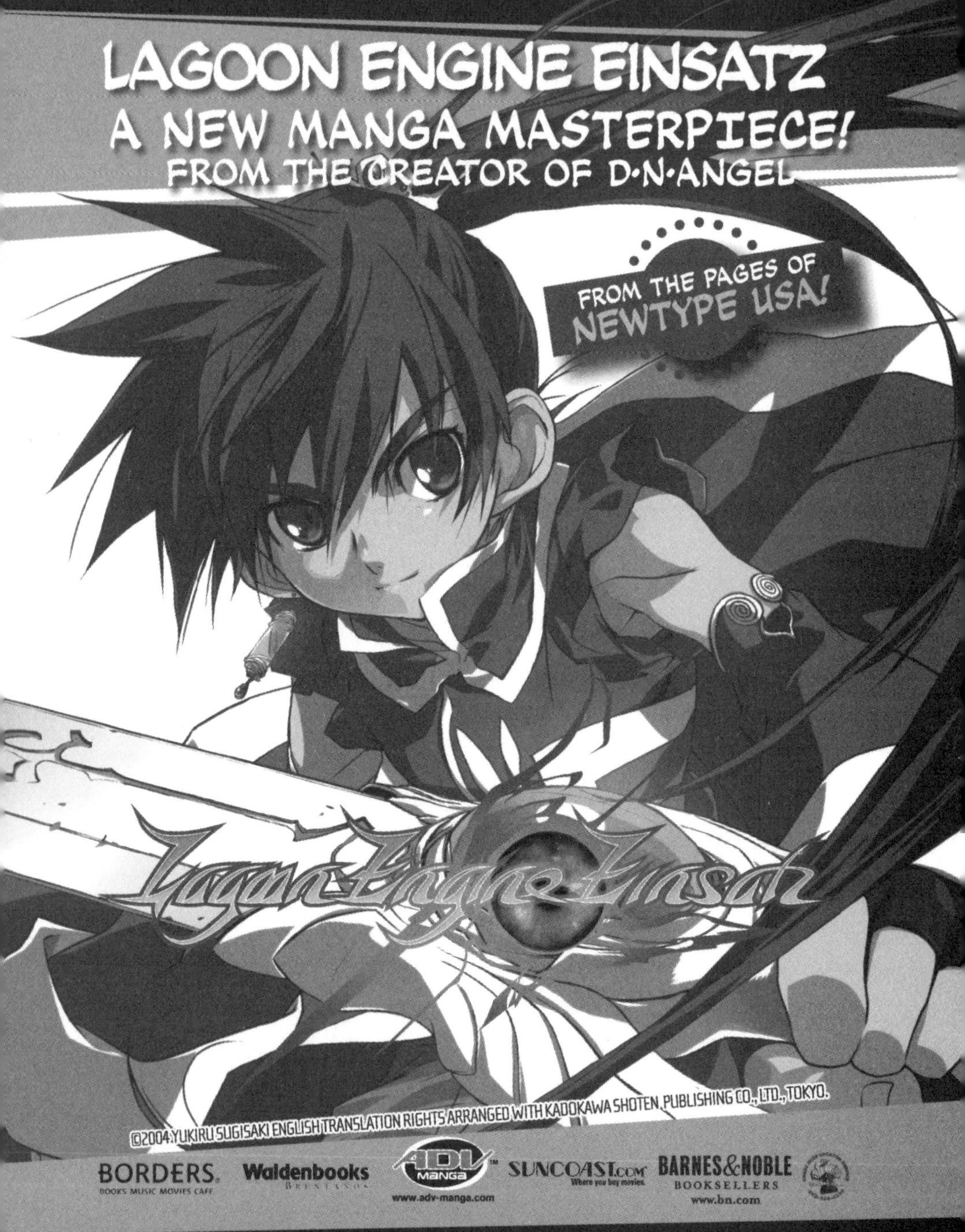

LAGOON ENGINE EINSATZ
A NEW MANGA MASTERPIECE!
FROM THE CREATOR OF D·N·ANGEL
FROM THE PAGES OF NEWTYPE USA!
©2004 YUKIRU SUGISAKI ENGLISH TRANSLATION RIGHTS ARRANGED WITH KADOKAWA SHOTEN PUBLISHING CO., LTD., TOKYO.
BORDERS.
BOOKS MUSIC MOVIES CAFE
Waldenbooks
ADV MANGA
www.adv-manga.com
SUNCOAST.com
Where you buy movies.
BARNES&NOBLE
BOOKSELLERS
www.bn.com

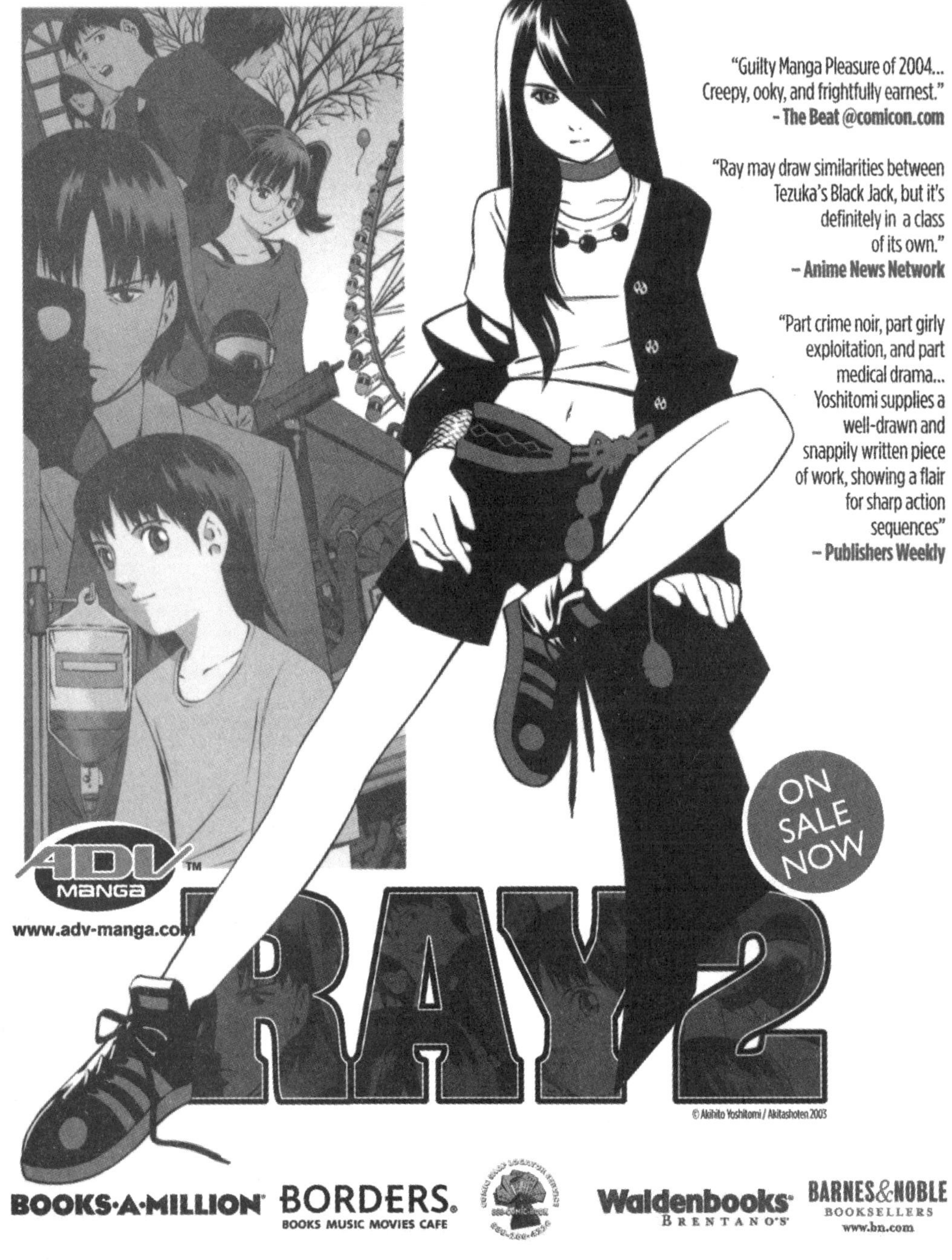
"Guilty Manga Pleasure of 2004... Creepy, ooky, and frightfully earnest."
– The Beat @comicon.com
"Ray may draw similarities between Tezuka's Black Jack, but it's definitely in a class of its own."
– Anime News Network
"Part crime noir, part girly exploitation, and part medical drama... Yoshitomi supplies a well-drawn and snappily written piece of work, showing a flair for sharp action sequences"
– Publishers Weekly
ON SALE NOW
ADV Manga
www.adv-manga.com
RAY 2
© Akihito Yoshitomi / Akitashoten 2003
BOOKS-A-MILLION
BORDERS.
BOOKS MUSIC MOVIES CAFE
Waldenbooks
BRENTANO'S
BARNES&NOBLE
BOOKSELLERS
www.bn.com

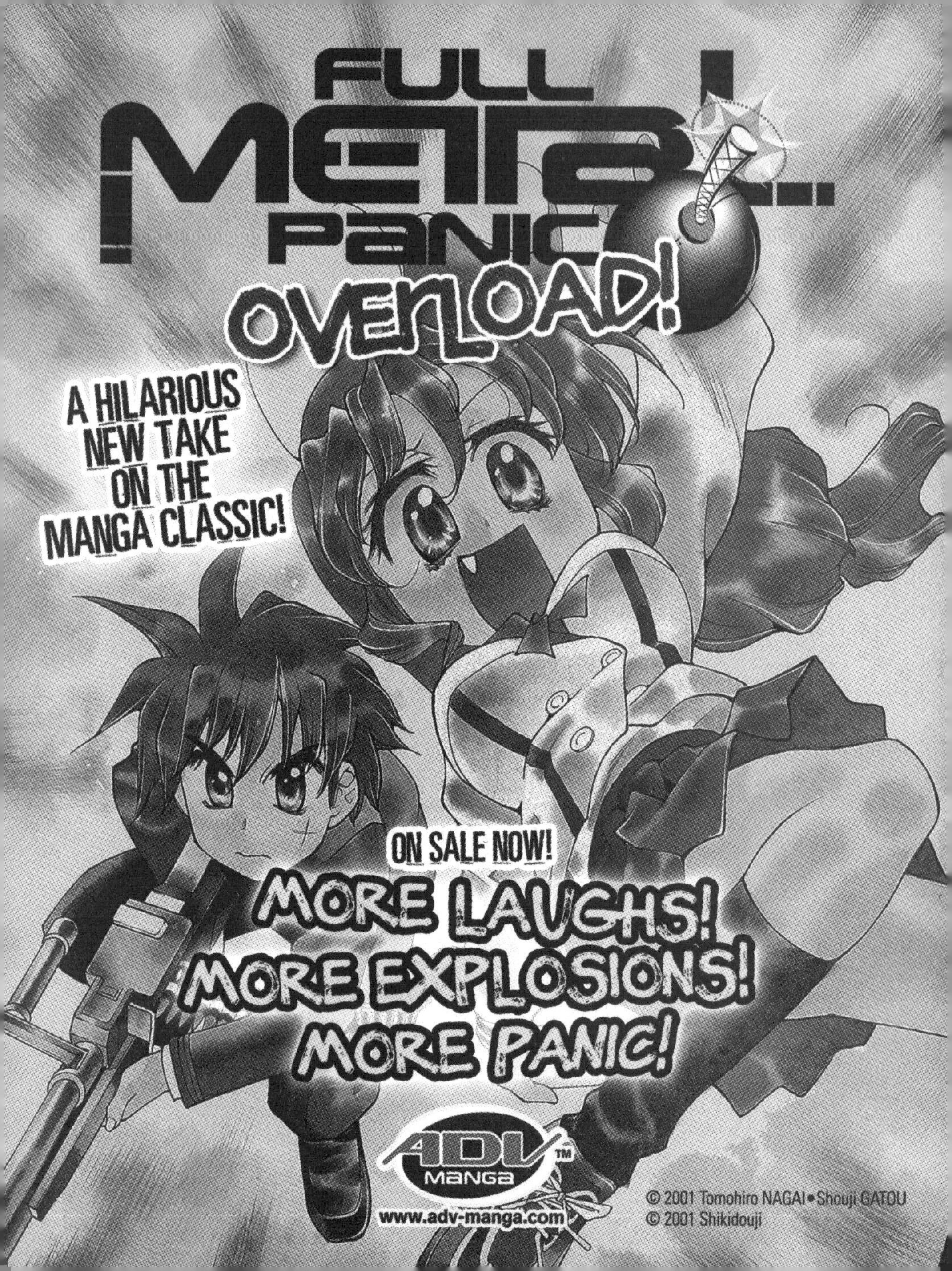

FULL METAL PANIC
OVERLOAD!
A HILARIOUS NEW TAKE ON THE MANGA CLASSIC!
ON SALE NOW!
MORE LAUGHS!
MORE EXPLOSIONS!
MORE PANIC!
ADV MANGA
www.adv-manga.com
© 2001 Tomohiro NAGAI • Shouji GATOU
© 2001 Shikidouji

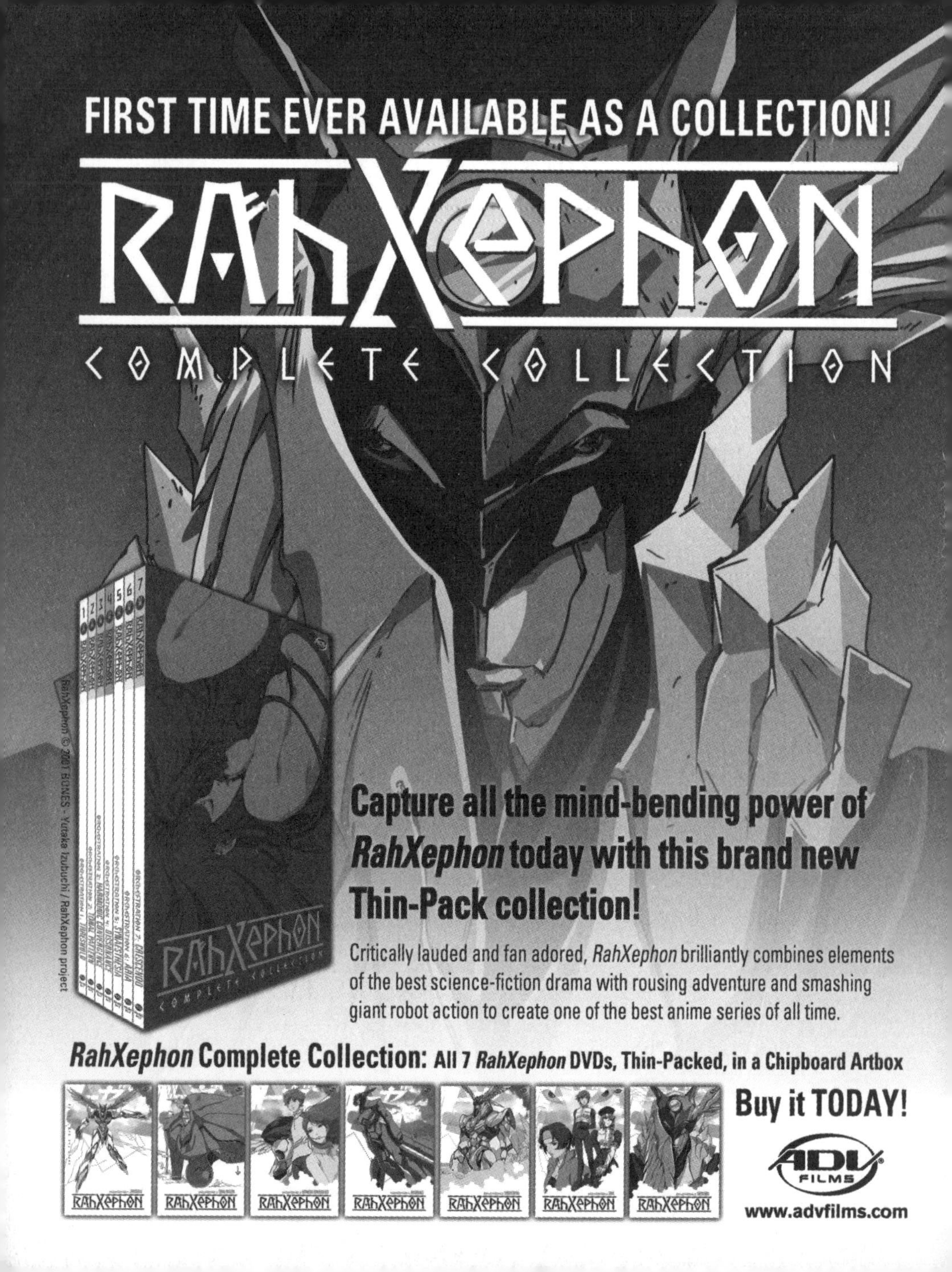

FIRST TIME EVER AVAILABLE AS A COLLECTION!
RAHXEPHON
COMPLETE COLLECTION
Capture all the mind-bending power of *RahXephon* today with this brand new Thin-Pack collection!
Critically lauded and fan adored, *RahXephon* brilliantly combines elements of the best science-fiction drama with rousing adventure and smashing giant robot action to create one of the best anime series of all time.
*RahXephon* Complete Collection: All 7 *RahXephon* DVDs, Thin-Packed, in a Chipboard Artbox
Buy it TODAY!
ADV FILMS
www.advfilms.com
RahXephon © 2001 BONES · Yutaka Izubuchi / RahXephon project

 **MANGA SURVEY**

**PLEASE MAIL THE COMPLETED FORM TO:** EDITOR – ADV MANGA
℅ A.D. Vision, Inc. 5750 Bintliff Drive, Suite 210, Houston, Texas 77036

Name:_____

Address:_____

City, State, Zip:_____

_____

E-Mail: _____

Male ☐   Female ☐          Age:_____

☐ *CHECK HERE IF YOU WOULD LIKE TO RECEIVE OTHER INFORMATION OR FUTURE OFFERS FROM ADV.*

*All information provided will be used for internal purposes only. We promise not to sell or otherwise divulge your information.*

**1. Annual Household Income** (*Check only one*)
- ☐ Under $25,000
- ☐ $25,000 to $50,000
- ☐ $50,000 to $75,000
- ☐ Over $75,000

**2. How do you hear about new Manga releases?** (*Check all that apply*)
- ☐ Browsing in Store
- ☐ Internet Reviews
- ☐ Anime News Websites
- ☐ Direct Email Campaigns
- ☐ Magazine Ad
- ☐ Online Advertising
- ☐ Conventions
- ☐ TV Advertising
- ☐ Online forums (message boards and chat rooms)
- ☐ Carrier pigeon
- ☐ Other:_____

**3. Which magazines do you read?** (*Check all that apply*)
- ☐ Wizard
- ☐ SPIN
- ☐ Animerica
- ☐ Rolling Stone
- ☐ Maxim
- ☐ DC Comics
- ☐ URB
- ☐ Polygon
- ☐ Official PlayStation Magazine
- ☐ Entertainment Weekly
- ☐ YRB
- ☐ EGM
- ☐ Newtype USA
- ☐ SciFi
- ☐ Starlog
- ☐ Wired
- ☐ Vice
- ☐ BPM
- ☐ I hate reading
- ☐ Other:_____

**4. Have you visited the ADV Manga website?**

- ☐ Yes
- ☐ No

**5. Have you made any manga purchases online from the ADV website?**

- ☐ Yes
- ☐ No

**6. If you have visited the ADV Manga website, how would you rate your online experience?**

- ☐ Excellent
- ☐ Good
- ☐ Average
- ☐ Poor

**7. What genre of manga do you prefer?**
*(Check all that apply)*

- ☐ adventure
- ☐ romance
- ☐ detective
- ☐ action
- ☐ horror
- ☐ sci-fi/fantasy
- ☐ sports
- ☐ comedy

**8. How many manga titles have you purchased in the last 6 months?**

- ☐ none
- ☐ 1-4
- ☐ 5-10
- ☐ 11+

**9. Where do you make your manga purchases?** *(Check all that apply)*

- ☐ comic store
- ☐ bookstore
- ☐ newsstand
- ☐ online
- ☐ other:___________________
- ☐ department store
- ☐ grocery store
- ☐ video store
- ☐ video game store

**10. Which bookstores do you usually make your manga purchases at?**
*(Check all that apply)*

- ☐ Barnes & Noble
- ☐ Walden Books
- ☐ Suncoast
- ☐ Best Buy
- ☐ Amazon.com
- ☐ Borders
- ☐ Books-A-Million
- ☐ Toys "Я" Us
- ☐ Other bookstore: ________________________

**11. What's your favorite anime/manga website?** *(Check all that apply)*

- ☐ adv-manga.com
- ☐ advfilms.com
- ☐ rightstuf.com
- ☐ animenewsservice.com
- ☐ animenewsnetwork.com
- ☐ Other:___________________
- ☐ animeondvd.com
- ☐ anipike.com
- ☐ animeonline.net
- ☐ planetanime.com
- ☐ animenation.com

*All information provided will be used for internal purposes only. We promise not to sell or otherwise divulge your information.*